REPOSITIONING CLASS

Social Inequality in Industrial Societies

GORDON MARSHALL

SAGE Publications
London • Thousand Oaks • New Delhi

© Gordon Marshall 1997

First published 1997

 SAGE Publications Ltd
6 Bonhill Street
London EC2A 4PU

SAGE Publications Inc.
2455 Teller Road
Thousand Oaks, California 91320

SAGE Publications India Pvt Ltd
32, M-Block Market
Greater Kailash – I
New Delhi 110 048

British Library Cataloguing in Publication data

A catalogue record for this book is available
from the British Library

ISBN 0 7619 5557 7
ISBN 0 7619 5558 5 (pbk)

Library of Congress catalog card number 97–066779

Typeset by Mayhew Typesetting, Rhayader, Powys
Printed in Great Britain by Biddles Ltd, Guildford, Surrey

Contents

List of Tables

Preface

The chapters that are gathered together in this volume were written over a ten-year period, during the course of which the death of social class was regularly reported, in popular and scholarly publications alike. Such pronouncements were as exaggerated as they were untimely. In fact, social class is as important to the understanding of late-twentieth-century industrial societies as it was to their early capitalist counterparts, and class analysis is probably now in a healthier state than at any previous time in its long sociological history. These essays attempt to explain why.

The collection is intended for an international (though English-speaking) academic audience. Several of the chapters are explicitly comparative, and examine the British experience in relation to that of the United States, communist Europe, or Scandinavia. In those cases where Britain provides the exclusive focus for discussion, the evidence for this country is used to make more general points, either about class itself or about how (in my view at least) sociologists might most usefully pursue class analyses in future.

A number of common substantive themes, pertaining broadly to the relationship between social stratification and social order, serve to link the various studies across the years. Specific issues include the debate about the unit of class composition, the question of meritocracy, the relationship between class and gender, crossnational similarities and differences in mobility regimes, and arguments about proletarianization, distributional struggles, collective identities, and the nature of the so-called underclass in advanced societies.

In a wider sense, the collection as a whole is intended as an illustration of those methodological principles by which I have tried to be guided in my work; namely, suspicion of grand theory and a preference for theories of the middle range, hostility to the historicism of the political left and right alike, and the attempt to match testable (middle-range) propositions to appropriate empirical data. This might suggest, at the risk of my appearing arrogant, that the volume could be situated within the tradition of studies in sociology exemplified by the work of Tom Marshall, David Lockwood, A.H. Halsey, John Goldthorpe and others. Verifiable conjecture about social class and social status, and in particular their implications for social integration, is at the heart of this literature.

The essays have diverse origins. Many were co-authored, and emerged from research related to the Essex Class and British Social Justice Projects, in which I was one of several participating investigators. Most attempt to develop the ideas first expressed in *Social Class in Modern Britain* (Marshall et al., 1988) and can be read as a companion to that earlier collaborative volume. I am, therefore, indebted to a number of close friends and colleagues, not only for their diverse contributions to the original texts, but also for the unconditional generosity with which they have responded to my requests for permission to reprint. Howard Newby, David Rose and Carolyn Vogler were fellow researchers in the Class Study; Carole Burgoyne, Stephen Roberts, David Routh and Adam Swift have at different times been part of the Social Justice team. John Goldthorpe and I first worked together when he supervised my doctoral thesis (which has nothing whatsoever to say about social class or social justice in modern societies) during the mid 1970s. In the mid 1980s he was good enough to provide specialist advice (not all of which was taken) to the Essex team in general and myself in particular. As will be obvious from the contents of Chapter 5, we continue to disagree about some specific issues, but share the same general understanding of the research agenda for class analysis (which is described at some length in Chapter 2).

The chapters have been reprinted as originally published, although the style of referencing and use of subheadings have been standardized for aesthetic reasons, and a consolidated list of references has been prepared in order to avoid duplication. A few redundant notes, making the same technical points but in relation to different chapters, have been removed. I have resisted the temptation to tinker with the text itself, mainly because this strikes me as being intellectually dishonest, but also because to do so at this juncture would be unfair to my co-authors.

Finally, I should record my gratitude to a number of individuals for helpful advice or encouragement, and for confirming in this particular way my own beliefs about the benefits of collaborative work. Chris Rojek first suggested that I compile the text and then devised its title. John Goldthorpe, Anthony Heath and Adam Swift read an earlier draft of the introductory chapter, and offered useful comments and criticisms. The nature of my output has, as always, been greatly improved by the quality of their input.

Gordon Marshall
Bradford-on-Avon

Acknowledgements

Due acknowledgement of permission to reproduce the chapters in this volume is made to my co-authors and the following publishers (the place of first publication is shown in brackets):

Chapter 1: Carolyn Vogler, David Rose and Howard Newby. The British Sociological Association (*Sociology*, 21, 1987)

Chapter 2: John H. Goldthorpe. The British Sociological Association (*Sociology*, 26, 1992)

Chapter 3: Oxford University Press (*European Sociological Review*, 4, 1988)

Chapter 4: Stephen Roberts and Carole Burgoyne. Routledge/LSE (*British Journal of Sociology*, 47, 1996)

Chapter 5: Stephen Roberts, Carole Burgoyne, Adan Swift and David Routh. Oxford University Press (*European Sociological Review*, 11, 1995)

Chapter 6: David Rose. Routledge/LSE (*British Journal of Sociology*, 39, 1988)

Chapter 7: Svetlana Sydorenko and Stephen Roberts. The British Sociological Association (*Work, Employment and Society*, 9, 1995)

Chapter 8: Stephen Roberts. The British Sociological Association (*Sociology*, 29, 1995)

Chapter 9: Adam Swift. Routledge/LSE (*British Journal of Sociology*, 44, 1993)

Chapter 10: Routledge/LSE (*British Journal of Sociology*, 47, 1996)

An earlier version of some parts of the Introduction originally appeared in an article entitled 'Social mobility – plus ça change . . .', co-authored with Adam Swift, and published in the second issue of *Prospect* Magazine (November 1995).

Introduction: Class and Class Analysis in the 1990s

Which of the following statements is true? British society is no more open now than it was at the time of the First World War. The chances of social mobility in Britain are almost the same as those to be found in Germany. Education plays a similar role in linking class origins to class destinations in both Britain and Poland. The impact of class on voting behaviour has shown no signs of weakening in either Britain or the United States for more than a quarter of a century.

The perhaps surprising answer is that they are *all* true. These are only a few of the remarkable findings to have emerged during the past twenty or so years, from an intensive programme of research, centred mainly on the activities of the International Sociological Association's Research Committee 28 on Social Stratification. The researchers involved, although quite independent and scattered across several continents, form a loose academic network based on a shared interest in class processes within industrialized societies. Until recently their discussions featured a good deal of disagreement – mainly about methods and techniques. Now, however, there are clear signs of an emerging consensus about results that will overturn much of what we thought we knew about social class in Britain and elsewhere.

The essays that are gathered together here are my own modest contribution to this revolution in class analysis. Like other investigators I have found that, despite such changes as the rising general levels of education, increased participation of women in paid employment, and expansion of newer nonmanual forms of work at the expense of traditional proletarian occupations, class inequalities in the industrialized countries have remained more or less constant throughout most of the twentieth century. The central problem for class theory is not therefore, as generations of critics have supposed, to account for the demise of social class in advanced societies. The real challenge is to explain why class has persisted as such a potent social force.

The Goldthorpe social class schema

What do we mean by social class? Class is, of course, a contested concept. Sometimes, classes are defined by occupational prestige scores, arranged in hierarchical fashion; or, more loosely, in terms of generalized social standing in the community. American observers (as well as popular writers from Nancy Mitford to Jilly Cooper in the UK) have tended to distinguish classes according to what Europeans conventionally think of as lifestyles – or what we might call 'social status'. (I pursue the distinction between class and status in Chapter 1.) Increasingly, however, the sociological debate has featured the class categories devised by John Goldthorpe and his colleagues for the Oxford Social Mobility Study of England and Wales during the 1970s. This particular approach to the study of social classes is explained fully in later chapters. Briefly, the Goldthorpe classification (see Table 4.1) differentiates positions within labour markets in terms of employment relations. More specifically, distinctions are made between individuals having relatively advantaged and disadvantaged conditions of employment; between those involved in agricultural and non-agricultural activities; and those having different employment statuses (notably the self-employed and employees).[1]

People in so-called service-class or *salariat* occupations render service to their employers in exchange for a particular form of remuneration. Professionals, administrators, and managers are required to exercise delegated authority or specialized knowledge and expertise on behalf of their employing organization, in return for which they enjoy relatively high incomes, security of employment, incremental advancement, enhanced pension rights, and a good deal of autonomy at work.[2] *Skilled manual* and *unskilled manual wage-workers*, on the other hand, supply discrete amounts of labour in a relatively short-term and specific exchange of money for effort. Working-class occupations tend also to be subject to more intensive supervision or control from above. The *routine clerical class* is defined by employment relationships that take a mixed form between the extremes of the service relationship and the pure labour contract – sometimes evident in employer versus employee conflict over issues such as time-keeping, chances of promotion, and methods of remuneration. Organizations themselves are often ambivalent about whether these personnel are 'staff' or 'labour'. *Small proprietors* (including the self-employed) also share conditions of employment that take an intermediate form, experiencing a degree of autonomy that is characteristic of the salariat, but also the necessity of exchanging money for effort on a 'piece' or time basis. Finally, *farmers* and *agricultural workers* are distinguished from other proprietors and employees, because of distinctive elements in the conditions of employment found in the primary sector, arising from the holding of property in land, the organization of production being often family-based, and the substitution of payments-in-kind for at least part of the monetary wage.

This schema may or may not correspond with our common-sense understandings of the term 'social class'. What is certain is that, over the years, it has been subject to intensive scrutiny by investigators in different countries, each of whom has refined the process of allocating occupations to classes according to the conditions of employment found in their society at the time, so that we can be increasingly confident of crossnational comparability in measurement. This alone has been a major achievement of the research programme, since previous attempts at crossnational study have been hampered by lack of consistency in different countries as to what constitutes (for example) 'manual work', or how one defines 'the working class'.

In other words, the Goldthorpe classification possesses a high degree of so-called 'criterion validity', since relatively homogeneous and distinctive groupings can be distinguished using the criteria spelled out in the underlying theory of class. Within each social class the constituent occupations will generally be found to share similar conditions and relations of employment. This mode of class analysis therefore features prominently in the chapters that follow. Of course, the schema is not entirely without its measurement problems, especially where crossnational comparisons are involved. Some of these are discussed below (notably in Chapters 4 and 7). However, they are markedly less serious than the many methodological difficulties that afflict alternative class schemes, especially (as I attempt to show in Chapter 3) those having an overtly Marxist pedigree.

Social fluidity and the 'FJH hypothesis'

How has social mobility been measured? There are two types of mobility research. On the one hand, it is possible to think in terms of *intra*generational or career mobility, viewing movement between classes as a work history – from, say, first to present employment. Alternatively, someone's current circumstances may be considered in relation to those of his or her parents, or in terms of class background. Arguments about crossnational differences or trends in mobility rates – including those pursued here in Chapters 7 and 10 – are centred largely on the interpretation of survey evidence relating to this type of *inter*generational movement between social origins and class destinations.

Much of the debate about social mobility in advanced societies has dealt with technical issues surrounding the measurement of class, quality of survey evidence, and statistical modelling of the relevant data. At times the discussion has been fairly arcane – even to other sociologists. However, the substantive dispute has increasingly been focused on a simple proposition about 'relative mobility chances' (class differences in the distribution of opportunities for intergenerational social mobility) first advanced by David Featherman, Frank Lancaster Jones and Robert Hauser in the mid 1970s. They argued that the overall pattern of mobility chances – or what has since become known as the degree of social fluidity – 'in industrial societies with a market economy and a nuclear family system is basically the same' (Featherman et al., 1975: 340). It is the research stimulated by this 'FJH hypothesis' that now challenges many popular beliefs about intergenerational social mobility in the industrialized world.

The terms in which the argument is expressed are not entirely unambiguous. One immediate problem was to determine whether or not it is intended to apply to societies without a market economy – such as, for example, the communist states of Central and Eastern Europe. This question was easily resolved. Featherman and his colleagues themselves raise the possibility that their arguments might also apply in non-capitalist countries. In any case, whatever were the intentions of its authors, it is certainly possible to test the hypothesis in this way. Other researchers therefore extended the original formulation so that data for communist (and formerly communist) countries were routinely included in their investigations.

Another issue of note is that the thesis distinguishes between total or absolute mobility rates (including mobility facilitated by shifts in the occupational structure) and relative mobility chances (the distribution of opportunities for mobility across classes). This distinction may not be readily apparent to anyone not involved in researching social class. Since the difference between absolute rates and relative chances is central to the arguments of this book it will be explained further below (and returned to at length in Chapters 7, 9 and 10).

However, the major difficulties associated with the FJH hypothesis probably stemmed from the loose verbal formulation of the thesis itself. What, precisely, are the criteria for judging mobility regimes (the degree of social fluidity or openness in societies) to be 'basically' the same? Does 'basically the same' mean 'identical'? Where nations have slightly different *patterns* of mobility, but the same overall *degree* of fluidity, does this count as evidence to support the argument? (The short answer to the second and third questions would appear to be 'no' and 'yes' respectively.) Lately, the dust seems to have settled on even this most troublesome aspect of the debate, revealing a new orthodoxy which contradicts commonplace assumptions about the generally progressive tendencies inherent in the social structures of industrial economies.

One main finding is of a remarkable similarity in the distribution of intergenerational class mobility chances across industrial nations. For example, European – mainly British, Swedish and German – researchers involved in the CASMIN (Comparative Analysis of Social Mobility in Industrial Nations) Project during the 1980s conducted an exhaustive study of social mobility patterns in fifteen of the world's major industrial societies, including the United Kingdom. They concluded that 'the total amount of the association between class origins and destinations that is cross-nationally variable is . . . only very small relative to the amount that is cross-nationally common' (Erikson and Goldthorpe, 1992a: 389).

This is not to say that there are no variations whatsoever in social fluidity across societies – merely that, as earlier American researchers also found, 'the cross-nationally common element heavily predominates over the cross-nationally variable one' (Grusky and Hauser, 1984: 26). In fact, according to the CASMIN data at least, the degree of 'common social fluidity' is such that something like 95 per cent of all of the association between class of origin and class destinations was found to be identical across the countries that were examined. Even those who were initially sceptical (notably some prominent Dutch researchers) now seem to accept that there is a basic crossnational similarity in mobility chances within nations – although they still want to emphasize that the between-country variations mean that mobility regimes are not *literally* the same across all industrialized societies (see Ganzeboom et al., 1989: 3–4, 47–8).

Researchers have also demonstrated an impressive stability in the pattern of mobility chances over time. The CASMIN team examined class mobility among different birth cohorts within countries but were unable to find any tendency towards greater openness in class structures. Their results demonstrate instead a 'trendless fluctuation' in mobility chances across successive birth cohorts spanning the past three-quarters of a century (Erikson and Goldthorpe, 1992a: ch. 3). This finding is also widely reported in other studies. Perhaps surprisingly, not only has there been no significant reduction in class inequalities of mobility chances in Britain, but the same is true also of the supposedly more open societies of the United States, Australia and Japan.[3]

It is clear that, in much of the industrialized world, the pattern of unequal social mobility chances has remained basically the same throughout most of the twentieth century – despite the advent of welfare states, universal free education, and redistributive tax regimes. This finding may seem implausible to those of us who grew up in the affluent 1950s, the swinging 1960s, or even the entrepreneurial 1980s, but it has now been reproduced so often, and across so many countries and data-sets, that it can no longer seriously be in dispute.

It seems that we may have mistaken changes in the *shape* of the class structure for changes in social fluidity or the degree of *openness*. In most advanced societies, the post-war years from the 1950s onwards saw rapid economic expansion, and a transformation in the occupational division of labour. With the shift from manufacturing to services, the proportion of the workforce involved in manual labouring declined, and there was a growth of professional, managerial and administrative positions. This helped generate substantial rates of mobility (especially upward mobility) overall. But more 'room at the top' has not been accompanied by greater equality in the opportunities to get there. All that has happened is that proportionately more of the new salariat jobs have gone to the children of parents already holding privileged class locations. In sum, the growth of skilled white-collar work has increased opportunities for mobility generally, but the distribution of those opportunities across the classes has stayed the same.

These results carry profound implications for social policy. Not only has the past half-century been a period of rapid economic growth. During this time, social reforms have also increased access to education, and tempered the worst effects of poverty. In other words, as the authors of the Oxford study put it, 'the project of creating a more open society was undertaken, and in circumstances which might be regarded as highly favourable to it'

(Goldthorpe, 1987: 327). However, despite this attempt to minimize the influence of class on processes of social selection, the degree of openness in advanced societies has remained unchanged, so that the relative chances of being mobile between classes were much the same in the 1980s as they had been more than half a century earlier. Only Sweden, it seems, has moved towards diminishing inequality in class mobility chances – and then only marginally – perhaps because social policy in that country (including the tax and welfare system) has actually succeeded in reducing the inequalities of condition that are found between classes (see Erikson, 1990).

What this programme of sociological research seems therefore to have discovered is the 'bed-rock' of class inequalities in industrial societies. Swedish exceptionalism tends to suggest that governments who pursue increasing social fluidity as an objective of social policy will find this bed-rock difficult to penetrate unless they also take sustained action to reduce inequalities of class position, since an important aspect of class advantage is precisely the ability it gives people to confer further advantage on their children, either directly via the transmission of wealth or indirectly through the medium of enhanced opportunities for educational achievement.[4]

Social mobility and social justice

The debate about social mobility shows no signs of slackening but now seems to be advancing in a number of different directions. Since the present volume makes no pretence of being a textbook on class analysis I will not attempt a systematic review of the latest mobility studies here.[5] However, two aspects of the discussion are worth mentioning in outline, by way of introduction to arguments that will be developed in the chapters that follow. The first of these concerns the attempt to explain such crossnational differences in social fluidity as can be detected in the mobility data. The second deals with the implications of these data for arguments about social justice in the late twentieth century.

Some researchers have pursued the residual issues surrounding the FJH hypothesis by attempting to model the variation that clearly does exist across societies; or, in the case of the CASMIN team, by arguing that such differences are best explained historically rather than sociologically. For example, Robert Erikson and John Goldthorpe (1992a: 379–89) maintain that the unexplained dissimilarities can be understood only by reference to historical particulars within each society (such as Swedish social policy), rather than in terms of systematic macro-sociological variables (type of political regime or national culture, level of economic or educational development) of the sort that have been suggested by others (compare Treiman and Yip, 1989).

One aspect of this crossnational variation is evident in Table (i). These results have been calculated from data made available through my own involvement in the large-scale social surveys comprising the 1991

Table (i)   *Salariat versus working-class odds ratios by sex for eleven nations*

Males		Females	
East Germany	2.11	East Germany	2.27
Estonia	2.21	Estonia	2.27
Bulgaria	2.51	Russia	2.79
Russia	3.09	United States	2.98
Czechoslovakia	3.17	Czechoslovakia	4.37
United States	3.72	West Germany	4.46
West Germany	5.39	Bulgaria	5.28
Great Britain	5.48	Great Britain	6.25
Slovenia	6.67	Poland	6.67
Japan	7.68	Japan	12.78
Poland	7.90	Slovenia	12.88

International Social Justice Project.[6] For each of eleven countries shown the table reports salariat versus working-class odds ratios by sex. Odds ratios are a simple means of measuring comparative mobility chances and are, therefore, well suited to addressing issues of social fluidity. In this case, they show the chances of someone whose father held a salariat position being themselves found in such a position rather than in the working class, as compared with the corresponding chances of someone from a working-class background – or, in other words, the ratio of the former to the latter set of odds. In this way, odds ratios are the outcome (as it were) of a competition between individuals of different class origins, seeking to achieve or avoid one rather than another destination in the overall structure. Where such competitions are perfectly equal, the odds for the particular movement in question are even, and the odds ratio will be one to one (or simply one). Odds ratios that are greater than one are a measure of the advantage held by one class over another in the competition to achieve (and avoid) particular class destinations.[7]

The findings reported in the table suggest that, in Britain for example, boys and girls from salariat homes are five or six times more likely to achieve salariat employment (and to avoid working-class destinations) than are their peers who come from working-class backgrounds. The relevant odds ratios are 5.48 (to one) and 6.25 (to one) respectively. Note also, however, that countries which were early industrialized and those which industrialized later appear throughout the table. The same is true of both democratic capitalist and erstwhile state socialist societies. The United States – the capitalist land of opportunity – fares rather badly when compared with some nations comprising the Evil Empire of the former Soviet Union. Mobility between the salariat and the working class in class-ridden and backward-looking Britain turns out to be more or less the same as in corporate and progressive West Germany. As the CASMIN researchers argue, it is hard to see how these figures can be explained in terms of any simple macro-sociological variable, such as 'level of industrial development'.

Table (ii) *Overall social fluidity (beta value) by sex for eleven nations*

Males		Females	
Estonia	−0.49	United States	−0.46
East Germany	−0.35	East Germany	−0.42
Czechoslovakia	−0.30	Russia	−0.26
Russia	−0.21	Estonia	−0.23
Bulgaria	−0.19	Czechoslovakia	−0.15
United States	0.05	Great Britain	−0.09
Poland	0.11	West Germany	0.18
Slovenia	0.15	Poland	0.19
Great Britain	0.25	Bulgaria	0.21
West Germany	0.48	Japan	0.49
Japan	0.50	Slovenia	0.53

Similarly, using some of the now standard modelling techniques developed by mobility researchers, we can order these nations in terms of overall fluidity, separately for each sex, as in Table (ii). The model being tested here is one which uses a very sensitive criterion of openness (explained fully in Chapter 7) to rank countries in terms of their distance from a strict model of common (identical) social fluidity.[8] Among males, Japan and the former West Germany are at one extreme (as the least fluid societies overall), and Estonia is at the other (as the most open). These results are generally consistent with those found in earlier research. For example, they show that British men confront a class structure that is somewhat less open than that found in (say) the United States, and that social fluidity among American men is in turn rather less than among their Russian counterparts. In the case of female mobility, not only the United States but also the former German Democratic Republic appear among the most fluid nations, while both Slovenia and Japan are found to be among the most closed.

Remember, however, that these are *minor* differences when set against the background of a 'basic similarity' in fluidity. Still, they do illustrate the point that it is hard to decipher any obvious pattern in such variation as does occur across nations, and it is by no means the case that the most advanced capitalist societies are uniformly more open than their post-communist neighbours. It does seem likely, therefore, that the differences between nations are to be explained by some combination of modest historical particulars – rather than in terms of an overarching sociological theory about the supposed logic of societal development.

Recent academic and public controversy about issues of social justice has also added a new twist to the debate. Clearly, the evidence from social mobility studies indicates a substantial association between class origins and destinations, and one that is largely stable across both countries and time. Can we therefore conclude that these are unjust societies? Does information about class disparities in the likelihood of social mobility license inferences about inequality of opportunity?

Some, like the authors of the Oxford study (see Goldthorpe, 1980: 252), have concluded that the persistent variation in mobility chances among individuals from different social origins points to inequalities of opportunity that are rooted in class structures. In other words, we can assume that class differentials in the propensity for mobility and immobility are not simply the result of the uneven exploitation of equal opportunities by individuals having distinctive abilities or talents, perhaps because of genetic or moral qualities that are unrelated to their social origins. Others, such as Peter Saunders (1990a: 51, 82–3) in Britain or Richard Herrnstein and Charles Murray (1994: 25–115) in the United States, have argued in reply that, since mobility researchers have tended not to gather evidence about the abilities of those whose occupational trajectories they examine, this can indeed only be a presumption. It is therefore possible that unequal mobility chances and unchanging social fluidity reflect instead the simple fact that talent is unequally distributed, with the most gifted people tending to rise to the highest social positions, and passing on their (perhaps genetic) endowments to their children. Justice as meritocracy, and equality of opportunity, are from this point of view quite consistent with the evidence on class mobility regimes.

This critique suggests that, before they can reasonably conclude that these societies are indeed unjust, researchers must examine data, not only on people's origins and destinations, but also on their relevant 'merits'. There is no other way to tell whether the indisputably differing statistical chances of class mobility reflect differing actual chances or merely differences in people's ability to take advantage of what are essentially equal opportunities.

My own research into this issue shows that children from salariat backgrounds are more likely to arrive at salariat destinations than are children whose social origins lie in the working class – even when those children have attained the same level of education. (For the moment I am assuming that educational achievement is a plausible indicator of ability.) One such analysis for Britain, in which Adam Swift and I examined the data from the Essex Class Project of the mid 1980s, is reported in full in Chapter 9. Our results suggest that (for example), at low levels of attainment (up to CSE grade 5), 23 per cent of men and women from salariat origins arrive at salariat destinations, as compared with only 7 per cent of those from working-class backgrounds. Similarly, among people holding medium-level qualifications (such as O levels and A levels), 39 per cent of those from salariat backgrounds themselves achieve salariat destinations, while 20 per cent are downwardly mobile into the working class. The corresponding figures among individuals with working-class origins holding the same educational qualifications are 17 and 36 per cent respectively. Among respondents with university degrees or equivalent professional qualifications, 86 per cent of those from salariat backgrounds arrived at salariat destinations, as compared with 76 per cent who grew up in working-class homes.

Independent research by Anthony Heath and his colleagues, who measure educational attainment with greater refinement, has generated analogous results. Their study also shows that, although the direct effect of social origin on class destination declines marginally between 1973 and 1985, the change is small and not statistically significant (Heath et al., 1991a). Similar findings in relation to what we may call 'trends in educational merit selection' – or, more accurately perhaps, the apparent lack of any trend towards educational merit selection – have also been produced for other industrialized countries as diverse as Ireland, Japan, and the United States.[9]

Class inequalities in the late-twentieth century

All of this research points unambiguously to the same conclusion; namely, that social class exerts a powerful influence on mobility outcomes, and one which shows no signs of having diminished in importance during the course of the twentieth century. In this way, an international network of researchers has transformed our understanding of social inequality, and debunked a series of powerful political myths – of the United States as an 'open society', of 'classless Japan', and of the former communist states as being either particularly fluid or especially closed (depending upon the Cold War ideology being touted at the time). The reality seems to be that, although all industrial nations do not have identical mobility regimes, the distribution of mobility chances within industrialized societies is not only 'basically similar' but also 'basically unchanging'. Whatever else they may be, it seems highly probable that the allegedly novel post-industrial societies of the late twentieth century will also be old-fashioned class societies, at least in so far as inequalities of opportunity are concerned.

The pervasive influence of class on other aspects of life in the advanced industrial world is demonstrated by the research that is summarized in Chapter 2. There, John Goldthorpe and I review the many studies which demonstrate the persistence of class differentials in educational attainment, not only in Britain but elsewhere. We further maintain that the best evidence from studies of voting behaviour, collective identification, and social attitudes and values demonstrates clearly that classes in Britain show no signs of being eroded in terms of either their ideological distinctiveness or their social cohesion. More recently, Goldthorpe (1996a) has reviewed the literature on class and politics in a variety of advanced industrial nations (including the United States, France, Italy and the Netherlands), showing both that the class–vote link retains a good deal of stability (or provides another example of a 'trendless fluctuation') over recent decades and that class retains its force as a factor shaping democratic politics; Evans (1996b) has provided evidence on the growing efficacy of class as a source of inequality and interest formation in post-communist societies; and Heath and Clifford (1996) have updated an earlier study of class inequalities in educational attainment in Britain, confirming that there has been no significant change in class relativities from the 1900–9 birth cohort to the 1960–9 birth cohort, despite such educational reforms as the 1944 Education Act, comprehensive reorganization of the 1960s, raising of the school leaving age to 16 years in 1974, and gradual spread of the Certificate of Secondary Education. (The 1907 Free Place Regulations may have reduced class inequalities in the competition to obtain selective secondary schooling, although this calculation is fraught with methodological difficulties, but it can be said with some confidence that subsequent reforms seem to have had no measurable impact on class relativities.) In earlier publications I also argued that Goldthorpe's particular approach provides a more useful measure of social class differences than do alternative schemes – including that currently utilized by the British government for the purposes of producing official statistics (the Registrar-General's social classes).[10]

One shorthand way of describing this material is to say that the Goldthorpe schema displays an impressive degree of 'construct validity'. It reveals not only statistically significant but also sociologically interesting differences in those dependent variables that one would expect to be class related. This can be illustrated further by looking at another substantive issue that has been drawn increasingly into the debate; namely, that of class inequalities in health, or of (literal) 'life-chances'. Of course, in the case of Britain it has long been recognized that death rates, sickness absence, and a wide range of pathological conditions (including deaths from lung cancer, other cancers, coronary heart disease, cerebrovascular disease, chronic bronchitis, other respiratory diseases, gastrointestinal disease and genitourinary disease) are all associated with social class differences.[11] In recent years, however, the evidence from other advanced societies has become no less compelling.

During the past decade or so, for example, the conventional view that health inequalities in Sweden were a thing of the past has largely been overturned. One series of studies, conducted by Denny Vågerö and his associates, shows that manual working classes perceive their general health to be worse than do nonmanual classes. They also report more symptoms and illness episodes, and have higher mortality in childhood, adult life and retirement, among both men and women. This general pattern of working classes having worse health than others is not entirely invariant. In Sweden, for example, the incidence of cancer is lowest among the farming population, and higher among both the manual and nonmanual classes alike. Nevertheless, in broad terms class mortality chances (however these are measured) tend to be lowest among members of the salariat and highest in the manual working classes, with intermediate classes ranged between these extremes. This holds true across a great variety of cause-specific mortality rates, including ischaemic heart disease, respiratory diseases, accidents and violent deaths. Moreover, there has been a widening of relative class differences in mortality in Sweden among those aged 35–69, in the case of both sexes.[12]

How does this compare with the evidence for other advanced societies? The usual difficulties associated with crossnational studies in other areas tend also to hinder reliable research into health and illness: independent investigators and official government agencies alike have gathered data-sets pertaining to different periods, in dissimilar ways, and for disparate purposes. Despite the problems that this poses for sociological analysis, it does seem safe to conclude that class differentials in adult mortality are smaller in (say) Sweden, Norway and Denmark than in Britain, Finland and France. One inquiry, by Vågerö and Östberg, examined class differences in life-chances among children aged 1 to 14 in Sweden and Britain during the 1960s and 1970s. The authors compare Goldthorpe manual classes against all others – a crude but robust classification that is aimed at minimizing the measurement error in the analysis. They find that the excess risk for the former group, among boys, was 30 per cent in Britain and 25 per cent in Sweden. The corresponding figures among girls were 20 per cent in Britain and 10 per cent in Sweden. In short, recent absolute mortality rates in Sweden have been low in comparison with earlier times and other countries, but relative class differentials remain substantial. Moreover, there is no evidence that these class relativities have declined in Sweden (or indeed elsewhere including Britain) during the course of the twentieth century.[13]

At least one recent inquiry (Bartley et al., 1996) has pursued this issue further, by investigating the relationship between mortality and social class as measured by both the (conventional) Registrar-General's categories and those devised by John Goldthorpe, within the confines of a single study. A cohort analysis of men aged 15/16–64, taken from the Office of Population Censuses and Surveys' Longitudinal Studies for 1971 and 1981 (consisting of an approximate 1 per cent random sample of the population of England and Wales), shows similar class mortality differentials using both classifications in the two periods. For example, in the case of the Registrar-General's categories, the age-adjusted relative risk of death among professionals, skilled nonmanual workers and unskilled manual workers respectively is 0.65, 1.02 and 1.28 for the 1971 cohort. The corresponding figures for the 1981 cohort were found to be 0.66, 0.99 and 1.30. Looked at in terms of Goldthorpe social classes, the results for the earlier cohort are 0.72 (higher salariat), 1.02 (routine clerical workers) and 1.16 (semi-skilled and unskilled manual workers). For the 1981 cohort the corresponding relative risk of death by social class is calculated to be 0.71, 1.00 and 1.18.[14]

The importance of this particular study is not that it demonstrates one measure of social class to be superior to another – at least in the sense of having a 'stronger' relationship to mortality. To the contrary, as the authors of the report themselves acknowledge, it can reasonably be argued that the appropriateness of any summary measure depends upon the purposes for which it is being used. Rather, what is of especial interest here is the clear demonstration that the Goldthorpe classes – which are rooted in a theory about the importance of such employment characteristics as the nature of the labour contract, career structure, and security of tenure – reveal mortality patterns showing that these aspects of the work situation and labour-market experience are significantly related to certain types of health risk, despite the fact that this class scheme was itself designed without reference to health outcomes. Since one acknowledged weakness of the Registrar-General's categories (at least as a vehicle for the study of inequalities in public health) is that they were designed precisely in order to display social gradients in mortality risk, what we have here is then a clear demonstration that important differences in mortality by social class do not in fact rely upon the use of the Registrar-General's classification, which in turn suggests that these class differentials are real rather than merely artefactual.

Moreover, as we shall see shortly, because we know what it is that the Goldthorpe classes are measuring (aspects of the work situation and of the contract between employer and employee) we can begin to construct causal narratives which specify the intervening variables that link social class locations to particular health outcomes. What *precisely* is it about the work situation that forms a pathway between social class and (let us say) a relatively higher risk of heart disease? Readers who are familiar with the history of the Registrar-General's classification will know that it does not facilitate this sort of aetiological interrogation, because its categories represent a largely commonsensical grouping of occupational titles into classes, supposedly on the basis of 'level of occupational skill' (although an earlier justification refers to the principle of 'general standing in the community'). Given this widely acknowledged ambiguity about what the schema actually measures, it has proved difficult to move beyond the demonstration of mere association, and to develop causal explanations of those social differences and trends in health outcomes to which the classification itself points. One further achievement of the class analysis research programme during the past two decades has been a growing convergence upon a measurement device (the Goldthorpe classification) that promises precisely this opportunity for aetiological analysis.

Postmodernism, reflexive modernity and other unconvincing critiques

This brief sketch does little more than outline a still developing but already substantial body of research that demonstrates the failure of post-war social policy in almost all industrial nations to achieve its declared aim of diminishing class differentials in distributive outcomes. These studies point consistently to the conclusion that social class remains an axial principle for the organization of social inequality and social integration in advanced societies.

Of course, this reasoning has not gone unchallenged, and some prominent critics have nevertheless insisted that class is a declining if not yet wholly spent social force. They maintain that the concept itself is largely irrelevant to the sociological understanding of the contemporary industrialized world, and that its continued use in research is to be attributed mainly to the failure of class analysts to confront the exhaustion of their paradigm, probably for reasons of political partisanship.

Much of this sceptical material is summarized in Chapters 1 and 2. An early version of the argument surfaced in the various accounts of embourgeoisement that were offered during the 1950s. On that occasion, class differences were deemed to have been abolished because manual workers were supposedly aspiring to a middle-class standard and style of life, and espousing middle-class values and norms. Twenty years later, during the recessionary 1970s and 1980s, arguments for affluence and assimilation seemed less convincing than those that emphasized social exclusion and sectionalism. In this version of events, the demise of class was seemingly no less obvious, but was rooted not in a consensus about an established social order but rather in new forms of distributional conflict – the unemployed as against employees, families trapped in economically depressed regions as compared with those enjoying buoyant labour markets, home-owners versus residents in public housing, and so forth. I have discussed both of these literatures at length elsewhere, and can see no virtue in repeating myself here, especially in view of the mass of contrary evidence (showing that class retains its social and sociological importance) that has been accrued during the past decade.[15] However, another variation on the familiar theme that class analysis is a bankrupt enterprise has now been advanced in the wake of arguments about postmodernity and reflexive modernization, and since these are a relatively recent innovation they perhaps require separate comment.

Postmodernist social theory is notoriously fragmented. A concise summary cannot easily be devised.[16] However, in whatever guise it appears, postmodernity implies the disintegration of modernist symbolic orders. It denies the existence of all 'universals', including the philosophy of the transcendental self, on the grounds that the discourse and referential categories of modernity (the subject, community, the state, use value, social class and so forth) are no longer appropriate to the description of disorganized capitalism.[17] According to one leading authority, for example, the postmodern condition represents the demise of the Enlightenment narratives of rationality, progress, liberation, truth and justice, and the consequent 'atomization' of the social into flexible networks of 'language games'. This is a new culture of 'paralogy' – of imagination, inventiveness, dissensus, the search for paradox, toleration of the incommensurable, and above all else of 'incredulity toward metanarratives' (see Lyotard, 1986). Postmodernism is therefore characterized by, as Bryan Turner (1990: 250) puts it, 'a pluralisation of life-worlds' resulting from 'the complex differentiation of societies'. Its most conspicuous features are 'variety, contingency and ambivalence', the 'permanent and irreducible *pluralism* of cultures, communal traditions, ideologies, "forms of life" or "language games"' (Bauman, 1992: 102, 187).

At this abstract level the concrete implications of the theory for class analysis may be somewhat opaque, but (fortunately) these have been spelled out clearly and at some length, most notably in a series of critical essays by Jan Pakulski and others.[18] These authors maintain that, even under organized capitalism, the various class categories begin to decompose and fragment, as social inequalities come progressively to be structured more by patterns of consumption than production. This results, in the later stages of capitalism, in a 'hypercommodification of products in which they are consumed not in terms of use values but in terms of their semiotic capacity to establish unequal relationships'; and then, under conditions of postmodernity, in a 'simulation of multiple and cross-cutting identities which are situated in equally multiple "imagined communities" . . . membership of [which] is a function of taste, choice and commitment [so that] the categories are therefore fluid in relation to one another and indeterminate at the boundaries' (Crook et al., 1992: 222).

Nowadays, therefore, we are experiencing a process whereby 'classes are dissolving and the most advanced societies are no longer class societies.' One allegedly obvious aspect of this change is 'an attenuation of the class identities, class ideologies, and class organizations that framed West European corporatist politics in the middle of the century'. Equally, 'the communal aspects of class, class subcultures and milieus, have long since disappeared.' The decomposition of economic class mechanisms, though perhaps proceeding more slowly, is steadily being accomplished via 'the wide redistribution of property; the proliferation of indirect and small ownership; the credentialization of skills and the professionalization of occupations; the multiple segmentation and globalization of markets; and an increasing role for consumption as a status and lifestyle generator' (Pakulski and Waters, 1996: 4). In this way, according to Pakulski and his colleagues, we have arrived at a social condition and at forms of everyday life that are the very antithesis of a class society.

Ulrich Beck's (1992) celebrated account of so-called reflexive modernization is widely regarded as a critique of postmodernist social theory. (He argues that the perverse and dysfunctional effects of rationalization for social life can be understood and managed through a 'radicalization of rationality' rather than its negation.) Beck nevertheless predicts a similar future for class and class analysis. He argues that reflexive modernity – an intermingling of continuity and discontinuity that is evident, for example, in the critique of science developed by the Green movement – dissolves those 'forms of the *conscience collective*' (not only class culture and consciousness but also gender and family roles) 'on which depend and to which refer the social and political organizations and institutions in industrial society'. The notion of a class society remains useful, therefore, only as an image of the past – and because we have not yet found a more appropriate label for the current more complex reality (1992: 87, 91).

More specifically, according to Beck, during the 1950s 'the unstable unity of shared life experiences mediated by the market and shaped by status, which Max Weber brought together in the concept of social class, began to break apart. Its different elements (such as material conditions dependent upon specific market opportunities, the effectiveness of tradition and of precapitalist lifestyles, the consciousness of communal bonds and of barriers to mobility, as well as networks of contact) have slowly disintegrated.' This 'individualization of social inequality' means that, 'under the conditions of a welfare state, class biographies, which are somehow ascribed, become transformed into reflexive biographies which depend on the decisions of the actor.' Increasingly, therefore, everyone must take the risk of choosing between a huge array of disparate social identities, lifestyles, opinions, and groups or subcultures. Attachments to social classes become weaker, people are separated from the traditional support networks provided by family or neighbourhood, and work loses its importance as a focus of conflict and identity formation. Ascribed differences – of ethnicity, gender, age and nationality – provide the basis for new lifestyles and self-conceptions that replace class solidarities. In Marxist terms, this is capitalism without classes, but with new and still emerging forms of differentiation and inequality (1992: 91–101).

Naturally, I would argue (citing the empirical studies discussed in earlier sections of this chapter) that these new pronouncements of the death of social class are no less premature than were their predecessors, and would predict that this critique (since it consists largely of what one might not unreasonably call 'data-free sociology') will ultimately succumb to the same weight of evidence as falsified the earlier theories of embourgeoisement and recessionary sectionalism. In this context it is perhaps worth noting that even outside observers who are not unsympathetic have been compelled to comment upon the resolutely programmatic nature of much of the postmodernist project in social theory.[19]

More obviously, one can point to the numerous ways in which this latest generation of critics misrepresents the evidence in order to substantiate their arguments, on those occasions when factual information is entertained. For example, in their account of *The Death of Class*, Pakulski and Waters (1996: 34) underline the claim that 'the notion of "consumption sectors" is proving remarkably attractive both in empirical analyses of political attitudes and in further theorizing the salience of consumption, lifestyle and taste' by referring the reader to Peter Saunders's work on the social and cultural implications of the division between privatized and collectivized modes of housing. This rather conveniently overlooks the fact that Saunders himself (1990b: 242–3), after an exhaustive analysis of the impact of consumption sectoral locations and housing tenure on political mobilization in Britain, was forced to reject his own hypothesis and concluded 'that the critics of consumption and tenure theories of voting are correct and that the erosion of the class basis of electoral politics has been exaggerated'. In sum, as he puts it, 'class remains the key variable associated with voting.' Similarly, Pakulski and Waters (1996: 48) point to the recognized social class differences in height at the beginning of this century (working-class boys in London and Glasgow were on average 2.5 inches shorter than their middle-class contemporaries), and insist (although no evidence is cited in support of this claim) that we are witnessing 'an amelioration of these dramatic inequalities'. In fact, however, research shows clearly that the difference in average height between the working and middle classes in Britain is still around two inches (rather more than this if Scottish and London regional effects are also taken into account), and that this gap is established largely before the age of 7 (compare Mascie-Taylor, 1990: 135–9). Nor is it true to assert, as these critics do, that 'the distribution and acquisition of education have become increasingly autonomous relative to class location' (Pakulski and Waters, 1996: 45). On the contrary, as a host of studies in a range of industrial nations has repeatedly confirmed, class differentials in educational attainment display a truly remarkable degree of temporal stability (compare, for example, Blossfeld and Shavit, 1992).

These illustrations confirm that the postmodernist critique of class analysis has largely detached itself from empirical reality. Much of the argument proceeds by mere assertion alone. Conceptual confusions also abound. Pakulski and Waters's text again provides a plentiful supply of examples. It is difficult to know how to respond to a critique of class analysis which manages to reverse the FJH hypothesis, so that it becomes a claim that 'while . . . the overall pattern of mobility is similar in industrialized Western societies, relative mobility rates vary' (1996: 51). Nor is it true that class analysts in general (and John Goldthorpe and I in particular) have ignored gender inequalities and the implications of increased female participation in employment. This charge is hard to reconcile with the protracted debates about the unit of class composition (individual or family?) in which we and others have been extensively involved. My own views on this matter are made clear in Chapters 5 and 8. The larger point that seems to have escaped the attention of our critics on this matter is that class analysis is precisely that: it is the study of the relationships between class structures, class mobility, class inequalities and class action. This neither precludes investigation of other forms of social stratification nor makes any assumptions whatsoever about their importance in relation to social class (compare Pakulski and Waters, 1996: 26, 40–3).

At this point, one is tempted simply to conclude that all pretence at conducting social science has been abandoned, and (to be fair to postmodernism) this may be entirely what its proponents intend. If postmodernity does indeed entail 'the final erosion of boundaries between the knowledges and practices of science and those of other domains', then it follows that the truth claims of social science 'enjoy no guaranteed salience or guaranteed cognitive privilege', that 'sociology is quite free to tell what stories it likes about change or any other matter', and that 'these stories are part of a more general economy of discourse in which they must fight to find an audience and establish a salience in competition with other stories, and in the absence of guarantees' (Crook et al., 1992: 223, 238). In other words sociology has the same epistemological status as do (say) New Age beliefs in reincarnation. However, if we are expected to take this critique seriously, then we must be clear that it commits us irrevocably to the world of the cultural madhouse. We should also recall that when the resolution of language games is linked solely to the exercise of power, then the result is invariably a totalitarianism in which the definitions that stick belong to those who wield the biggest stick, and in earlier times this has included both the Church and the Party. No class analyst – at least outside of orthodox Marxist-Leninism – has ever pursued his or her truth claims with quite such intransigence.

Attempts to document the fragmentation of identities and pluralization of lifestyles that are associated with the supposedly new reflexive forms of modernity are scarcely more convincing. Possibly the most sustained of these – Harriet Bradley's *Fractured Identities* – amounts to not much more than a lengthy restatement of the truism that 'class, gender, "race", ethnicity and age . . . refer to different aspects of lived social relationships, although they interweave together to produce an integrated structure of inequality' (1996: 20). For example, no class analyst would be surprised to be told that 'racialized minority members in Britain and America are likely to be disproportionately concentrated in working-class locations', or that 'age is both an important aspect of individual identity and of more transient but recurrent generational conflicts' (1996: 139, 177). However, they might well ask what critical implications these observations are intended to convey for *class* analysis, especially since the empirical material that Bradley cites in order to illustrate precisely how the various dimensions of stratification are interwoven in particular instances tends mainly to underline the continuing salience of class itself.[20]

The argument that societies are becoming more fragmented and identities more fluid seems also to be in large part programmatic and rhetorical. To suggest, as Bradley does (1996: 78, 112), that 'the lived relations of gender are complex and volatile, operating at all levels of society', or that we 'need to develop a more adequate and multi-dimensional theory of gendered power, which may be used to integrate the discussion of the diverse aspects of gendered reality', or that 'research needs to be done to ascertain exactly how class meanings and identities relate to other aspects of social identi- fication', is scarcely to make a compelling case for believing that social life has taken a more reflexive form in contemporary societies – far less for concluding that such reflexivity is systematically undermining social class differences and processes. Ironically, Bradley herself recognizes that 'accounts employing concepts such as multiple identities and focusing on consumption, mass media and information technologies move beyond economism, but remain at the level of speculation and assertion. Post- modernism offers the promise of a plural account of inequality which it has not yet fulfilled' (1996: 43). One can only add that it is hard to see why this conclusion should not be extended to include the various pronouncements of reflexive modernity itself.

New directions in the class analysis programme

I have argued that the class analysis programme of research, as this is explained in Chapter 2, has transformed our understanding of social inequality in advanced societies during the past twenty or so years. What then should be the direction for future study in this area? Here, I would make only two suggestions, the first of which (if acted upon) would greatly facilitate pursuit of the second.

The former concerns the question of how we differentiate between the various social classes. A number of observers have pointed out that, especially in view of the increasingly widespread use of the Goldthorpe schema as a research instrument in crossnational comparative analysis, we should seek additional guarantees of its internal (or criterion) validity as a measure of the class characteristics of occupations (see, for example, Savage et al., 1992: ch. 1; Baxter et al., 1991: ch. 4). The theoretical basis of the scheme itself is clear enough and was explained above: it aims to distinguish class positions in terms of the employment relations they entail. The outstanding issues are operational rather than conceptual.

Specialists will know that, in translating their theory about the importance of the labour contract and conditions of employment into concrete research practice, Goldthorpe and his colleagues generally refer to an individual's occupational title (for example electrician or lawyer) and employment status (self-employed with employees, manager in large establishment, and so forth) as indicators of (or proxies for) the market situation and work situation characteristics that are central to the classification. When devising this procedure, in the first instance for the purposes of the Oxford Social Mobility Project, they allocated an appropriate class standing to each combination of occupational title and employment status 'in the light of the available information from official statistics, monographic sources etc., regarding the typical market and work situations of the individuals comprised: e.g. on levels of income, other monetary and non-monetary benefits, degree of economic security, chances of economic advancement, and location in systems of authority and control' (Goldthorpe and Payne, 1986: 21). This information was naturally of uneven quality and in any case is now some twenty years old. It is true that the algorithm for creating the class categories from occupational titles and employment status information has been revised periodically during the interim. Nevertheless, the relative lack of systematic contemporary evidence about employment relations, yielding data which could routinely inform the process of updating the algorithm, does tend to create, as Geoffrey Evans (1992: 212) has put it, a 'methodological lacuna' that, in the long run at least, is potentially damaging from the point of view of preserving the validity of the schema as a measure of social class.

Evans himself has conducted an exhaustive validity test which shows that the scheme, as currently constituted, is indeed highly predictive of the characteristics that are central to Goldthorpe's concept of class; namely, employment and payment conditions, authority relations, levels of pay, and control over work activities. Using survey data for Britain, collected by myself and my colleagues as part of the Essex Class Project, Evans examines the association between Goldthorpe class and some eighteen separate items describing the regulation of work, including security of employment, supervisory responsibilities, routes to increased pay, rules governing attendance at the workplace, control over work tasks, and salary guarantees. The results show unambiguously that class membership is strongly predictive of these characteristics; or, as Evans (1992: 227) concludes, that 'the substantial association between class and indicators of a service relationship versus a labour contract confirms empirically the main distinction embodied in the schema.' The analysis also verifies that the various aggregation procedures adopted for collapsing the class categories do not reduce the validity of the shorter versions of the classification, and provides substantial evidence to support its use as a valid measure of class position for both women and men alike (1992: 226; 1996a: 209).

But the Essex data themselves relate to the mid 1980s. More recently, the development of so-called flexible labour markets and post-Fordist organizations is thought by some observers to have had a major impact on the regulation of employment (at least in Britain and the United States), for example by encouraging firms to hire even professional staff on short-term contracts offering non-standard terms (such as reduced entitlement to pensions), payment according to results, and greatly diminished levels of discretion or autonomy at work. In other words, the relatively advantaged conditions of employment that characterize the service relationship are perhaps being diluted, as managerial and higher-administrative occupations come increasingly to be governed by labour contracts that embody the short-term and specific exchange of effort for money (see Brown and Scase, 1994). There is some evidence to support these arguments (much of it anecdotal rather than sociological), although some also suggests that the supposed impact of flexible employment on actual conditions of work has been greatly exaggerated, and is certainly uneven across the industrially advanced nations. (For an overview see Procter et al., 1994.) However, if indeed it could be shown that the move from bureaucratic to adaptive forms of work organization had taken place on a large scale and with the consequences that have been claimed for changing employment relations, then one would also have to examine whether or not classes could still reliably be distinguished according to such criteria as forms of remuneration, opportunities for promotion, and autonomy (especially as regards the use of time) at work. In any event, it would clearly be useful to obtain confirmation that these are robust indicators, which continue to discriminate between the classes as effectively now as they demonstrably have done in the past.

This is not merely a technical issue about the finer points of operationalizing a social-scientific concept in the field. One of the recognized advantages of the Goldthorpe schema (especially as compared with, say, the Registrar-General's class categories) is that we know what it is that the classification is measuring. This brings me neatly to my second suggestion, which is that class researchers should now embrace Richard Breen and David Rottman's advice (1995b: 467) to 'hypothesize and test a number of different intervening variables that would represent alternative mechanisms linking class and outcome'; or, in other words, to pursue more vigorously the issue of constructing explanatory causal narratives within the class analysis programme.

An impressive start has already been made in this direction. For example, in the area of health and illness, there is epidemiological evidence to support the idea that autonomy and control at work are important factors in the aetiology of heart disease. What has been called the 'effort–reward imbalance' – a work situation involving high demands but with low career prospects, job security, and financial reward – may also be implicated here. Similarly, reductions in opportunities for career advancement and differences in control over work have been linked to a number of other adverse consequences for health, and some studies show that pension rights may be important in explaining mortality differentials among adult and retired men and women from different class backgrounds.[21]

In one analysis that offers a model for future investigators, Evans (1993) has attempted to explain the association between social class and political preferences by regressing voting intention on to both aspects of social class itself and also a wide variety of other structural variables, such as welfare dependency, home ownership and education. He demonstrates convincingly that class predicts political preferences in expected ways and that a substantial proportion of the class effect can be traced to the individual's promotion prospects. Differences in left–right partisanship are primarily the result of class differences in expectations concerning future occupational rewards (although this role diminishes over time, so that among older respondents, it is one's present rather than anticipated rewards that are important). In Evans's judgement, this finding reinforces the emphasis that Goldthorpe places on the prospective elements of the service relationship, such as having assurances of security both in employment and (through pension rights) in retirement, salary increments on an established scale, and well-defined career opportunities (compare Erikson and Goldthorpe, 1992a: 41–2).

A number of studies have also examined alternative explanations for the persisting class differentials in educational attainment. One interpretation, originating broadly within the tradition of rational action theory, suggests that, because of the dissimilar opportunities and constraints facing children from working-class and middle-class backgrounds, they (and their parents) are involved in different calculations of the possible costs and benefits of particular educational strategies. As children reach distinct transition points in the educational system, families must make choices (for example, to encourage sons and daughters to leave school or stay on, or to take vocational rather than academic courses) that are influenced by the structural constraints arising from the relationship between their different class origins and the destinations they envisage for their offspring. From this point of view, aspirations (say) to attend university on the part of working-class children are rather more ambitious than would be those same desires when expressed by their middle-class peers, and also involve the increased risks implied by the attempt to travel a greater social distance. Any tendency among working-class children to pursue less demanding courses of study, or to obtain more modest qualifications and credentials, might therefore be the result of a rational evaluation of the probable gains and losses to be made from different educational strategies.

Thus, for some skilled working-class families containing bright children, the best option might appear to be a vocational course leading to a skilled manual job, offering relatively high initial wages, a fairly low risk of relegation into the ranks of the unskilled or unemployed, and a high probability of early promotion to a supervisory position – rather than an academic course, requiring not only continued investment in the child's education, but also investment of a more hazardous kind (since downward mobility is perceived to be a likely consequence of a failed attempt to obtain academic qualifications). By comparison, middle-class families confronting the same decision about the future of their children would perhaps be more likely to choose the more ambitious option, since they have access to greater resources that might mitigate against the consequences of educational failure – for example the ability to purchase extra tuition, or links into personal networks that could offer direct access to the labour market at a reasonably attractive level, despite the lack of formal qualifications.[22]

What these otherwise diverse studies have in common is that they embody the sorts of multivariate analyses that are required in order to determine how the effects of class are mediated by specific intervening variables. As John Goldthorpe and I note in Chapter 2, replying to some of the critics of class analysis, no one would suppose that the proximate causes of voting for a particular political party, of failure to achieve certain educational credentials, and of contracting a specific type of respiratory disease are the same. But, in so far as causal links can be traced back from each of these outcomes, via intervening variables, to the location of individuals or families in disadvantaged class positions, then the importance of class is enhanced by this unravelling of the different causal narratives involved. The evidence is not yet compelling, but these and other similar studies have tended – thus far at least – simply to underline the importance of class in modern societies, and they strike me as being rather more convincing in this respect than have been the many recent critiques of the class analysis programme.

A summary of chapter contents

What then are the specific arguments that I and my co-authors make in the following chapters?

Part I of the book describes a research agenda for class analysis and explains its relationship to studies of social stratification more generally. Chapter 1 challenges the widely held view that novel and fundamental changes in the structure of social hierarchy have altered the basis of distributional conflict in modern Britain. By looking back to the nineteenth century we can see that sectionalism, egoism, and privatism are not peculiar to the modern era. It is then argued that commentators on both the political left and right have oversimplified the relationship between the distributional order of societies on the one hand, and the specific forms taken by distributional conflict on the other. This means that the implications of the lack of a capitalist *Sittlichkeit* (morality or moral order) for social integration may be quite different from those commonly drawn by many prominent social theorists.

Chapter 2 then acknowledges that the research programme of class analysis has been criticized from a variety of standpoints, but argues that much of this criticism is misplaced, and that the promise of class analysis is far from exhausted. The first part of the chapter clarifies the nature and purpose of class analysis, which are often misunderstood by its critics, and in particular distinguishes the modern enterprise from the class analysis of Marxist sociology. The second part then makes the case for the continuing relevance of class analysis by reviewing findings from three central areas of current research.

Some care is taken, in making these arguments, to distinguish social classes from status groups. It will be clear that I disagree with those such as Witz who argue that 'the very nature of contemporary occupational change and mobility regimes, as well as of patterns of family/household formation, seems to defy sociological attempts to differentiate cleanly between "class" and "gender" processes' (1995: 56). On the contrary, the advent of loglinear techniques has made it possible for the first time to identify how (if at all) and to what extent social class does or does not interact empirically with the conceptually distinct status attributes of gender or ethnicity, as I attempt to show elsewhere in this volume. It is for this reason that I would disagree with the suggestion, made in broadly the same terms by Bradley and by Pakulski and Waters, that class analysis is somehow inherently flawed because it does not incorporate ('theorize') gender and ethnicity as part of a *class* analysis programme. This also explains why I am not much attracted by the alternative social classification devised by Blackburn, Prandy and their colleagues in Cambridge, since the scale of 'social advantage' that they have constructed purports to indicate both class and status simultaneously in a single scale score, thus sacrificing conceptual precision and explanatory power for the dubious methodological gains that are said to accrue from measurement using a continuous variable (compare Marsh and Blackburn, 1992: 188–9).

Of course, matters of method and measurement loom large in contemporary class analysis, and rightly so. One of the major achievements of researchers in this field during the past twenty years has been to improve dramatically the quality of data, for example by paying more attention to the apparently mundane concerns of coding, and the standardizing of data-collection procedures and protocols. Another has been the development of new statistical techniques for the analysis of cross-tabulated data, notably those associated with loglinear analysis, which have facilitated theoretical innovation by allowing for the isolation and study of complex interaction effects between variables. The chapters in Part II discuss a range of such methodological issues.

Chapter 3 extends some of the findings of the Essex Class Project, specifically in relation to class structure and socio-political class formation, and relates these to comparable studies in Sweden and the United States. It raises conceptual, operational, and substantive problems with regard to the neo-Marxist class theory of Erik Olin Wright by contrasting his class schema, which forms the principal comparative tool for the studies in question, with an alternative in which routine clerical workers are distinguished from proletarians. As I have argued elsewhere (see, for example, Marshall et al., 1988: ch. 3), those of us involved in the Essex project undoubtedly shared Wright's interest in crossnational differences in the overall shape of class structures, but we were never convinced that these could be explained in terms of systematic variation in one (or a very few) sociological variables (rather than historically) – especially when, as this chapter seeks to make clear, serious doubts could be entertained about the reliability of the class-mapping exercise itself.[23]

Chapter 4 addresses the popular argument that the research programme of class analysis is undermined by its apparent neglect of large numbers of economically inactive adults who are not included within the empirical studies, but are affected by class processes, and form distinctive elements within any class structure. It disputes the claim that welfare dependants, the retired, and domestic housekeepers show distinctive patterns of socio-political class formation. In part, therefore, the chapter is a response to the feminist critique of class analysis. However, it also seeks to address a quite separate issue about social exclusion, by demonstrating that the class-related attributes of the supposed underclass are not so distinct that this group requires separate treatment in a class analysis. Evidence to support the orthodox strategy of sampling economically active men and women is taken from the International Social Justice Project (ISJP) sample surveys of adults in Britain and the United States.

Chapter 5 reviews three further and interconnected issues that have been central to the controversial problem of describing the relationship between class and gender. The first is the matter of taxonomy, and whether or not extant class schemes are suitable for the study of women's employment. The second is the question of how sex segregation in the occupational structure relates to regimes of class inequality and class mobility; more specifically, of the nature of the connections between absolute mobility rates and relative mobility chances. The third is the attempt to identify the unit of class composition, in particular the so-called asymmetry hypothesis concerning the pattern of relationships among the class positions of spouses and the attributes that are said to comprise socio-political class formation. The chapter argues that the last of these provides the most important strand to the debate, and presents new crossnational data on the relationships between class identities, voting behaviour, and the social class standing of male and female partners. The findings for advanced capitalist societies support the conventional view that the unit of class composition is the household. However, those for post-communist states are contrary to conventional expectations, suggesting that processes of socio-political class formation may be different in East and West.

Issues of social mobility more generally are addressed in the chapters comprising Part III. Four different versions of the thesis of proletarianization in the class structures of advanced societies are identified in Chapter 6. These are then tested empirically against the class mobility experiences of a representative sample of men and women in Britain. An appropriate shift-share analysis confirms that, though there are some differences between the sexes, a net upgrading rather than a degrading of the class structure has occurred. On these grounds the thesis of proletarianization is rejected as it applies in this country. Because of the limitations of the data, the specific argument about deskilling of particular types of job is not pursued in this chapter, although it is worth noting that studies elsewhere provide no support for the deskilling thesis (see, for example, Gallie, 1994a).

Occupational and class mobility data for Britain will in part reflect the fact that this was the first industrialized capitalist society. Chapter 7 again looks at male and female social mobility – but this time in the context of the oldest industrial communist power. Until the researchers from the ISJP conducted their survey of Russia, little was known about patterns of intergenerational social mobility in the former Soviet Union, since extant studies were unrepresentative or methodologically problematic. Using data from the ISJP national samples, this chapter examines absolute mobility rates for each sex, and relative rates for Russia in relation to Britain. It argues that, contrary to the conclusions reached by many Soviet sociologists during the communist era, Russia was not a 'remarkably open' society. Relative mobility chances were in fact rather similar to those found in Britain. Even more strikingly, perhaps, this conclusion is little undermined when educational attainment is taken into account.

Chapter 8 then weaves together the themes of mobility and gender by examining the implications of intergenerational social mobility among women for processes of socio-political class formation. I have already noted (in relation to the contents of Chapter 5) that the asymmetry hypothesis is central to the controversy about the unit of class composition. It is argued by those who support a conventional approach to class analysis that marital partners themselves recognize that it is the occupational position of the husband that confers status on the household in modern industrial societies. This chapter confirms that the conventional approach better explains observed patterns of socio-political class formation among partnered females in Britain than does an alternative individualist strategy. However, the recent suggestion that this household composition effect can be attributed mainly to intergenerational class processes is shown to be unwarranted, irrespective of the degree of labour-market participation among women. These findings are based on pooled data obtained from three large-scale social surveys. In a limited way, they illustrate the type of multivariate research that now needs to be done, in order to establish which intervening variables and mechanisms link social classes to particular causal (in this case socio-political) outcomes.

Finally, in Part IV, I examine the implications of social class for social justice. As was noted above, this is one of the newest and most controversial debates in class analysis, and at the time of writing is the research issue in which I am most heavily involved (see, for example, Marshall and Swift, 1996).

Chapter 9 poses the issue of distributive justice in terms of the relationship between social class, social mobility and educational attainment in contemporary Britain. Having discussed various conceptions of justice which might vindicate class inequality, it investigates empirically the specifically meritocratic defence, and reports survey data suggesting that the effect of class origins on class destinations is only partially mediated by educational achievement. Class privilege can compensate for educational failure. Gender is also significant since women tend to fare worse than men with similar class origins and credentials. It concludes that this evidence tends to undermine the claim that Britain is a meritocratic society; and, further, that it supports the suggestion that only by political intervention can equality of opportunity be rendered compatible with significant and structured inequality of outcome.

Chapter 10 then considers this issue in a crossnational context by analysing social inequality in the former Federal and Democratic Republics of Germany. Social policy in the GDR reflected a conflict between egalitarian and meritocratic conceptions of justice. Against this background, I attempt to determine whether or not half a century of communism reduced class inequalities of opportunity in East Germany, relative to those in the Federal Republic. The study of social mobility data suggests that little progress was made towards achieving this goal. I also argue that attitudinal data indicate that the perceived failure of the East German authorities to create a more open society may have exacerbated the problem of regime legitimation. This chapter was first presented as a conference paper, at a symposium held to celebrate the career of David Lockwood, and I hope that, in some measure, it reflects his enthusiasm for comparative studies of social inequality and social integration.

Of course this is not all that there is to the study of social class. Surveying the field in the mid 1990s, Rosemary Crompton (1995: 59-60) could detect no fewer than three 'levels of class analysis', only one of which (the so-called 'employment-aggregate approach') is represented here. I offer no historical analyses of social change (in the manner of, say, Edward

Thompson's studies of the eighteenth-century working class), and no contemporary case-studies of specific groups, along the lines of Howard
Newby's research into the 'deferential' farm worker. Undoubtedly, as with
the employment-aggregate approach itself, some such investigations
illuminate the processes of demographic and socio-political class formation;
others (if I may mix my metaphors) simply muddy the water. There are
versions of class analysis from which I would positively wish to be
disassociated. I do not think, for example, that there is much to be gained
by phenomenological or cultural approaches that define classes in terms of
the discourse of social movements, especially when every public issue (such
as that of preserving the environment) is 'theorized' to be 'in the last
instance shaped by class politics', a stance which characterizes all forms of
collective action as – by definition – 'potential class conflicts' (compare
Eder, 1993: 191). But this is not the occasion on which to review the entire
field critically. The following chapters may contribute to only one version
of the class analysis programme, but it is that version which has proved
most illuminating during these past two decades, and shows greatest
promise for further sociological understanding of the processes by which
social class inequalities are likely to be perpetuated in the advanced
societies of the twenty-first century.

Notes

1 Because of its complex genealogy, this class scheme has variously been described in the
literature as the Goldthorpe, EGP (Erikson-Goldthorpe-Portocarero) and CASMIN
(Comparative Analysis of Social Mobility in Industrial Nations) typology. The original
schema (indicated by the roman numerals in the left-hand column of Table 4.1) was designed
by Goldthorpe for the Oxford Social Mobility Study of England and Wales in 1972. In the late
1970s, an expanded version was produced (by Goldthorpe, working together with Robert
Erikson and Lucienne Portocarero), specifically for a crossnational comparative analysis
involving France and Sweden. A number of the classes were subdivided, mainly to allow for
important differences in the relations of employment governing workers in the agricultural
sector, of whom there were relatively large proportions in these other societies (at least in
relation to Britain). However, as crossnational comparison was extended, it became necessary
for pragmatic purposes to collapse some of the categories. These are the so-called CASMIN
classes (see the right-hand column of Table 4.1). For example, it was not possible to
differentiate reliably between the upper and lower elements of the salariat in all cases, given
the quality of the data-sets available to the researchers. Likewise, skilled workers (class VI)
could not always be distinguished from supervisors (class V), and in some countries there was
inadequate information on whether or not self-employed workers had employees (so that
classes IVa and IVb had also to be combined). In Britain, the conventional terminology for all
instantiations of the scheme is 'Goldthorpe classes', and at the risk of offending Goldthorpe's
collaborators I have followed this usage in the chapters that follow. I also explain, as the need
arises, why particular versions of the classification have been adopted for specific analyses.

2 For practical reasons large employers are also placed in this class. Erikson and
Goldthorpe (1992a: 40–1) have explained their reasoning on this issue at some length. They
argue that a randomly selected national sample of respondents – of the type that forms the
basis for most empirical studies of class inequality and social mobility – is not an appropriate
strategy for investigating top industrialists. Very few such individuals will be selected for
analysis in even the largest of surveys. Moreover, those few large proprietors that are selected

are typically the owners of garages, hotels, transportation firms and suchlike, rather than the captains of industry and finance. They are therefore included in the service class, not because of their entrepreneurial activities, but because proprietors of such businesses tend also to be extensively involved in management. In this respect, they are rather similar to salaried managers, many of whom also have shares in the ownership of the enterprises in which they are employed. Finally, the distinction between employee, self-employed and employer is at this relatively privileged level often rather ambiguous and sometimes merely formal, being artificially induced for reasons of legal or fiscal convenience. In short, even if it were possible to identify genuinely large employers accurately, their numbers would be too small to allow separate study in a class analysis of this type.

3 See also, for example, Jones et al. (1994), Ishida (1993: ch. 6) and Goldthorpe (1995).

4 This is a point that social scientists across the political spectrum often fail to grasp, when they enthusiastically endorse what they take to be an unequal but fair form of society (for example a 'meritocracy'), but without examining the implications of unchanging class inequalities of outcome for their arguments in favour of enhanced equality of opportunity. See, for example, the recent accounts in Wooldridge (1995) and Saunders (1996).

5 A comprehensive overview of the relevant publications will be found in Breen and Rottman (1995a).

6 Details of this study are given later in this volume, in those chapters that make further use of its data-sets, and in Kluegel et al. (1995).

7 For a full account of the logic of odds ratios, and of their importance in studies of social mobility, see Marshall et al. (1997: Appendix B).

8 Note that the beta statistic is a measure only of *general* fluidity. It does not imply that adjacent nations in the table will also have similar mobility *patterns*.

9 These studies, and their implications for arguments about social justice, are discussed fully in Marshall et al. (1997).

10 See, for example, Marshall et al. (1988) and Marshall and Rose (1990).

11 For overviews, and two rather different but equally convincing empirical analyses (one based on a study of British civil servants, the other using national data from the British General Household Survey for 1991–2), see Marmot (1994) and Arber (1996).

12 Details of the most important of these studies, together with a discussion of the central findings about trends in (Goldthorpe) class differentials in mortality levels in Sweden, will be found in Vågerö and Lundberg (1995).

13 For a useful summary of this literature, and an insightful commentary on its implications for crossnational comparative analysis, see Östberg (1996).

14 Relative risks, expressed as percentages, are very similar to the familiar standardized mortality ratios reported by other researchers. As will be seen from the results reported in the text, the absolute range of these statistics tends to be somewhat larger for the Registrar-General's classification than for the Goldthorpe classes, but this is mainly because the former embraces more extreme categories ('professional occupations' and 'unskilled occupations') at either end of the taxonomy. These relatively small classes tend to stretch the distribution of health risks artefactually. (Goldthorpe classes I and VII comprise a proportionately much larger percentage of places in the class structure.) For the complete results, covering all social classes, and a discussion of their significance for class analysis, see Bartley et al. (1996).

15 The debate about embourgeoisement is reviewed in Marshall (1990: ch. 6). The many different theories about the possible sociological consequences of the economic recessions of the 1970s and 1980s are discussed extensively in Marshall et al. (1985). These spawned a version of the thesis that class had been all but abolished in advanced societies which took my own earlier work (among that of others) as a particular target for criticism. See, for example, the discussions in Saunders (1990a), Pawson (1990) and Emmison and Western (1990), and – for a reply – Marshall and Rose (1990) and Marshall (1991).

16 See Bauman (1992: vii). A flourishing intellectual industry has grown up around attempts to define postmodernism, although there are few signs of agreement, even about such fundamental issues as whether postmodernity describes a type of society, a cultural paradigm, a particular theoretical discourse, or a state of mind (compare, for example, Lash, 1990: 3–4

and Bauman, 1992: vii–xi). Proponents seem undecided as to whether they should construct a 'postmodern sociology' or merely a 'sociology of the postmodern'. Bauman (1988: 812) has argued for the latter, insisting that sociologists should be engaged in 'deploying the strategy of systemic, rational discourse to the task of constructing a theoretical model of postmodern society'. However, this sits uncomfortably alongside attempts to deconstruct fundamental concepts (including those of 'rationality' and 'society'), on the basis that all claims about social life and criteria of truth and validity are linked to strategies of power (compare Nicholson, 1992: 83). Similarly, and despite the appearance of convenient check-lists which purport to itemize the diametrically opposed characteristics of modernity and postmodernity (for an example see Rose, 1991: 49–50), it is hard to determine whether the latter is to be understood as a revolutionary theoretical and historical rupture or merely a carrying to their logical extremes of some of the secular tendencies of modernism itself. Postmodernity may be a 'system in its own right' – or it may just be the latest in a long line of evolutionary shifts in the surface appearance of organized capitalism (compare, for example, the contrasting interpretations offered by Murphy, 1988 and Harvey, 1990). Perhaps, as some have noted ironically, it is entirely appropriate that a movement which celebrates eclecticism, relativism and fragmentation is itself so incoherent.

17 According to Callinicos (1990: 100–1) the argument has at least three identifiable strands. The first is the poststructuralism of French theorists such as Michel Foucault, Jacques Derrida and Gilles Deleuze, who have argued (in quite different ways) that modern notions of truth, meaning and subjectivity are inadequate to the analysis of late-twentieth-century capitalism. The second is the theory of post-industrialism usually associated with the names of Daniel Bell and Alain Touraine, the argument here being that advanced societies are organized around the development and dissemination of scientific knowledge rather than the production of material goods, and are characterized by cultural contradictions between the ascetic norms of work and new norms of hedonistic consumption. Finally, and perhaps most obviously, there is the cultural postmodernism evident in the movement against abstraction in painting and the International Style in architecture. The leading theorists of postmodernity, such as Jean Baudrillard and Jean-François Lyotard, have attempted to link these separate but parallel developments in a diagnosis of a generalized 'postmodern condition'.

18 See, for example, Pakulski (1993), Crook et al. (1992) and Pakulski and Waters (1996). See also Bauman (1992: xvii–xxiv, 191), who argues that the postmodern social world appears to the individual as an uncontrolled market of endless choices, a seamless web of 'imagined communities' based on a 'rampant tribalism' of fleeting affiliations and competing allurements, none of which can sustain our attention or retain our loyalties, yielding an existential insecurity that dissolves the orthodox categories of modernity, specifically those of 'society, normative group (like class or community), socialization and control'. Similarly, Scott Lash depicts postmodern culture as 'two processes of de-centring of identity – that is, of both (1) individual and (2) collective identity'. The metanarratives of the Enlightenment have vanished, and as postmodernist spectacle has displaced realism and narrative, class culture has given way to mass culture. The end result, at least in the view of Lash and others, is 'instrumentalist individualism and mindless consumerism'. The overall effect is to create a 'soft', flat, ahistorical, and undifferentiated culture of eclectic textualism, of 'universalized particulars, existing in a state of "metaphysical equality"' (see Lash, 1990: 27–30; Seligman, 1990: 131; Wexler, 1990: 169). The critical, reflexive, political (and class-constituted) individual is thus replaced by a diffuse, fragmented and decentred subject. In short, and in plain language, stable conceptions of collective identities (and therefore shared interests) disappear – including, most obviously, those associated with social class.

19 See, for example, Featherstone (1991: 10–11) who notes that 'The concept of post-modernism is not . . . merely an empty sign which can be manipulated by artists, intellectuals and academics as part of the power struggles and interdependencies within their particular fields. Part of its appeal is that it . . . also purports to illuminate changes in the day-to-day experiences and cultural practices of broader groups in society. It is here that the evidence is weakest . . . we possess little systematic evidence about day-to-day practices, and we need information in terms of the stock sociological questions "who? when? where? how many?" if

we are to impress colleagues that postmodernism is more than a fad.' One need only add that little has changed in the five or so years since this assessment was penned.

20 Passages such as the following hardly point to the demise of social class: 'In the contemporary world . . . Women from the service and capitalist classes are able to use the "qualifications lever" to pursue managerial and professional careers, thereby achieving financial independence and near equality with men. They can use their wealth to buy out of the "double shift" of paid labour and housework through employing cleaners and childminders. By contrast working-class women are encumbered by increasing workloads in the home and in employment; their labour market opportunities are often restricted to low-paid service work. It is more difficult for them to gain full financial independence from their menfolk, which leaves them more vulnerable to violence in the home. Recent decades have seen increasing polarization between a middle-class professional elite and working-class women' (Bradley, 1996: 109–10). Not surprisingly, Bradley (1996: 79) concedes that 'neither class, as a set of lived economic relationships, nor class analysis, as a set of social categories, is dead', although she adds the rider that 'there must be a recognition of how class relations are shaped by other forms of inequality.' In other words, like most theorists of reflexive modernity (see also Giddens, 1991: 5–6, 82, 228), Bradley implies that social class differences are of decreasing salience in advanced societies, but also acknowledges that class is not yet dead – and so offers a critique of class analysis that, in sum, promises much more than it delivers (since it is conducted mainly at the level of unsubstantiated declaration).

21 For a discussion of this literature, and of the problems involved in conducting multivariate analyses of this kind, see Bartley et al. (1996: 467–70) and Vågerö and Illsley (1995).

22 Examples of studies in this general mould include Gambetta (1987), Goldthorpe (1996b) and Erikson and Jonsson (1996).

23 For a contrasting view of the significance of Wright's International Project on Class Structure and Class Consciousness, and a discussion of the implications of its major findings for debates in class analysis, see Myles and Turegun (1994).

Part I
SOCIAL THEORY

1

Distributional Struggle and Moral Order in a Market Society*

There are clear signs of a developing consensus among social scientists about the changing basis and form of distributional conflict in the United Kingdom. It is commonly argued that fundamental shifts in the structure of social hierarchy have generated a new sectionalism that displaces formerly solidaristic struggles. At the same time complementary swings in values have allegedly intensified individualism and privatism. Structural shifts tend to be linked in some way to altered values, and both are said to be evident in the decline of class-based politics in Britain since 1979.

In Eric Hobsbawm's (1981) version of this argument the solidarity of shared lifestyle and political objectives among the 'traditional' British working class has been undermined since the 1950s by the growth of public sector employment and multinational corporations. The majority of employees now bargain for wages under conditions other than those of the free market. This, together with the increased but uneven participation of women in paid labour, expansion of nonmanual employment, and post-war immigration from the New Commonwealth, has encouraged 'a growing division of workers into sections and groups, each pursuing its own economic interest irrespective of the rest'. Everywhere, according to Hobsbawm, solidaristic forms of political consciousness have given way to 'the values of consumer-society individualism and the search for private and personal satisfactions above all else'.

In similar vein, Steven Lukes (1984) has concluded from his review of the social and occupational structures of Britain in the 1980s that 'the . . . distinction between manual and nonmanual labour is less and less relevant . . . Labour or work itself, and the sphere of production, seems to be becoming less central to the identity and consciousness of workers, while consumption, especially with respect to housing and transport, has become more central to the definition of their basic interests.' Britain is a society divided against itself in new ways: those with a stake in property markets and those without; the self-sufficient on wages versus welfare claimants; the populations of declining regions against those resident in economically buoyant areas; and so on. These changes are reflected in the extent to which the *mentalité* of the market has been given free rein. 'There appears,' in Lukes's view, 'to have been a reactive growth (encouraged by a combination of recession and inflation) of instrumental, pecuniary, egoistic, in short capitalist values and attitudes, and a disintegration of various moral frameworks within which these had a subordinate place and faced various countervailing forms of commitment, loyalty and discipline – whether based on unionism, locality or class.' The majority of people are now convinced that there is no alternative to the morality of the acquisitive society; that Britain's seemingly intractable economic problems are quite beyond human control; that inequalities are therefore unalterable; and so have settled down in a mood of quiet disillusionment to seek their private satisfactions and pursue conflicting sectional demands.

Both Hobsbawm and Lukes attribute the breakdown of class politics, and in particular the poor showing of Labour at the polls, to the new sectionalism and self-interest. In this they would seem to be supported by a number of studies which claim that the electorate is now fragmented politically along unfamiliar lines. There is some disagreement as to whether working-class support for Labour has been undermined specifically by partisan dealignment, the disaggregation of economic interests, cognitive consumer voting, or the development of sectoral consumption cleavages, but in every case structural shifts in the ordering of stratification are seen to generate new conceptions of self-interest and intensify the vigour with which these are then pursued.[1]

Recent research in the fields of human geography, social policy and industrial sociology is widely cited in corroboration of this version of events.[2] It is then given additional credibility by the consensus that exists among post-Parsonsian social theorists to the effect that capitalism possesses, to use Fred Hirsch's (1977) celebrated phrase, a 'depleting moral legacy'. Again this process is characterized as one of growing and excessive individualism. Daniel Bell, for example, maintains that the 'cultural contradiction' of Western society

> is a widening disjunction between the social structure (the economy, technology, and occupational system) and the culture (the symbolic expression of meanings), each of which is ruled by a different axial principle. The social structure is rooted in functional rationality and efficiency, the culture in the antinomian justification of the enhancement of the self . . . In the organization of production and work, the system demands provident behaviour, industriousness and self control, dedication to a career and success. In the realm of consumption it fosters the attitudes of *carpe diem*, prodigality and display, and the compulsive search for play. But in both realms the system is completely mundane, for any transcendent ethic has vanished. (1976: 477–8; see also Bell, 1979)

Similarly, Jurgen Habermas (1975; 1979) speaks of a 'motivation crisis' in advanced capitalist societies, the effect of a contradiction between exorbitant demands for individual enhancement generated in the socio-cultural system, and the strictly limited redistributive aspirations of the bourgeois state, even in its welfare-reformist guise.

Contemporary pluralist societies thus emerge as the domain of materialistic citizens progressively inclined towards instrumental pursuit of growing expectations for personal satisfaction. Those on the political left (Offe, 1976; 1984) chart this as a depletion in the moral legacy willed to capitalism by earlier eras and lay bare the (as they see it) increasingly precarious residue of the cash nexus. Economic liberals (Brittan, 1978; Hayek, 1976), on the other hand, bemoan the revolution of rising expectations, pervasive envy and irresponsible egoism that generate seemingly endless and, to them, irrational demands for pay increases and better living conditions. For one group heightened distributional dissent is an expression of the moral bankruptcy of the old order and brings the system to the threshold of a new age of egalitarianism. For the other it marks a lamentable decline of traditional values, *civitas*, and responsible unionism into the anarchy of gang loyalties. Nevertheless, the common conclusion of commentators as diverse theoretically and politically as Habermas, Offe, Hirsch, Bell, Brittan, and Hayek is that dysfunctional effects of the market are no longer offset in advanced capitalist societies by consensus about a concrete morality for rendering distributive issues principled. Western liberal democracies lack *Sittlichkeit* (morality or moral order). In the 'legitimation vacuum' thus created, distributional struggles become increasingly fragmented and intense, raising in due course serious problems of social integration.

The role of ideology

There are good reasons to suppose that these structural and attitudinal features of British society are considerably less novel than proponents of the thesis of restructured distributional conflict would have us believe.

Sociological research on lower-class meaning systems has consistently identified a heterogeneity of circumstances, interests and beliefs among manual workers during the period since 1945. Numerous accounts of post-war class segmentation identify a variety of 'new' and 'old' working classes based on a diversity of market and work situations. These structural cleavages have generally supported some form of intraclass schism. Moreover, it has also been argued that, during the so-called years of affluence in the 1950s and 1960s, 'expressive' orientations to manual work largely gave way to more narrow 'economistic' calculations, usually in association with declining job satisfaction, an increase in home-centredness and family-centredness, and corresponding 'privatization' of hitherto communitarian working-class lifestyles. It would seem, therefore, that neither sectionalism nor privatism is newly arrived among the proletariat.[3]

In fact, sustained research into the 'social consciousness' of British workers reached an impasse in the 1970s, when the various studies con-

verged on the conclusion that the great majority of respondents were
normatively ambivalent and therefore content to make contradictory
statements and act in inconsistent ways. Since, as Michael Mann (1970)
puts it, 'only those actually sharing in societal power need develop consistent societal values', the dispossessed majority adopt a pragmatic stance
towards existing socio-political arrangements. Their immediate concerns are
contingent matters of everyday life. Normative attachments are to the
proximate structures of family and community rather than the distant state.
Lower-class meaning systems are correspondingly ambiguous and volatile.
The social cohesion of liberal democracies therefore rests on the lack of
consensus rather than its achievement.[4]

These findings have led some critics to argue that modern social theory
places too much importance on the role of dominant ideologies and too
little on the pressing necessities of material existence. That is, they question
the assumption that there exists in most societies a set of dominant beliefs,
propagated by the ruling classes, which are absorbed into the consciousness
of subordinate strata and so help block the development of radical political
dissent.

For example, Bryan Turner and his colleagues (Abercrombie et al.,
1980; Turner, 1983) maintain that dominant ideologies are rarely
transmitted effectively throughout social structures, and that their principal
effects are on superordinate rather than subordinate classes. In feudal and
early capitalist societies such ideologies functioned to maintain the control
of the dominant class over wealth – but at the level of the elites themselves. Both the feudal manor and the capitalist family firm depended on
the conservation and accumulation of property. Private possession of land
and capital required a stable marriage system, with unambiguous rules
about inheritance, legitimacy and remarriage. The 'dominant ideology' was
a complex of legal, moral, and religious values which had the required
effect of preserving wealth. Among feudal ruling classes, for example,
Catholicism and the system of honour provided ideological guarantees that
children would remain loyal to family holdings. By comparison the
peasantry (and in early capitalism the factory workforce) were co-opted by
the sheer exigencies of labouring to live – the 'dull compulsion of economic relations'. Even in late capitalism the 'iron cage' of everyday life
offers a better explanation of working-class quiescence than does ideological incorporation. Moral pluralism and a great diversity of political,
social and cultural deviance can readily be tolerated because the com-
pliance of subordinate strata is secured by economic constraint, political
coercion, and the bureaucratic mechanisms of school, family, workplace
and prison. The 'structuralist' or 'materialist' position thus concurs with
the perceived lack of *Sittlichkeit* in modern capitalist societies, but concludes that this raises no real problems for social integration since the
meaning systems of subordinate classes have never been more than
'dualistic', embracing only a much modified version of any particular
dominant ideology.[5]

Forms of distributional conflict

It is beyond the scope of this chapter to explore in detail the full-blown and diverse theories of social solidarity and schism encompassed by economic liberalism, Marxism, and the new versions of structuralism – far less arbitrate between these. Nevertheless, we would challenge two aspects of recent liberal and Marxist thinking, as this bears on the issue of distributional conflict in contemporary Britain. We shall argue, first of all, that left and right alike have exaggerated the extent to which current forms of distributional dissent can be said to be novel. Neither proletarian sectionalism nor pecuniary privatism are recent inventions of economic recession or restructuring. Moreover, it seems to us, the tendency to connect changes in electoral behaviour directly to swings in values and/or shifts in the occupational structure greatly oversimplifies the relationship between the distributional order of societies on the one hand, and the specific forms taken by distributional conflict on the other. In particular it omits important issues that arise at the level of organizational capacity and collective action.

Before pressing these objections in terms of the evidence from distributional struggles in Britain, we can clarify the issues involved by considering the structure of distributional conflict in a more general sense. In principle, such conflict can be organized along inclusionary or exclusionary lines, and on the terrain of class or status orders. Four types of distributional conflict are then possible, as can be seen from Table 1.1. This table represents one possible, though by no means the only, interpretation of Weber's remarks on class and status. In particular it embraces the central idea that social classes and status groups are 'phenomena of the distribution of power within a community' (Weber, 1968: 302–7, 926–39).

In abstracto classes may be said to have their origins at the level of production so that 'property and lack of property are, therefore, the basic categories of all class situations' (1968: 927). Organized on an inclusionary basis, class conflict would involve two collective actors: owners of capital and sellers of labour power. The obvious example is that of the solidaristic class struggle between bourgeoisie and proletariat as analysed by Marx. However, at the level of what Marxists have termed 'social formation', certain complications appear. Principal among these are the complexities explored by Weber in terms of market situation, and by subsequent neo-Weberians (such as Lockwood, 1958) via the model of market, work and status situations. Empirically, class conflicts are mediated through and modified by particular circumstances of market, work and status factors. The market, as shaped by legal and conventional norms, serves to distribute life-chances differentially and, therefore, to circumscribe broad social classes. However, these social classes are themselves further cross-cut by work and status factors. For example, the technical, sectoral and social divisions of labour create a highly differentiated structure of roles and tasks. These divisions are made effective via market exchanges of the same

Table 1.1 *Types of distributional struggle*

		Principle of conflict	
		Class	Status
Principle of organization	Exclusion	Sectional	Conventional
	Inclusion	Solidaristic	Legal

order as those which actuate the distribution of property and, consequently, create a hierarchy of groups distinguished by the different types of skills and resources that each possesses or controls. Obviously, such considerations serve to render social classes less coherent empirically than they are theoretically, since they give rise to numerous sectional disputes. These disputes emerge as those differently placed in sectoral and technical terms attempt to maximize whatever advantages their particular position puts at their disposal. The wage advantage sought by workers strategically placed in a particular economy or process of production is one characteristically sectional form of class action.

Distributional struggles organized on the terrain of social class issues, whether sectional or solidaristic in tenor, contest in some way the control of property or allocation of rewards for marketable skills. Status conflicts also contest the structure of differential access to power and advantage. Again it is the allocation of life-chances that is in dispute, and again such conflicts can be organized according to exclusionary or inclusionary principles. However, status conflicts are rooted in the moral rather than material order of society. Exclusionary struggles occur when a group or groups of people differentiated from the wider society according to some conventional or symbolic criterion claim for themselves specific privileges of an honorific nature. All social relationships based on institutionalized deference are examples of status conflicts organized in this manner. Most commonly these are structured along lines of racial, ethnic, cultural or lifestyle differences. Similarly, where inclusionary class struggles are an attempt to incorporate whole societies under a system of undifferentiated substantive rewards, status conflicts, organized on the same principle, seek to achieve universal membership in the privileges and responsibilities of citizenship. These may be oriented towards legal, political, or social equality.

Though analytically distinct, class and status struggles are, in practice, invariably intertwined, and their precise relationship at any time becomes a matter for empirical research. Because the capitalist market has no moral dimension, sociologists have sometimes seen the importance of the status order as that of legitimating the structure of power and advantage created by the system of production and exchange.[6] Conventional status inequalities based on race, gender and lifestyle, for example, are perceived by some as emergent properties of the class structure itself. Others have observed, however, that in present-day plural democracies legal rights of citizenship have been widely recognized, so that as long as these societies continue also to be organized economically on the basis of market exchanges they are subject to conflicts, arising out of the contradiction between axial principles governing class relationships on the one hand, and the status order on the other. Since the rights of citizenship determine the welfare of individuals independently of their market capacity, and in an egalitarian manner, they act as a barrier to the free play of exclusively capitalist social relations and are a constant reminder that the fundamental conflict between social justice and market value has not been resolved (see Goldthorpe, 1978; Lockwood, 1974).

One of the earliest commentators to appreciate the significance of this tension was T.H. Marshall (1973) writing about the 'realization of citizenship' in Western democracies. Citizenship for Marshall embraces civil, political, and social elements. The civil element is composed of individual rights to freedom of person, speech, association, and the right to justice in civil courts. Political citizenship is extended by participation in the exercise of political power via the universal franchise. By the social element Marshall means that form of economic welfare and social security that is accorded members of a society as a right and irrespective of their ability to pay. The various educational, health, and income-maintaining services of a welfare state, for example, are designed to ensure that all members of a society can 'live the life of a civilized being according to the standards prevailing in the society', and to this end diminish inequalities that are specifically grounded in the market relations of a capitalist order.

There are two aspects of this argument that are particularly important in the British context. The first is that citizenship rights tend not to have advanced in tandem. In the course of British history, for example, civil and political rights were secured for males in the eighteenth and nineteenth centuries, and for females during the present century, while the rights to social citizenship have been a matter of contention for more than three-quarters of a century and remain so today.[7] The other important feature of Marshall's argument in relation to the British situation is the centrality of trades unions to struggles both for greater class equality and for the extension of citizenship rights themselves. Marshall notes that the confirmation of civil rights in the economic sphere created a secondary system of 'industrial citizenship' complementary to that found in the realm of politics. Moreover, when exercised by workers, rights to collective bargaining became 'an instrument for raising their social and economic status, that is to say, for establishing the claim that they, as citizens, were entitled to certain social rights' (1973: 94). In other words, collective bargaining presents the anomaly of civil rights, normally settled on individuals, being exercised collectively, as if such action were political in intent. Historically, of course, it is only political rights that have been so established – through elections to parliament and local councils.

For this reason trades unions have been involved from the outset, not only in class, but also in status conflicts:

To have to bargain for a living wage in a society which accepts the living wage as a social right is as absurd as to have to haggle for a vote in a society which accepts the vote as a political right. Yet the early twentieth century attempted to make sense of this absurdity. It fully endorsed collective bargaining as a normal and peaceful market operation, while recognizing in principle the right of the citizen to a minimum standard of living, which was precisely what the trade unions believed, and with good reason, that they were trying to win for their members with the weapon of the bargain. (1973: 111)

Wage disputes can pursue sectional or class interest by extracting whatever returns the market will bear at a given moment. But they can also appeal to conceptions of social justice based on common citizenship – the notion of what constitutes a 'fair wage' for example. Indeed, the hierarchical wage structure of British society today is as much a reflection of differentially successful appeals to social rights as it is a gradation according to strict market value. Conversely, from positions of market strength unions have bargained for the extension of rights of industrial citizenship itself, pursuing such objectives as security of employment, minimum wage guarantees, pension rights, and social service support during periods of ill-health.

In recent times, therefore, it has been the trades union movement which has formed the interface between class and status conflicts in this country. On many occasions trades unions have organized themselves along exclusionary lines and secured sectional gains at the expense of the working class as a whole. At other times more inclusionary class objectives have been to the fore. At one moment the struggle has been couched in class terms, at another in status terms, and often both simultaneously. In the following section we shall illustrate this argument by reference to the emergence of the so-called labour aristocracy in mid-nineteenth-century England. Though necessarily sketched in broad terms, this example does confirm that working-class sectionalism and pecuniary privatism are not specific to the present recession, and so casts doubt on the thesis that distributional conflict in Britain today has recently taken these novel forms. It also confirms that neither changes in the occupational structure nor shifts in individual values constitute adequate explanations for the patterning of distributional dissent.

The labour aristocracy in nineteenth-century Britain

The watchwords in the thesis of restructured distributional conflict are sectionalism, egoism, and privatism. Although proponents of the argument interrelate these in different ways their common perception is one of recent changes in social hierarchy (in particular the occupational structure) and in social values, each associated with the rise of a diffuse individualism embracing lifestyles, politics and ideology. The heterogeneous working class of contemporary Britain has absorbed capitalist economic values; it takes an instrumental stance towards class organizations so that pecuniary collectivism based on sectional self-interest has undermined worker solidarity; and it has retreated from class politics into the privatized world of home and family. Distributional dissent now centres on consumption and status rather than production and class. In this way sectionalism and privatism emerge as the obverse of class consciousness. The assumption is that they are not and cannot be associated with solidaristic or inclusionary forms of class-based distributional conflict. (For a detailed review of this literature see Newby et al., 1985.)

This contrast forces the history of British labour into an implausible dualistic mould: solidaristic and class versus sectional and privatized. The reality is more complex. Consider, for example, the evidence from studies of the mid-nineteenth-century workforce in rapidly industrializing Britain. Sectionalism is already evident, most obviously in the existence of a 'labour aristocracy' of traditional artisans and skilled manual workers, but for both groups the emergence of a culture of domesticity centred on the home and on privatized lifestyles coexisted with solidaristic and class-based political activity in the context of the trades union movement.

It is true that there is little or no consensus about how to marshal these data under particular theoretical banners. At one extreme are those such as Foster (1974) who accept an undiluted version of the classical Marxist theory of the labour aristocracy. At the other are critics who deny this term any analytical value and maintain that its retention, since it carries the implication of explanation, actually hinders the development of alternative frameworks within which to place changes in the social structure of Victorian Britain (Joyce, 1980). But the so-called debate about the labour aristocracy is largely concerned with the circumstances surrounding its emergence and the precise parameters of the stratum itself. Why was the overt antagonism expressed in Chartism replaced in the mid nineteenth century by a working-class politics of moderate reformism? Precisely how deep were the divisions in political outlook between the different grades of factory workers?[8] If one suspends judgement on the various attempts to locate the documented changes in lifestyles, politics and ideology within some wider theory of social order, it soon becomes apparent that there exists considerable overlap between the apparently competing accounts, at least in so far as the substance of the changes themselves is concerned.[9]

A common starting point is the observation that the culture of the artisan in the immediate pre-industrial era was trade-based, work-centred, and male-dominated. During the first half of the nineteenth century, for example, most London trades worked a twelve-hour day, six days each week, with people residing in the immediate vicinity of their work. Spare-time association, conviviality and political discussion were centred on the workplace or an associated local hostelry, which served also as a house of call and centre of craft organization. Trade feasts, carnivals, intermarriage and hereditary apprenticeships all served to reinforce trade solidarity.

Homes were cramped, uncomfortable and, where they were not places of work, served as little more than somewhere to eat and sleep.

During the second half of the century, however, home and family became increasingly important for both artisans and the newly emerging skilled workers in the capital goods sector. For those who enjoyed secure employment, and were able to restrict entry to the trade via apprenticeships, the mid-Victorian economic boom brought a new prosperity. Rising real wages and falling prices saw the emergence of a margin of comfort over subsistence. The rise in living standards was, in turn, associated with a shortening of the working week, improved housing, suburbanization, home-centred patterns of consumption, and new forms of 'family leisure', all of which increased the importance of home and family in working men's lives. Robert Gray, for example, documents the emergence of a 'culture of domesticity', of 'domestic respectability', and the shifting focus of artisanal life away from work towards home-centred and family-centred lifestyles. This period also sees the emergence of specifically artisanal housing areas as skilled workers moved away from the courts and alleys of the slums, where they shared facilities with unskilled and casual labour, to the often badly built but nevertheless self-contained houses in superior suburbs. By 1870 the majority of skilled workers already commuted to work by tram or workers' train.

The concern for better housing was not simply a reflection of the desire for improved physical amenities. It was also an attempt to escape identification with inhabitants of the older central slums, and reflected the revaluation of home and family as a haven from work, source of dignity and centre of recreation. Geoffrey Crossick, for example, describes the artisan elite as

> separated from lower strata by a complex of social, economic and cultural characteristics, and to some extent divided internally amongst precisely demarcated crafts. This aristocracy of labour, and the skilled workers who shared its aspirations if not its achievements, was defined by more than income alone. Social status, opportunity and behaviour reinforced the elitist potential offered by a stable and relatively adequate income. These artisans were conscious of their superiority over other sections of the working class, especially their labourers and the 'dishonourable' sections of their own trades, and they held an ambiguous position at the very time when they were the only organised section of the working class, organised within trade unions and, with those white-collar and *petit-bourgeois* groups with which they were seen by contemporaries to merge, dominating the benefit societies, building societies, co-operatives and working men's clubs. (1978: 60–1)

This does not mean that there was wholesale conformity to middle-class ideals of domesticity. The outlook of the labour aristocracy was an ambivalent one. 'Dominant values changed their meaning as they became adapted to the conditions of the artisan world and mediated through autonomous artisan institutions' (Gray, 1974: 26). But a distinctively working-class conception of respectability did emerge and this was closely tied to a developing domestic ideal.

One consequence of this revaluation of family life that did in fact diffuse down the class structure was the emergence of a much stricter sexual division of labour, under which married women withdrew from paid employment outside the home. Men bargained for, and in effect secured, a family wage. Wives who remained in paid labour shifted to genteel occupations like shopkeeping or did home-work such as laundering. The new division of labour was reinforced by the Education Act of 1870 which forced children into schools and left all household tasks in the hands of adult women. In due course the interiors of skilled working-class homes were transformed by cheap factory-produced commodities for home-based consumption. Wallpaper, floor coverings, furniture and ornaments turned front parlours everywhere into shrines of respectability. Finally, rising living standards and shorter working hours saw the development of new forms of family-centred recreation, including excursions and seaside holidays, although there remained considerable regional variation in this sphere, with mining and heavy-industry areas tending to retain more traditional sex-segregated patterns of associational activity.

These evolving home-centred and privatized lifestyles nevertheless coexisted with high levels of participation in a range of voluntary associations, from sports clubs and churches to working men's clubs and trades unions. The labour aristocrats were unified outside family and workshop through their participation in local associations that were linked to claims for both respectability and citizenship rights. Skilled workers in particular were dependent on collective forms of organization and especially on the trades unions.

These could be, and were, simultaneously exclusionary and inclusionary in their activities. At one level, for example, the craft unions were concerned to protect the standard of living of their members by restricting apprenticeships and bargaining for higher wages. The instrumental use of trades unions by the skilled elite of manual workers differed from the individualistic instrumentality typical of the Victorian middle class, in that the latter was concerned solely with personal or family benefit, whereas the former rested principally on collective self-help. There was, in other words, an identification with craft or stratum, a feeling of mutuality and collective strength, a shared aspiration for economic betterment and social respectability to be achieved by the group as a whole. But instrumentalism this was, all the same. Many trades union struggles during the period were therefore exclusionary; that is, sectional and conventional. Their objective was to advance the interests of members in the areas of pay, hours, craft privileges, conditions of work and social benefits. At another level, however, these same craft unions were engaged in strenuous attempts to extend industrial and social citizenship by petitioning parliament on such issues as the ten-hour day, health and safety at work, formal rights for trades unions, and the vote for working men. Narrowly instrumental in pursuing sectional wage demands, the labour aristocracy in mid-Victorian Britain was also considerably more radical than any other section of the working class, in both its class and its status aspirations. Of course it was the radicalism of social reform rather than revolution. As Crossick has observed:

> This radicalism was circumscribed by a broad social acquiescence; an acquiescence not in this law or that law, not in this employer or that employer, not in this level of wages or that level of wages, but in the existing system of law, in the existence of employers, in the methods of wage determination. The oppositional efforts of working-class radicals in Kentish London during this period were based on an analysis of social ills that placed political inequality at its heart . . . This radical position dovetailed with the social values of its adherents. Their liberalism concerned independence and respectability, acknowledgement of moral worth and value as citizens, and concern for justice and the ending of privilege . . . Its central concerns can be summarized as universal suffrage, excessive taxation, opposition to the privileged establishment – especially the Church of England – and an opposition to landed privilege and the power of the great landowners that produced demands for reform of tax law and the ending of the national debt. To these must be added a Painite anti-authoritarianism built upon a traditional conception of an Englishman's liberties. (1978: 230–1)

Elsewhere in Britain, as studies by Foster, Tholfsen and others have shown, working men's organizations developed at different times a labour-conscious, a class-conscious and, according to some, even a socialist politics. Yet these were coincidental with a constant concern for respectability and the defence of craft privileges.

Among nineteenth-century labour aristocrats, therefore, sectionalism and privatism coexisted with solidarism and the growth of class institutions (trades unions, trades councils, the Trades Union Congress) which were commonly engaged in pursuit of civil, political, and social rights of citizenship that extended beyond particular crafts to the working class as a whole. As Gray concludes:

> The importance of craft control on the job meant that skilled trade unionists were often divided, not just from the unskilled, but also against each other. Such sectionalism can be found throughout the history of the working class . . . [But] . . . the struggle to legalise union activity, and to achieve a wider recognition of the working class presence in the community, fostered a common sense of identity among these skilled trades . . . If the identity of trade unionists was narrowly based, it still reflected some common interests beyond immediate craft sectionalism. As at other times in the history of the movement, there was an uneasy coexistence of sectional and broader types of activity. (1981: 49)

Despite the apparent existence of great regional and sectoral variations, most unions were simultaneously (or at least sequentially) involved in what were earlier termed sectional, solidaristic, conventional and legal forms of distributional struggle. At times they acted against the interests of unskilled and unorganized workers by defending craft privileges. But there is little doubt that, in their status aspirations, they were consistently the most forceful representatives of the interests of the working class as a whole – or, at least, the male portion of it. Neither the pecuniary motivations nor the burgeoning 'privatized' lifestyles of their members seem to have precluded solidaristic forms of collective action.[10]

Conclusion

Those who would argue that sectionalism, egoism, and privatism are novel aspects of contemporary British working-class life, somehow peculiar to the recent years of economic recession, are therefore mistaken.

It is true that the occupational structure has undergone considerable reshaping as a consequence of the decline in the manual workforce, proportionate expansion of white-collar employment, and growth of widespread and long-term joblessness. The evidence further suggests that the impact of this process, and of the recession itself, is indeed uneven. Certain regions, occupations and sectors of the economy have fared markedly better than others. Lines of cleavage between those in public and private sectors, between men and women, between those employed in multinational and in national enterprises, merely compound this unevenness. But such sectionalism is no less apparent in data from the mid nineteenth century. The 'working class' has always been stratified according to industry, locality, grade and occupation. Today the owner-occupier may find it difficult to find common cause with the council tenant. The British Steel furnace-men in Sheffield may not see interests shared with the women assembling computer keyboards for Burroughs in Cumbernauld. But was it not ever so? The craftworkers, casual labourers, skilled and unskilled employees in the factories, small workshops, docks and quarries of mid-Victorian Britain were no less segmented yet no less members of the same working class.

Nor are privatism – home-centredness and family-centredness – and pecuniary instrumentalism inventions of the last decade. In the 'affluent' 1960s, for example, Goldthorpe and Lockwood dismissed the thesis of working-class 'embourgeoisement' after research in Luton had shown the majority of workers to be 'privatized instrumentalists'. Attempting to put this world-view into its social context, David Lockwood wrote that:

> The social environment of the privatised worker is conducive to the development of what may be called a 'pecuniary' model of society. The essential difference of this ideology is that class divisions are seen mainly in terms of differences in income and material possessions . . . Basically, the pecuniary model of society is an ideological reflection of work attachments that are instrumental and of community relationships that are privatised. It is a model which is only possible when social relationships that might provide prototypical experiences for the construction of ideas of conflicting power classes, or of hierarchically independent status groups, are either absent or devoid of their significance. (1975: 21–2)

As such it explains the lack of class consciousness among these workers and their obviously instrumental attitude towards both trades unions and the Labour Party (see Goldthorpe et al., 1969). Lockwood, of course, argued further that the privatized instrumentalists of the age of post-war affluence were 'prototypical' of workers in general in advanced capitalist societies, and that their world-view was gradually replacing those of the traditional proletarians and deferentials of earlier eras. The evidence of the mid-Victorian labour aristocrats suggests, however, that the three 'images of society' have long coexisted among employees who, at one moment, have supported collective action on behalf of the class or stratum, yet, at another, subscribed to the conventional status politics of the privatized craftsman.

The constant discovery and rediscovery of money-mindedness, sectionalism and privatism among British workers by successive generations of researchers is largely a product of the tendency to treat class consciousness (the elusive quarry of most studies) as an attribute of individuals rather than collective actors. In fact, as we have seen, the substantial literature on working-class consciousness is sufficiently open-ended for one to be able to read into studies of proletarian ambivalence, volatility, pragmatism and instrumentalism whatever theoretical – or political – conclusions one so desires. Thus, to cite only one rather obvious example from the literature on Britain, a wave of post-Braverman studies of the labour process has persistently drawn attention to what is taken to be resistance against managerial strategies of control at the point of production. Even in the face of the inexorable logic of capital accumulation, it is argued, labour cannot routinely be degraded and deskilled. In fact, the research in question confirms that the terrain of the workplace is still firmly in the grasp of the capitalist class, but the emphasis of the analysis is invariably placed on the extent to which this is contested by sections of the workforce.[11] Thus, working-class kids might 'learn to labour', and so move painlessly from classroom to factory, but even then, in their subcultural beliefs and rituals, they transform dominant values and recapture – if only symbolically – those of 'traditional' proletarians. The kids may appear to you and me to be racist, sexist, apolitical, and self-centred in both speech and behaviour – but they're still all right. They are still the rising class (Willis, 1979).

The fallacy of explaining class consciousness solely in terms of workers' beliefs, attitudes or values is then compounded by strenuous attempts to locate structural sources for the particular variant of consciousness that has been identified. A strict dualism is practised, whereby social consciousness becomes a spiritual reflection of social location. The analytical deficiencies of this position are only too evident in the convergence about the electoral consequences of affluence and recession. During the long post-war boom, as during the more recent recessions, it was tempting to see the various economic and political tendencies of the day in a tidy relationship of cause and effect. Butler and Rose (1960: 15) linked changes in the occupational and social structure directly to patterns of voting behaviour and concluded of the 1959 general election that 'the swing to the Conservatives cannot be dismissed as an ephemeral veering of the electoral breeze. Long-term factors were also involved. Traditional working-class attitudes had been eroded by the steady growth of prosperity.' Twenty-five years later Sarlvik and Crewe (1983) were to herald the decade of dealignment in almost identical terms. Again changes in the occupational structure (this time induced by recession rather than affluence) were the deep-rooted cause of electoral upheaval, and again this was associated with a 'new' growth of sectionalism, privatism and instrumentalism.

Those who, in this manner, reason directly from shifts in the social or occupational structure to swings in values or electoral behaviour oversimplify the relationship between the distributional order of society itself, and the specific forms of distributional conflict evident at any particular time. To do so is to neglect the lesson taught by Michels (1962); namely, that organizations count. Between the shared consciousness of commonly held beliefs or values, and joint pursuit of these in co-ordinated action, lies the necessity of collective organization. But the dynamics of organization itself intervene between the shared experience or consciousness and the collective actions of particular members. Leaders may pursue ends that are personal and differ from those of the membership in general. Bureaucratic procedures can stifle the objectives sought by the rank and file. Conversely, those at the top of the organizational hierarchy may invoke democratic principles to impose the wishes of the majority on a reluctant or dissenting minority. In this way organizational process intervenes between tendencies immanent in social structures and whatever patterns of social action are consequent upon these.

We have already argued that, in the context of mid-Victorian Britain, one such organizational entity – the trades union – was crucial in giving direction to struggles both for sectional and for class gains on behalf of British working men. Moreover the exclusionary or inclusionary nature of these conflicts was, as far as the evidence permits us to judge, largely independent of the 'social consciousness' of the craftworkers themselves. Privatized in lifestyle and fiercely sectional in defence of craft interests though they were, their unions nevertheless pursued radical social and political objectives, not only on their members' behalf, but also in the name of the wider community of workers as a whole.

The additional analytical purchase that is gained on the phenomenon of class consciousness by shifting the focus of study from the individual, and his or her attitudes, to the dynamics of the collectivity is evident in the debate about the significance of the apparent disintegration of the moral order of late capitalist societies for the maintenance of social consensus. When class consciousness, that is collective action in pursuit of a coherent ideological strategy, is seen properly – as an attribute of organizations rather than individuals – then the lack of *Sittlichkeit* in capitalist societies carries few immediate implications for social integration. What is important, rather, is the ability of class organizations to mobilize members behind centrally organized initiatives on behalf of class rather than particular interests; and, once mobilized, to hold in check groups who would 'free-ride' or pursue sectional gains at the expense of the collectivity as a whole. The fact is, of course, that the British Labour Party and trades unions have been relatively unsuccessful (compared with their counterparts in Sweden for example) in constituting and mobilizing class interests by presenting issues in class terms, and reinforcing the formation of collectivities with shared class identities (Korpi, 1983; Scase, 1977).

We suspect it is this realization that has led at least one leading participant in the debate to revise his position radically during the past decade. John Goldthorpe in some of his writings closely follows the arguments of Fred Hirsch and maintains that working-class sectionalism, with its allied intensification of distributional struggles, is a major threat to the stability of capitalist societies. His characterization of working-class consciousness as 'pecuniary instrumentalism' derives, of course, from the Affluent Worker Studies. It echoes David Lockwood's suggestions as to the 'prototypicality' of the new 'privatized instrumentalists' among post-war British workers by settling this mantle upon the proletariat as a whole. The decline of locality-based status orders, extension of the sphere of citizenship, demographic and socio-political maturity of the working class, have encouraged members to exploit to the full such market advantages as they may possess. Workers are thus pecuniary in their attitude to labour, instrumental in support of working-class organizations such as the trades unions and Labour Party, and privatized in their role as consumers. Central life-interests lie outside the workplace in the home. Pushful wage demands may be pursued aggressively, but they testify only to the economic rationality of workers, and imply nothing in the way of discontent that can be channelled in the direction of specifically socialist or even class objectives. Nevertheless, militant wage demands can generate uncontrolled distributional dissent and, in the form of inflationary pressure on the economy, bring the system to the point of crisis (Goldthorpe, 1978).

In more recent publications however, and without altering this conception of the pecuniary and privatized instrumentalism of his working-class subjects, Goldthorpe has also argued that, under certain circumstances, sectionalism among employees operates to the advantage rather than the obvious disadvantage of the capitalist classes. Indeed it may even be actively encouraged by them. Faced with the problems of managing the economy under conditions of heightened distributional dissent, governments can choose to pursue corporatist solutions by organizing private economic interest groups and classes into the political arena, and according them a role in the formation of (and responsibility for implementing) public policy. The problem is that, in societies such as Sweden, Austria and Norway which exhibit relatively stable corporatist arrangements, effective political bargaining to counter the economically dysfunctional effects of the market has required institutional recognition of real power shifts in the social structure. In short, the major interest groups, notably the centralized union movements, have become increasingly powerful and made real gains on behalf of their working-class constituents. Faced with the political costs of corporatist inclusion, therefore, governments and employers can opt instead to pursue an exclusionary strategy by creating disprivileged and disorganized collectivities of economic actors within the sphere of production itself. In other words they attempt to divide and rule. Economic dualism, such as is evident in the segmentation of labour markets and maintenance of 'industrial reserve armies', undermines organized labour by providing flexible, cheap, and organizationally weak workforces engaged according to 'non-standard' employment arrangements, standing outside systems of industrial citizenship, and disposable as and when needs arise. From this perspective, which we ourselves would share, it is not lack of capitalist *Sittlichkeit* that poses the greater threat to pluralist democracies, but its achievement, since corporatist arrangements tend, where they have persisted, both progressively to undermine the free play of the capitalist labour market, and to reinforce class-based as opposed to sectional identities. Collectivism may still be instrumental, but the collectivity is now the class as a whole, rather than some fragment thereof (Goldthorpe, 1984a).

If, therefore, we accept the readily available data which suggest that there is little evidence of British working-class participation in a consensus about agreed principles governing distributional issues (be that testimony to instrumentalism, pragmatism, sectionalism, privatism, or whatever), this would seem to lend support to Turner and his colleagues in their claim that social order in capitalist societies does not depend on agreement about a dominant ideology. But we would also argue the obverse: lack of *Sittlichkeit* need not imply the absence of solidaristic and highly structured distributional conflict. Privatized instrumentalism – so-called narcissism, egoism, individualism and status awareness – can be consistent with collective action, with social identities based on class, and therefore with class consciousness. The changing forms of distributional struggle are not a matter, at least primarily, of altering individual awareness but are, instead, more a question of straightforward organizational capacity. Lower-class meaning systems carry no particular implications for social integration unless these are seen in their changing organizational contexts. Modern British society lacks capitalist *Sittlichkeit* but it is not for this reason that social order will – or will not – be secured.

Notes

* Gordon Marshall, Carolyn Vogler, David Rose and Howard Newby. The authors acknowledge the support of the Economic and Social Research Council (grant number HR 8633).

1 See, for example, Sarlvik and Crewe (1983), Robertson (1984), Himmelweit et al. (1985) and Dunleavy (1980a).

2 For example see the studies by Massey (1984), Duke and Edgell (1984) and Daniel and Millward (1983). For additional references and a summary of these studies see Marshall et al. (1985) and Rose et al. (1984).

3 For an overview of this literature see Marshall (1983).

4 See also the papers collected in Bulmer (1975).

5 Moreover, the argument continues, in late capitalist societies changes in the forms of ownership and control of wealth (in particular the rise of multinational corporations and expansion of the state) mean that ideology ceases to be crucial for the coherence of the ruling

class itself. Monopoly firms are not family firms and generally do not rely on inherited wealth for finance. Modern market economies do not depend on a coherent ruling class which retains capital within the family and there is correspondingly less need for coherent 'ruling ideas'.

6 See, for example, Kuhn and Wolpe (1978), Miles (1982), Parkin (1972) and Westergaard and Resler (1976).

7 Of course, this does not mean that civil and political rights are irrevocable, once gained; or that they are automatically bestowed on those entitled to them; or that they have ceased to be matters of dispute. The events of the miners' strike in Britain during 1984 offer sufficient proof of all three qualifications.

8 See, for example, the discussion in the journal *Social History*: Moorhouse (1978; 1979; 1981), Reid (1978) and McLennan (1981).

9 The following paragraphs are based principally on the studies by Alexander (1976), Crossick (1978), Davidoff (1979), Daunton (1983), Gray (1976), Harrison (1965), Hobsbawm (1964), Kirk (1985), Pelling (1972), Tholfsen (1976) and Walton (1981).

10 See also Jones (1983), who tends to locate the 'remaking' of the (mass of the) working class during the final quarter rather than the third quarter of the nineteenth century. Nevertheless, his substantive conclusions tend also to support our argument, in so far as he sees sectionalism and privatism antedating the mid-Victorian period. Moreover, reviewing the interrelationships between the growth of trades unionism and that of working-class leisure, he describes the working-class culture of the 1880s and 1890s as defensive, stoical, fatalistic and politically sceptical. Yet, at the same time, the solidarity and organizational strength achieved in earlier struggles was channelled into union activity and, eventually, into support for a political party committed to union objectives. Unions, co-operatives, friendly societies and the music-hall all indicated 'a *de facto* recognition of the existing social order as the inevitable framework of action', and the rise of a 'culture of consolation' (1983: 236–7). Jones, like ourselves, points to the relative neglect of the organizational aspects of class analysis and goes so far as to suggest that it is not consciousness (or ideology) that produces politics but politics that produces consciousness. 'In general,' he observes, 'the temporality of periods of heightened *political* conflict and political mobilization is determined, in the *first* instance, not by the conditions of the local economy or by cultural factors, but by the activity of all those institutions of government and political order, both legislative and executive, central and local, which in short we call the state . . . What sort of political dimension it acquires, other things being equal, depends upon the existence of a political organization or current with a capacity convincingly to portray the particular sequence of events as an instance of a coherent general position on the character of the state and a strategy for its transformation' (1983: 10–11, 19). This, in turn, raises the issue of state activity: the other side of the coin in the discussion of organizational capacities. (We comment on this briefly below.)

11 See Littler and Salaman (1982), Wood (1982) and, for a particularly glaring example of political optimism belied by the sociological analysis on which it rests, Pollert (1981).

2

The Promising Future of Class Analysis: a Response to Recent Critiques*

What are the prospects for class analysis? Of late, the enterprise has been widely dismissed as unconvincing and unproductive by prominent critics writing from a variety of different standpoints. Our own work has been a frequent target. In the present chapter, however, our primary aim is not to reply to such charges on our own behalf, but rather to uphold the kind of class analysis that our work can be taken to represent – since it is our contention that its promise is far from exhausted.

The argument comprises two parts. In the first, we seek to clarify the nature and purpose of class analysis as we would understand it, and in particular to distinguish it from the class analysis of Marxist sociology. This is necessary because some critics – including Hindess (1987), Holton and Turner (1989) and Sørensen (1991) – have not, in our view, made this distinction adequately, while others, most notably Pahl (1989), have failed to make it at all. In addition, several instances can be noted of authors who, having lost faith in the Marxist class analysis that had once commanded their allegiance, or at least sympathy, now find evident difficulty in envisaging any other kind. Gorz (1982), Hobsbawm (1981), Bauman (1982), Lukes (1984) and Offe (1985) are obvious examples.

In the second part of the chapter we then go on to make the case for the continuing relevance of class analysis, in our own conception of it, by reviewing findings from three central areas of current research. Here we seek to take issue more specifically with the assertions made by Pahl (1989: 710) that, in modern societies, 'class as a concept is ceasing to do any useful work for sociology', and by Holton and Turner (1989: 196) that we are now 'in a situation where the persistence of the class idiom is explicable more in terms of the metaphorical character of class rhetoric than any clear intellectual persuasiveness'.

Class analysis as a research programme

Class analysis, in our sense, has as its central concern the study of relationships among class structures, class mobility, class-based inequalities, and class-based action. More specifically, it explores the interconnections between positions defined by employment relations in labour markets and production units in different sectors of national economies; the processes through which individuals and families are distributed and redistributed among these positions over time; and the consequences thereof for their life-chances and for the social identities that they adopt and the social values and interests that they pursue. Understood in this way, class analysis entails a commitment not to any particular theory of class but, rather, to a *research programme* – in, broadly, the sense of Lakatos (1970) – within which different, and indeed rival, theories may be formulated and then assessed in terms of their heuristic and explanatory performance.

It may be asked, and critics have indeed done so (see, for example, Holton and Turner, 1989: 173), why such a programme should be pursued in the first place. We would think the answer obvious enough. The programme is attractive in that it represents a specific way of investigating interconnections of the kind that have always engaged the sociological imagination: that is, between historically formed macrosocial structures, on the one hand, and, on the other, the everyday experience of individuals within their particular social milieux, together with the patterns of action that follow from this experience. These are precisely the sorts of interconnections that, in Wright Mills's (1959) words, allow one to relate biography to history and 'personal troubles' to 'public issues'. From an analytical standpoint, the programme also promises economy of explanation: the ability to use a few well-defined concepts such as class position, class origins, class mobility or immobility, in order to explain a good deal both of what happens, or does not happen, to individuals across different aspects of their social lives and of how they subsequently respond.

But *a priori* there is only attraction and promise. Whether the research programme of class analysis proves worthwhile – is progressive rather than degenerative – must be decided by the results it produces. No *assumption* of the pre-eminence of class is involved. To the contrary, it is integral to the research programme that specific consideration should also be given to theories holding that class relations are in fact of diminishing importance for life-chances and social action or that other relations and attributes – defined, for example, by income or consumption, status or lifestyle, ethnicity or gender – are, or are becoming, of greater consequence.

It ought to be readily apparent that class analysis, thus conceived, differs significantly from the class analysis of Marxist sociology. Nevertheless, in polemicizing against – or despairing of – the latter, several critics have evidently supposed that they were providing the quietus of class analysis *tout court*. Before proceeding further, therefore, we think it important to spell out four elements, in particular, that class analysis as we would understand it does *not* entail – although they are found in most Marxist versions.

First, our conception of class analysis entails no theory of history according to which class conflict serves as the engine of social change, so that at the crisis point of successive developmental stages a particular class (under capitalism the working class) takes on its 'mission' of transforming society through revolutionary action.[1] In fact, among those sociologists who have been actively engaged in what we would regard as the research programme of class analysis,[2] a strong opposition to all such historicism, whether of a Marxist or a liberal inspiration, can be found (see, for example, Esping-Andersen, 1990: ch. 1; Goldthorpe, 1971; 1988; 1992; Haller, 1990; Korpi, 1978; Marshall et al., 1988: ch. 10). The emphasis is, rather, on the diversity of the developmental paths that nations have followed to modernity and on the very variable – because essentially contingent – nature of the part played in this respect by class formation and action.

Secondly, class analysis as we understand it implies no theory of class exploitation, according to which all class relations must be necessarily and exclusively antagonistic, and from which the objective basis for a 'critical' economics and sociology can be directly obtained. Although exponents of class analysis in our sense would certainly see conflict as being inherent within class relations, this does not require them to adhere to a labour theory of value, or indeed any other doctrine entailing exploitation as understood in Marxist discourse. Nor must they suppose, as is suggested by Sørensen (1991: 73), that what is to the advantage of one class must *always* and *entirely* be to the disadvantage of another. In fact, much interest has of late centred on theoretical discussion of the conditions under which class relations may be better understood as a positive-sum (or negative-sum) rather than a simple zero-sum game. And this interest has then been reflected in substantive studies in a concern with the part that may be played by 'class compromises' in, for example, labour relations or the development of national political economies and welfare states (compare the papers collected in Goldthorpe, 1984c).

Furthermore, arguments advanced from a liberal standpoint, whether by functionalist sociologists or neo-classical economists, to the effect that class inequalities are, through various mechanisms, conducive to the greater welfare of all would be seen as calling for empirical investigation rather than mere ideological rejection. And, in turn, the results of such investigation would be recognized as directly relevant to any moral evaluation of class inequalities that might be made. In this regard, the influence of Marxist theories of exploitation would be surely far less than that of the 'difference principle', as formulated by Rawls (1972).[3]

Thirdly, the version of class analysis that we would endorse takes in no theory of class-based collective action, according to which individuals holding similar positions within the class structure will thereby automatically develop a shared consciousness of their situation and will, in turn, be prompted to act together in the pursuit of their common class interests. In fact, awareness of developments in the general theory of collective action, from the time of Olson's (1965) crucial study onwards, has led those engaged in class analysis as a research programme effectively to reverse the traditional Marxist perspective. Instead of expecting class-based collective action to occur (and then having to resort to 'false consciousness' arguments when it does not), they have concentrated on establishing the quite special conditions that must apply before such action can be thought probable – because rational for the individuals concerned – *even where* shared interests are in fact recognized. Thus, when Pahl (1989: 711) represents class analysts as mindlessly repeating the 'mantra' of 'structure–consciousness–agency', with the links in the chain being 'rarely seen as problematic', this is in fact essentially the opposite of what has happened over the last decade or more.

In turn, we may add, the models of class-based collective action with which critics such as Pahl or Holton and Turner operate are ones that recent work has largely transcended: that is, either the revolutionary 'storming-of-the-Winter-Palace' model, or the *gemeinschaftlich* model of working-class action based on the local solidarities of workplace or community. If a paradigm case of collective class action for 'post-Olson' analysis were to be given, it would surely have to be that of working classes under neo-corporatist political economies – for example the Swedish – which takes on a quite different, and indeed contrasting, character. Essentially, such action (or, some might wish to say, inaction) consists in workers accepting the participation of their union confederations in governmental policies of wage regulation, and in showing a class-wide solidarity by *abstaining* from the use of localized or sectional bargaining power, so that their leaders may better pursue the more generalized working-class goals of full employment and redistributive social welfare policies, as a *quid pro quo* for wage restraint (see Goldthorpe, 1984a; Korpi, 1983; Pizzorno, 1978; Scharpf, 1984; Stephens, 1979). From this new standpoint, then, the consciousness–agency link at least is radically rethought: class consciousness, to quote Elster's (1985: 347) formulation, is 'the ability to overcome the free-rider problem in realising class interests'.

Finally, class analysis as we understand it does not embrace a reductionist theory of political action – collective or individual – according to which such action can be understood simply as the unmediated expression of class relations and the pursuit of structurally given class interests. At the same time as they have come to a much changed understanding of the consciousness–agency link, so also have many class analysts sought to move to a new view of the relationship between consciousness (or at least consciousness of interests) and structure, again under the influence of more general theoretical developments (see, for example, Berger, 1981). What has been rejected is, precisely, the idea that an awareness of and concern with class interests follows directly and 'objectively' from class position. Rather, the occupancy of class positions is seen as creating only potential interests, such as may also arise from various other structural locations. Whether, then, it is class, rather than other, interests that individuals do in fact seek to realize, will depend in the first place on the social identities that they take up, since – to quote a maxim attributed to Pizzorno – 'identity precedes interest'. And although in the formation of such identities various social processes, for example those of mobility, will be important, it is emphasized that for class interests to become the basis of political mobilization, a crucial role must be played by political movements and parties themselves, through their ideologies, programmes and strategies (see Esping-Andersen, 1985; Heath et al., 1991b: ch. 5; Korpi, 1983; Marshall et al., 1988: ch. 7; Pizzorno, 1978).

Hindess (1987: ch. 6) has insisted, with reference to some of the authors cited above, that non-Marxist, no less than Marxist, class analysis remains beset with problems of reductionism in its treatment of politics. However, his case is hardly convincing, since he merely asserts that the authors in question are led into reductionist positions, without anywhere attempting to demonstrate this either by quotation or by specific reference. And, further, he offers no reason why non-Marxists, who have no theory of history as class struggle to defend, should be at all attracted to reductionism or have any difficulty in rejecting it outright. Although particular analyses may focus on the part that is played in class formation – or decomposition – by social rather than political processes, this in no way implies that the relevance of the latter is denied. Indeed, the authors to whom Hindess refers have all had occasion to emphasize the autonomy – even the primacy – of the political, as against what they would regard as an undue 'sociologism'.[4]

In the light of the foregoing disclaimers, class analysis in our sense may well then appear as a far more limited project, intellectually as well as politically, than in its Marxist form. And indeed in certain respects it is, most obviously in not deriving from or being directed by any one general theory of class, or in turn aspiring to form the basis of yet wider theories of society or history.[5] However, class analysis as we would wish to defend it has ambitions that lie in a different direction. While its proponents may adhere to different concepts and theories of class, they aim to put these to the test by pursuing issues of the kind posed at the start of this chapter, and through research of a methodological standard generally more adequate to their inherent difficulty than that previously undertaken. More specifically, if in the research programme of class analysis the leading concerns are those of examining the importance of class (relative to that of other factors) in shaping life-chances and patterns of social action, and of seeking to trace any shifts in this respect that may occur over time, then a number of requirements in conceptualization, data analysis and data collection alike must be met. Three such requirements at least call for attention here, both because of their inherent importance and because this would appear to have been often insufficiently appreciated by critics.

First, class concepts must be as sharply defined as is operationally feasible, in order to avoid any confounding of class with other factors of possible relevance. Holton and Turner argue (1989: 172) that 'status elements' often enter into 'class discourse', but they give little attention to efforts made over the last decade or so (from both Marxist and non-Marxist standpoints) to produce class concepts and categorizations of an analytically more satisfactory kind. Pahl (1989: 712–13) notes such efforts on the part of Wright and of Goldthorpe but then seeks to devalue them since 'sadly, they do not appear to be congruent.' That this should be the case is, however, in itself neither surprising nor disturbing. What Pahl fails to recognize is that it is precisely a concern of class analysts to evaluate rival conceptual approaches, and that there are indeed sound procedures for so doing (see Marsh, 1986a; Marshall, Chapter 3 in this volume; Marshall et al., 1988; Marshall and Rose, 1990). Class analysts have an obvious interest in determining which categorizations are the most effective in displaying variation in dependent variables under examination – and in part because those who have sought to play down class effects have often drawn on results derived from categorizations that are *least* satisfactory in analytical and empirical terms alike. Pahl himself (1989: 714) here provides a good example, while also suggesting (1991: 128), quite erroneously, that it makes little difference which approach is followed.[6]

A second requirement is that analyses should be undertaken that are of a genuinely multivariate character and that questions of causal 'texture' should be given careful consideration. For example, if it is contended that the explanatory power of class is waning and has been overtaken by that of, say, differences in consumption patterns or lifestyles, then such a claim obviously calls for multivariate analysis as the basis for its empirical assessment. It is notable, however, that although both Pahl (1989: 714) and Holton and Turner (1989: 185–92) address this issue – and, in Pahl's case, as if it were in fact already decided against class analysis – neither gives any serious consideration to results from studies in which relevant multi-variate analyses have figured.

Again, Pahl in particular sets great store on the argument that the simple demonstration that associations exist between class and dependent variables 'is probably conflating a number of quite distinct processes that should be kept analytically distinct' (1989: 716). But here he merely opens up a range of issues with which he is, apparently, not very familiar. One is that of just how far in any particular case it can actually be shown – as, say, by causal path analysis – that the effects of class are mediated through specified intervening variables. Another is that of the theoretical significance that should in any event be given to causal factors of a less and a more proximate kind. Contrary to what Pahl (1991: 128) appears to believe, even the completely successful 'unpacking' of class in the way he envisages would not necessarily reduce its sociological importance. Thus, no one would suppose that the *immediate* causes of, for example, low educational attainment, voting Labour, and suffering from chronic bronchitis are all the same. But, in so far as a linkage can be traced back from each of the different sets of immediate causes involved to the location of individuals or families in (let us say) unskilled working-class positions, then the import-ance of class is enhanced rather than diminished. The pervasiveness of the influence of class is underlined.

A final requirement is that class analyses, and in turn the data on which they draw, must in some way or other incorporate a time dimension. Pahl (1989: 715–16) and Holton and Turner (1989: 176–7) both seek to argue that class is losing its explanatory force in consequence of various current trends of economic and social change: the decline of heavy and manufacturing industry and the rise of services, the breakup of 'traditional' working-class communities, the growth of 'household privatism', and so on. But in so doing they move on from some changes that are reasonably well-documented to others that are not; and, as regards class effects *per se*, they make no reference whatever to findings from cohort analyses or longitudinal or panel studies of the kind that would be necessary to give their position adequate empirical support. Rather, they could be said to provide a good illustration of 'the tendency towards dualistic historical thinking' against which Marshall et al. (1988: 206) have explicitly warned: that is, a tendency 'whereby a communitarian and solidaristic proletariat of some bygone heyday of class antagonism is set against the atomised and consumer-oriented working class of today' – in a manner, however, that has little basis in either sociological or historical research.

Some illustrative results

In this second part of our argument we draw attention, albeit in a very summary way, to findings from three areas within the research programme of class analysis which, we would argue, any serious critique would need to address – and especially if its ultimate aim were to establish that class analysis no longer has a useful part to play in the study of modern societies. We will discuss in turn class mobility; class and education; and class and political partisanship.

Class mobility

To study social mobility within the context of a class structure, rather than, say, that of a status hierarchy, is a conceptual choice that must be made *a priori* (Goldthorpe, 1985). However, where this perspective has been taken, results have been produced that are of no little sociological significance.

For present purposes, what may chiefly be stressed is that, across diverse national settings, classes have been shown to display rather distinctive 'mobility characteristics': that is, in inflow perspective, in the homogeneity of the class origins of those individuals who make up their current membership; and in outflow perspective, in their degree of retentiveness or 'holding power', both over individual lifetimes and intergenerationally (Erikson and Goldthorpe, 1992a: ch. 6; Featherman and Selbee, 1988; Featherman et al., 1989; Jonsson, 1991b; Mayer et al., 1989). Thus, for example, the service classes, or salariats, of modern societies tend to be highly heterogeneous in their composition but tend also to have great retentiveness both intra- and intergenerationally. In comparison, working classes are more homogeneous in composition, and farm classes far more so, but both these classes reveal lower holding power, especially in intergenerational terms. In other classes, such as among the *petite bourgeoisie* and routine nonmanual employees, the combinations of homogeneity and of worklife and intergenerational retentiveness are different again.

Such mobility characteristics can be shown to have a twofold origin. First, they reflect the fact that classes – defined in terms of employment relations within different sectors of national economies – tend to follow rather distinctive trajectories, or 'natural histories', of growth or decline in relation to the structural development of these economies (in a way that strata defined in terms of status or prestige do not).[7] And secondly, they reflect the fact that different classes tend to be associated with specific 'propensities' for immobility or mobility independently of all structural effects. This last finding, it may be noted, is one made possible only by technical advances in the analysis of mobility tables, which have allowed the crucial conceptual distinction between 'absolute' and 'relative' rates to be drawn (compare Goldthorpe, 1980; Hauser et al., 1975; Hauser, 1978).

That classes can be shown to display such distinctive mobility characteristics would then in itself suggest that they are capable of being defined in a way that is more than merely arbitrary, and that the 'boundary problems' which some critics have sought to highlight are a good deal more tractable than they seek to imply. Certainly, one may question the grounds of assertions such as that made by Holton and Turner (1989: 174) that it is 'very hard to aggregate the multiplicity of class positions into categories, without having recourse to evaluative cultural criteria'.[8]

Furthermore, it is in terms of such mobility characteristics that class formation can be assessed at its basic 'demographic' level (Goldthorpe, 1980); that is, in terms of the extent and the nature of the association that exists between individuals or families and particular class positions over time. And this in turn may be seen as determining the potential for classes, as collectivities, also to develop distinctive subcultures and a 'capacity for socialization', which are themselves the key prerequisites for class identities to be created (Featherman et al., 1990).[9] In other words, an approach is here provided, and is being actively pursued, for investigating processes of class formation, or decomposition, through systematic empirical inquiry. It is not supposed, in the manner of dogmatic Marxism, that class formation is in some way historically scheduled. But neither, in the manner of Pahl or Holton and Turner, is it assumed that in modern societies class decomposition is a quite generalized phenomenon. And, as we have indicated, the evidence thus far produced does indeed point to the existence of a situation of a clearly more complex kind.

Class and education

The countervailing force that has most often been cited in arguments claiming that the influence of class on individual life-chances is in decline is that of education. According to those theories of industrial society which could, in Holton and Turner's phrase, be seen as posing 'the challenge of liberalism' to class analysis, the very 'logic' of industrialism requires both that the provision of, and access to, education should steadily widen, and further that educational attainment should become the key determinant of success in economic life. In turn, then, it is expected that the association between class origins and educational attainment will weaken, while that between educational attainment and class destinations strengthens, and itself mediates (and legitimates) most of whatever association between class origins and destinations may continue to exist (see, for example, Blau and Duncan, 1967; Kerr et al., 1960; Kerr, 1983; Treiman, 1970). In other words, there is a progressive movement away from a 'closed' class society towards a meritocratic society of a supposedly far more 'open' kind.

However, in the light of the research results that have so far accumulated, support for this liberal scenario can scarcely be thought impressive. Long-term changes in the interrelations between class and education of the kind envisaged turn out in most national societies to be scarcely, if at all, detectable (see especially Blossfeld and Shavit, 1992). Moreover, a further major problem is raised by another crossnationally robust finding from the side of mobility research: namely, that relative rates of intergenerational class mobility typically show a high degree of temporal stability (Erikson and Goldthorpe, 1992a: ch. 3). In the case of Britain, for example, at least four independent analyses have revealed little change at all in such rates over the course of the present century – and certainly none in the direction of greater fluidity (Goldthorpe, 1987: chs 3 and 9; Hope, 1981; Macdonald and Ridge, 1987; Marshall et al., 1988: ch. 5). Thus, even if it could be established that social selection has become more meritocratic, there is little indication of this having had any effect in producing more equal class mobility chances.

In the British case, where research on this issue has been perhaps more extensive than elsewhere, it was initially suggested by Halsey (1977) that although some evidence of a 'tightening bond' between education and worklife success was apparent over the middle decades of the century, this had been offset by widening class differentials in educational attainment, accompanied by little or no reduction in the strength of the 'direct' effects (those not mediated via education) of class origins on class destinations. In the light of subsequent research based on more extensive longitudinal data and more refined analytical techniques, the claim of actually widening class differentials in education would seem difficult to uphold; and the issue has rather become that of whether these differentials have remained essentially unaltered or have in some respects shown a degree of narrowing (Heath and Clifford, 1990; Jonsson and Mills, 1993).[10] But what then also emerges is greater doubt about the supposed secular tendency for educational attainment to become more important as a determinant of destination class. Increasing occupational selection by merit, at least in so far as this is defined by educational credentials, is not easy to discern (see Heath et al., 1991a and Jonsson, 1991a for similar results for Sweden).

In sum, the evidence for education operating as a force of 'class abatement' remains slight. Rather, what is suggested by the research to which we have referred is that a high degree of resistance can be expected to any tendency favouring a reduction of class inequalities via 'meritocracy'. If education does become somewhat more important in determining worklife chances, then members of relatively advantaged classes will seek to use their superior resources in order to ensure that their children maintain a competitive edge in educational attainment; or, as Halsey (1977: 184) puts it, 'ascriptive forces find ways of expressing themselves as "achievement".' Alternatively, and as seems perhaps the more likely occurrence, if class differentials in educational attainment are to some extent diminished, then within more advantaged classes family resources can be applied through *other* channels, in order to help children preserve their class prospects against the threat of meritocratic selection (see Marshall and Swift, Chapter 9 in this volume). We do not, we would stress, seek to argue here that class inequalities can *never* be mitigated through changes in educational systems and their functioning: only that there is no reason to suppose, as liberal theorists would wish to do, that this is likely to occur as the automatic and benign outcome of social processes that are in some way inherent in the development of industrial societies.[11]

Class and political partisanship

For those who believe that in modern societies the impact of class on life-chances is in decline, there is a natural progression to the further claim that class is also of reduced importance in shaping the response of individuals to their social situation, in particular through political action. During the 1950s and 1960s liberal sociologists were pleased to describe the partici-pation of citizens in the electoral politics of Western nations as representing 'the democratic translation of the class struggle' (Lipset, 1960: ch. 7). However, under the influence of political as much as of social developments from the later 1970s onwards, a much stronger position was taken up. Class, it was now held, was (finally) dissolving as the basis of political partisanship, and this was most evident in the declining support from the working class for parties of the left (see, for example, Lipset, 1981; Clark and Lipset, 1991). Moreover, such a diagnosis has also come to be accepted by many of the former leaders of *marxisant* social commentary, in their despairing *adieux* to the working class in particular and to class analysis in general.

In the British case, the thesis of 'class dealignment' in party politics has perhaps a longer history than elsewhere, and following the Conservative electoral triumphs of 1979 and 1983 it was enthusiastically revived by a series of authors (for example, Butler and Kavanagh, 1985; Crewe, 1984; Franklin, 1985; Robertson, 1984; Rose and McAllister, 1986).[12] Among the latter it was widely believed that the counterpart to the declining effect of class on vote was a tendency for party-political conflicts to become organized more around 'issues' than socially structured 'interests' of any kind. However, in the view of certain other commentators, class was giving way to new structural cleavages as the basis of party support – in particular, cleavages which divided individuals and families, considered as either producers or consumers, according to their location in the public or the private sector of the economy (see Duke and Edgell, 1984; Dunleavy, 1979; 1980a; 1980b; Dunleavy and Husbands, 1985; Saunders, 1984).

Critics of class analysis such as Pahl and Holton and Turner have, apparently, looked little beyond this range of literature. They write as if the thesis of class dealignment were securely established within electoral sociology and the 'new structuralism' now provides the paradigm to be reckoned with (Holton and Turner, 1989: 177, 186–90; Pahl, 1989: 713). What they quite fail to recognize, however, is the extent to which both the 'new structuralism' and the underlying claim of class dealignment have in fact been empirically challenged, and on the basis of research and analysis that has significantly raised technical standards in the field.

Most importantly, Heath and his associates have shown the necessity of introducing into the debate on dealignment a distinction between absolute and relative rates of class voting, analogous to that between absolute and relative rates of social mobility (Evans et al., 1991; Heath et al., 1985; 1991b). Applying this distinction to data on voting in British elections from 1964 to 1987, they are able to show that changes in absolute (or, that is, actually observed) class voting patterns are almost entirely attributable to two factors: on the one hand, changes in the 'shape' of the class structure, most importantly the growth of the service class or salariat and the decline in size of the industrial working class; and, on the other hand, changes in the number of political parties contesting elections and in their general effectiveness (that is, in their capacity to win support 'across the board', in equal degree from members of all classes alike). In contrast, changes in relative class voting – or, in other words, in the *net* association between class membership and vote – turn out to be rather slight. Moreover, in so far as such changes can be detected, they show no secular tendency for the class–vote association to decline, and appear more open to explanation in political than sociological terms (see especially Heath et al., 1991b: ch. 5). Although, for some, these findings have proved disturbingly counter-intuitive, it is important to note that they are confirmed in their essentials by those of a number of quite independent, if more restricted, analyses (see Hibbs, 1982; Marshall et al., 1988: ch. 9; Weakliem, 1989).[13]

As Heath and his colleagues then go on to argue, their results bring out clearly the dangers of 'dualistic historical thinking' on the issue of class formation, of the kind in which critics of class analysis have tended to engage. So far at least as the evidence of political partisanship is concerned, there is in fact no reason to suppose that over recent decades, classes in Britain – the working class included – have shown any weakening in either their social cohesion or their ideological distinctiveness. This conclusion is also consistent with a variety of other findings on, for example, trends (or their absence) in patterns of class mobility, in levels of class identification, and in class differences in political attitudes and values (Heath et al., 1991b: chs 5 and 6; compare also Heath, 1990).[14]

Furthermore, at the same time as the thesis of class dealignment has been called into question, so too have the claims of the 'new structuralism', at least in their more ambitious versions. It is important to recognize here that the argument that political partisanship may be influenced, over and above the effects of class, by such factors as whether an individual is employed in the public or private sector of the economy, or is a home-owner or council tenant, is in itself far from new and, in any event, creates no problem whatever for exponents of class analysis. For the latter have never supposed that class alone determines vote; and sources of differentiation in political orientations and action *within* classes have always been of interest to them. Class analysis is only challenged in so far as it is maintained that sectoral cleavages have by now superseded those of class in providing the major structural basis of partisanship across the electorate as a whole. It is, however, exactly this kind of argument that has been empirically undermined by the studies cited above (see especially Heath et al., 1991b: chs 6 and 7; also Marshall et al., 1988: 248–54).

Thus, for example, as regards 'production' cleavages, some effect on vote may be discerned within the salariat, according to whether individuals are employed in the private or different branches of the public sector – although it is likely that this reflects in part at least more specific *occupational* factors and also self-selection processes. But, for the present purposes, the important point is that no comparable effect is to be found within the working class. Conversely, as regards 'consumption' cleavages as represented by housing tenure, some effect on vote can be seen within the working class – though with the direction of causal influence being again questionable – but no such effect is apparent within the salariat.

In other words, there are two quite different features of sectoral cleavage being proposed, neither of which turns out to exert an influence on partisanship that has anything like the generality or the overall strength of that of class. Recently, one may observe, the weight of the empirical evidence would appear to have led some proponents of sectoral cleavage arguments to modify positions they earlier adopted. Thus, for example, Saunders (1990b: 234) states that his most recent research 'would seem to confirm previous studies which claim that the electoral significance of housing tenure is secondary to that of social class and that its effects may be more pronounced in some strata than in others'.[15]

From the standpoint of the research programme of class analysis, the relative weakness of sectoral effects is not in fact difficult to understand, especially in regard to consumption. For one thing, 'boundary problems' are here truly formidable, since many if not most individuals will be extensively engaged in both the public and the private sectors simultaneously. For another, the mobility regimes determining the degree of association over time between individuals or families and different sectoral locations would appear to be far more fluid than those that apply in the case of class.[16] Thus, one may point out, doubts of the kind that Pahl and Holton and Turner express concerning the formation of collective identities and a perceived commonality of interests on the basis of class should apply *a fortiori* so far as consumption cleavages are concerned – though this is in fact a point that they pass over in silence.

Conclusion

We have sought in this chapter to respond to recent critiques of class analysis on two principal grounds. First, we argued that critics have not adequately distinguished between class analysis in its Marxist versions and class analysis understood and engaged in as a research programme. Various objections that may be powerfully raised against the former simply do not apply to the latter. This is scarcely surprising, given the extent to which class analysis viewed as a field of empirical sociological inquiry freed from entanglements with the philosophy of history and 'critical theory' did in fact develop as a reaction against Marxism. Secondly, we have attempted to show, by reference to three central topics, that the research programme of class analysis has in fact yielded results permitting a flat rejection of the claims of Pahl and of Holton and Turner that class as a concept no longer does useful work, and retains only a rhetorical and not a scientific value.[17]

Finally, we may note that the two main lines of argument that we have pursued do in a sense converge. For Marxists, class analysis was the key to the understanding of long-term social change: class relations and specifically class conflict provided the engine of this change, and the study of their dynamics was crucial to obtaining the desired cognitive grasp on the movement of history. However, class analysis as a research programme not only is a quite different kind of intellectual undertaking from the class analysis of Marxism, but also generates results which give a new perspective on the substantive significance of class relations in contemporary society. A common theme in the research findings now accumulating is, as we have seen, that of the *stability* rather than the dynamism of class relations. What is revealed is a remarkable persistence of class-linked inequalities and of class-differentiated patterns of social action, even within periods of rapid change at the level of economic structure, social institutions, and political conjunctures. The disclosure of such stability – made possible largely by the advances in techniques of data analysis and in the construction of data-sets to which we have referred – would in turn appear to carry two major implications. Most obviously, problems are created for liberal theorists of industrial society who would anticipate the more or less spontaneous 'withering away' of class, and of class analysis likewise. But at the same time the need is indicated for the theoretical concerns of proponents of class analysis to be radically reoriented. They must focus, not on the explanation of social change via class relations, but rather on understanding the processes that underlie the profound resistance to change that such relations offer.

Notes

* John H. Goldthorpe and Gordon Marshall. The authors wish to thank Geoff Evans, A.H. Halsey and Ray Pahl for helpful comments on an earlier draft of this chapter.

1 Pahl can only be read as supposing that such a theory is involved in *any* kind of class analysis. Sørensen (1991: 73) argues that such a theory is integral to Marxist class analysis and *may* be present in 'Weberian' versions. Hindess (1987: 24) claims to find a historicist position in Goldthorpe (1980: 28–9) which he contrasts with that of Heath et al. (1985). The contrast is not, however, apparent either to Goldthorpe or to Heath and his associates (compare Heath et al., 1991b: ch. 5), and would appear to derive from a complete misreading by Hindess of the passage from Goldthorpe that he cites.

2 We should make it clear here that we do not wish to suggest that this programme is one of a formally organized kind. Rather, it is undertaken by a loosely textured network of quite independent researchers, with some institutional underpinning being provided by bodies such as ISA Research Committee 28 on Social Stratification. It should moreover again be said that a shared interest in the programme in no way implies consensus on theoretical or, for that matter, substantive issues. The idea of such a programme indeed implies significant areas of controversy.

3 Sørensen (1991: 73) argues that while the class schema developed by Goldthorpe and others – unlike that advanced by Marxists such as Wright – does not explicitly claim relations of exploitation between the classes distinguished, the idea of exploitation cannot be avoided by those using the schema, since Goldthorpe's analysis assumes 'a class theory of inequality that would seem to need an exploitation concept at its basis'. To this, we must respond that Sørensen nowhere shows just why this argument should hold. In fact, he subsequently shifts his ground to making a quite different criticism: namely that Goldthorpe and others have advanced no theory of the general relationship between class position and differential rewards. This, we would accept, is the case, and the relationship is one that undoubtedly calls for more systematic investigation – even though more of a start has perhaps been made than Sørensen acknowledges. Thus, for example, the idea of the 'efficiency wage' is not only prefigured in Wright's 'loyalty wage' concept, as Sørensen recognizes, but also, and more fully, in Renner's (1953) argument on the essential distinction between the 'service relationship' and the labour contract, which is developed in Goldthorpe (1982) and provides a key element in the class schema that he and his associates have developed (compare Erikson and Goldthorpe, 1992a: ch. 2).

4 Thus, for example, Hindess contends, with respect to Esping-Andersen and Korpi (1984), that 'class interests are seen as objectively given in the structure of capitalist relations' (1987: 99). There is simply no warrant for this statement, and indeed a diametrically opposing view is central to the argument of Esping-Andersen (1985).

5 To this extent, we would in fact concur with the conclusions reached by Wright (1989b: 313–23) in the course of providing a comparison of Marxist and non-Marxist class analysis, from the Marxist side.

6 For another instance, see Saunders (1990b: 221). One good illustration of the way in which the use of different class categorizations can produce results differing in their substantive implications – but also in their validity – is provided in note 14 below.

7 Prestige or status scales tend to bring together – quite properly on their own terms – occupational or other groupings that have widely disparate locations within labour markets, production units and economic sectors; and these groupings are then likely to be set on quite different trajectories of growth or decline (compare Erikson and Goldthorpe, 1992a: ch. 6; Westergaard and Resler, 1976: 287). Thus, where a prestige or status hierarchy is taken as the

conceptual context for the study of mobility, the full extent of effects deriving from structural change in the economy is likely to be obscured.

8 Note that we are *not* here arguing in favour of the procedure, advocated by Breiger (1981) and others as essentially 'Weberian', whereby class boundaries are *actually determined* on the basis of mobility analyses. Whether or not this approach can claim any serious endorsement in Weber's work, it is, in our view, excessively empiricist and likely to lead to major interpretive problems.

9 To repeat, however, the importance of political factors in this process must always be recognized. Note also that the mobility characteristics to which we here refer are defined in terms of *absolute* rates (though relative rates of course play a part in their determination).

10 Much seems to turn here (and also in analogous debates in the USA) on just how educational attainment is measured: that is, by reference simply to the number of years spent in education, or via more or less refined classifications of educational careers or of qualifications obtained.

11 Even among those who still believe that some association can be shown between industrialism and growing equality in educational attainment and relative mobility chances, the connection is now regarded not as deriving from developmental necessity but rather as the more contingent outcome of a variety of factors, including political ones. See, for example, Ganzeboom et al. (1989), Treiman and Yip (1989). Critical commentary on the data and analyses of these studies can be found in Erikson and Goldthorpe (1992a) and Jones (1991).

12 The main emphasis was of course on factors tending to reduce support for Labour among the working class – just as it was in the period after the third successive electoral defeat suffered by Labour in 1959. However, the 1970s version of 'class dealignment' concentrated, rather, on the causes of declining middle-class support for the Conservatives.

13 Critiques of the work of Heath and his associates on the class–vote association (for example Crewe, 1987; Dunleavy, 1987) have not, to say the least, been impressive, and have been given short shrift (compare Heath et al., 1987a; 1987b). Some subsequent commentaries on the debate (such as Edgell and Duke, 1991: 55–8) show a disturbing lack of comprehension of the procedures followed by Heath and his associates and of the issues involved. Also disturbing is the continuing use of the 'Alford Index' as a measure of 'class voting', as, for example, by Clark and Lipset (1991: Figure 1), when the grave deficiencies of this have for long been known (see, for example, Heath et al., 1985; Korpi, 1983: 87–9). One may set against the results reported by Clark and Lipset those presented by Weakliem (1991), which derive from far more appropriate analysis, and show that a more or less stable class–vote association is by no means a British peculiarity.

14 What was taken – at the level of Sunday newspaper sociology – to be the most obvious example of working-class decomposition was the distinctive propensity for 'skilled workers' to desert Labour for the Conservatives. However, evidence cited to support this claim would seem likely to be an artefact of the changing composition of the Market Research Society 'C2' category. Although usually referred to as that of skilled workers, the category is, in class terms, quite heterogeneous, comprising, in addition to rank-and-file wage-workers, manual supervisory grades and self-employed artisans. These latter groupings have always had a higher rate of Conservative voting than the former and, from the late 1970s on, would have been a growing component of the category as a whole. If a more adequately defined skilled working-class category is adopted, no clear tendency emerges for its members to become more likely than members of other classes to vote Conservative rather than Labour (compare Heath et al., 1986).

15 When undertaking appropriate multivariate analyses, Saunders is in fact unable to detect *any* significant effect of housing tenure on vote within his (very small) sample (1990b: Table 4.12). He argues that some more specific effects are indicated within the collapsed 'intermediate' classes of the Goldthorpe schema. However, it is extremely ill-advised to make such a collapse in any analysis concerning voting behaviour, since the voting patterns of the members of these classes are so different. Again, Edgell and Duke (1991: 69), after taking the 'new structuralism' with great seriousness, are obliged to acknowledge that 'class dealignment is a myth', and the most they can say for sectoral factors is that they influence variation in

voting behaviour from one election to another 'depending on particular historical circum-stances'. Moreover, even this conclusion does not follow in any compelling way from the analyses they report, which are quite inadequate to the issues they address.

16 That this is indeed so with housing has been shown by Savage et al. (1990) for an area of South-East England.

17 In this connection it is worth noting that we have cited over a score of recent books, monographs and research papers, exemplifying class analysis as we would understand it, which, for whatever reasons, received virtually no mention from these critics.

Part II
METHOD AND MEASUREMENT

3
Classes in Britain: Marxist and Official

This chapter reports some of the findings from an international comparative analysis of class structure and class consciousness. The project was initiated by Erik Olin Wright in the United States and involves academics in more than a dozen countries. The principal objective was straightforward enough: to organize strictly comparable surveys of class structure and class consciousness in different countries throughout the capitalist world and so provide a rigorously comparative analysis of class processes.[1]

The various teams participating in the project agreed to conduct a class analysis of their respective societies in terms of the class categories devised by Wright himself. The logic of Wright's schema (Table 3.1) has been explained at length elsewhere (Wright, 1979). He argues that, in each mode of production, certain basic social classes are defined by being completely polarized within the relevant relations of production. Under capitalism, for example, the working class is completely dispossessed of the means of production, and must sell its labour power to the bourgeoisie, so is both exploited and dominated by it. However, in the absence of wholesale polarization, contradictory locations within a mode of production also arise. Managers, for example, are simultaneously in two classes. They are workers, since they are exploited by capital (managerial work contributes to surplus value), yet capitalists in that they dominate workers (managers exercise control at the point of production).

Moreover, concrete social formations rarely comprise a single mode of production, so that capitalist societies, for example, will typically contain certain non-capitalist forms of production relations. Most obviously they inherit the legacy of simple commodity production in which direct producers own and control only their own productive means (including their own labour power). These are the *petite bourgeoisie* more common to feudal societies but also extant in capitalist societies as the 'self-employed' or 'own account workers'. Furthermore, certain class locations in fact interpenetrate both modes of production, and so constitute contradictory locations between them. The most important of these define small employers on the one hand, and semi-autonomous employees on the other. The former are simultaneously *petit bourgeois* and capitalist in that they are self-employed direct producers but also employers and therefore exploiters

Table 3.1   *The Wright class categories*[1]

Capitalist mode of production		Simple commodity production
Bourgeoisie		
	Small employers	
Managers and supervisors		Petite bourgeoisie
	Semi-autonomous employees	
Proletariat		

[1] Italicized classes are those holding contradictory locations within class relations (see text).

of labour. Semi-autonomous employees are non-owners of productive means but continue to exercise considerable control over their own activities within production. Employed professionals are the example most often cited by Wright.

Wright argues that the relational properties of exploitation and domination which underpin his scheme can be tapped by means of information about ownership of productive means, the degree of autonomy exercised by individuals at work, and their involvement in decision making and the supervision of other employees. These translate into concrete activities such as participation in decisions dealing with budgets and investment, the ability to design and execute work tasks, possession of authority to impose sanctions upon subordinates, and so forth. It is these questions – Wright's operationalization of his class framework – which form the common core of the survey research instruments used in the various national studies and so permit each to conduct a class analysis in terms of Wright's own categories.

The principal comparative effort thus far has examined the results for Sweden alongside those obtained for the United States (see, for example, Ahrne and Wright, 1983). This suggests that the class structures of the two societies are somewhat different (Table 3.2). Most noticeably, there are relatively more managers and supervisors in the United States than in Sweden, whereas the Swedish class structure contains a higher proportion of semi-autonomous employees. The differences are explained by political factors – notably the effects of the state and of differences in the constitution of authority relations at work (the 'political dimension' of production). Sweden has a proportionately much bigger state sector than the United States. Ahrne and Wright speculate that this might be due either to the limited possibilities for accumulation open to smaller countries within the capitalist world system or to the more successful forms of political struggle pursued by Swedish workers (or perhaps both). In any event, the effect of increasing state employment is to generate relatively larger numbers of semi-autonomous employees, since the public sector characteristically contains proportionately fewer proletarians than are involved in

Table 3.2 *The Wright class structures of Sweden, the United States, and Great Britain (% by column)*

Class	Sweden	United States	Britain
Bourgeoisie	0.7	1.8	2.0
Small employers	4.7	6.0	4.5
Petite bourgeoisie	5.4	6.9	6.0
Managers and supervisors:			
managers	11.1	12.3	12.4
advisory managers	3.2	4.6	4.5
supervisors	6.8	12.8	9.4
Semi-autonomous employees	17.4	9.5	11.6
Workers	50.7	46.2	49.6
Total	100.0	100.0	100.0
(N)	(1,180)	(1,491)	(1,315)

private enterprises. Moreover, in the United States, the supervisory aspects of managerial functions are more commonly delegated to class positions which would otherwise be proletarian, so increasing the numbers involved in supervisory activities in production. Somewhat paradoxically, Ahrne and Wright trace this tendency for American capitalists to integrate large numbers of routine wage-earners into lower management to the relative powerlessness and decentralization of the labour movement in that country. The long-standing weakness of the unions means that American management is usually excluded from the union bargaining unit by law. By comparison, the more powerful union movement in Sweden has eliminated restrictions on its organizational activities, and so embraces many supervisory and lower-level management positions within its scope. In an attempt to avoid obvious class polarization American management has 'incorporated' skilled clerical, craft, and service workers to perform routine supervisory activities. Such a strategy segments the working class and helps maintain the weakness of the union movement. This difference between the two countries is probably reinforced by the fact that the more centralized Swedish unions can themselves discipline their members and so make the social control activities of Swedish capitalists less imperative.

Whether or not one agrees with this kind of analysis, there can be no doubt that Wright's enterprise is one of the major attempts in class analysis to treat social class as an object of investigation in its own right; that is, as a structure to be explained rather than simply as another variable to be used in the explanation of particular outcomes. In most analyses class is an independent variable or explanans. Wright deserves considerable praise for addressing himself also to the question of class as a dependent variable or explanandum. He would be the first to admit that his attempt to explain the differences between the class structures of Sweden and the United States is somewhat speculative. The task of 'mapping' these structures to a common scale is itself a major preliminary exercise, and subsequent explanations for the observed similarities and differences are programmatic, rather than conclusive in nature.

Nevertheless, Ahrne and Wright are convinced that their results reflect 'real differences in the world and not simply differences in our measuring devices' (1983: 215). Every care was taken to ensure that the samples were fully representative of their respective populations; the same survey questions were used to operationalize the class categories in each country; and Wright's instructions for coding the data were followed scrupulously throughout. This close attention to the details of research design is an attempt to ensure that, as far as it is possible to facilitate this, the comparative results are *reliable*. That is, that the findings reported paint a reasonably robust picture of the class structures of Sweden and the United States, in terms of Wright's class categories. However, Ahrne and Wright fail to address themselves to the possibility that these categories themselves are suspect, and so yield a class map which cannot be said to give a *valid* representation of class realities. In other words, the categories of the schema do not measure what they are supposed to; that is, relatively homogeneous class locations.

This chapter matches the information from the British survey of class structure and class consciousness to the analytical datum provided by Wright himself in order to illustrate my reservations about the veracity of his findings. Two class groupings in particular are examined: the proletariat and the 'marginal working class' in the contradictory locations adjacent to it. The data suggest that Wright's working class contains large numbers of routine clerical workers whose proletarian credentials are suspect. There are good grounds for believing that these employees can more appropriately be aligned alongside the 'marginal middle classes' of Wright's model. Moreover, the marginal working-class categories are themselves so heterogeneous in their composition as to raise serious doubts about their integrity as class locations at all, certainly from Wright's own point of view which is that of determining their potential as 'class allies' of the proletariat in its long march towards socialism.

However, before proceeding to the details of this analysis, there is one preliminary complication that must briefly be dealt with. Those familiar with Wright's work will know that he has revised his class scheme and, indeed, abandoned altogether the theory of contradictory class locations which underpinned it. Perhaps, therefore, we should not take the original model that seriously? In fact matters are by no means as clear-cut as this. Most of Wright's colleagues within the comparative project seem convinced that the initial class scheme is in almost all respects superior to the revised version: it is more rigorously Marxist; it is more systematically operationalized (since the common survey research instrument was designed and fielded before Wright published his autocritique); and, finally, it is not contaminated by the inclusion of occupational data in a class algorithm supposedly expressing social, rather than technical, relations of production. (I shall pursue this last point below.) Consequently, most of the comparative projects have continued to base their analyses on the first rather than the second of Wright's class frameworks, although the British study actually reports the results for both (see Marshall et al., 1988). In fairness to Wright I shall examine the newer scheme later in this chapter. Nevertheless, since most of the criticisms to be made in respect of the original model apply equally to the revised version, it is appropriate to express my critique in terms of Wright's first, and more popular, formulation.

The British class structure

The basic data on the class structure of Britain, conceptualized in terms of Wright's original class categories, are summarized in Table 3.2. As far as the comparative analysis itself is concerned, there are two points that are worth making with regard to these results. First, and most obviously, the overall shape of the British class structure is similar to that reported by Ahrne for Sweden and Wright for the USA. About half of the labour force in each country will be found in proletarian locations with another 12–15 per cent in the various employer categories. Second, such differences as there are tend to arise in respect of contradictory, rather than basic class locations. While the variation in the range of the worker and capitalist positions is quite modest, that for managers and semi-autonomous employees is comparatively large, at around 8 per cent. Among the former, in fact, the countries are rather similar at the level of policy-making management: 11.1 per cent for Sweden, 12.3 per cent for the USA, and 12.4 per cent for Britain. Even at the level of advisory management the proportions in the various countries range only from 3.2 (Sweden) to 4.6 per cent (USA). Rather, the differences arise principally at the level of non-decision-making supervisory positions, where (as was noted by Ahrne and Wright) there is a full 6 per cent difference between Sweden and the United States. Britain falls almost exactly half-way between these two. In the case of semi-autonomous employees, by comparison, Britain is more like America than Sweden, having some 2 per cent more such class locations than the former country, but around 6 per cent less than the latter.

These results are certainly consistent with Ahrne and Wright's contention that the basic shape of class structures is broadly similar across capitalist countries and that the principal differences between them originate in the manner by which authority and autonomy are organized within production. But do the similarities in the sizes of basic classes, and the differences in the relative sizes of contradictory class locations, actually reflect meaningful differences in the real world of class relationships? No less than half of all employed respondents to the British survey are, following Wright's logic and research procedures, to be classified as proletarians. This is considerably out of step with the figures for socio-economic groups obtained in the closest (1981) British census, where the categories of skilled, semi-skilled, and unskilled manual employees together comprise a mere 36 per cent of the economically active population. So how plausible is Wright's account? Does his working class represent a homogeneous category of wage-earners or has it been artificially swollen as an artefact of his theory and methodology?

Clerks and proletarians

It is not difficult to establish why Wright's working class represents such a large percentage of the workforce. With Braverman, he suspects that 'the large majority of white-collar employees, especially clerical and secretarial employees, have – at most – trivial autonomy on the job and thus should be placed within the working class itself' (Wright, 1979: 81). For this reason the common questionnaire for the national surveys contains a sequence of questions designed to determine the extent to which particular groups of wage-labourers possess autonomy of conception and execution in their work tasks.[2] Semi-autonomous employees share in the knowledge of how the whole production process in which they are involved is organized and have the capacity to use such knowledge in their jobs. Workers are non-decision-making, non-supervisory employees, who have been 'deskilled'; that is, they perform simple routinized tasks, under close supervision, and at a pace determined by machinery or by decision makers elsewhere, rather than by themselves. According to these criteria, large numbers of routine clerical and secretarial staff have been proletarianized. It is the inclusion of these white-collar workers which – in the British data at least – swells the ranks of the working class beyond its conventional boundaries.

This is confirmed by an inspection of the distribution of occupations within the various class categories. The International Class Project codes occupations, for comparative purposes, to United States 1970 census categories collapsed by Wright, first to a 27-category typology, then to the 13 categories listed in Table 3.3. This exercise has failed to solve all of the problems associated with coding occupations from different national surveys to a common classification. (Some of the difficulties are discussed in Marshall et al., 1988.) But the scheme serves well enough for present purposes, since it can clearly be seen from this table that more than two-thirds of all routine clerical workers in the British sample are to be found in Wright's proletariat, where they comprise more than one-fifth of this class as a whole.

How valid is this reconceptualization of the working class? At one level, of course, the *internal* validity of Wright's procedure is entirely sound. Those respondents so classified all answered the autonomy questions (together with those on ownership, supervision and decision making) in the negative. But is this classification meaningful, given that Wright's stated objective is to resolve the ambiguities in the class structure according to the real processes of class relations in actually existing societies, and not simply

Table 3.3 Wright classes and occupational categories, Great Britain

(a) Distribution of occupations within classes (% by row)

Occupational categories	Class[1]									
	B	SE	PB	M	AM	S	SAE	W	Total	(N)
Professionals	5.2	7.8	5.2	20.9	7.8	17.4	15.7	20.0	100.0	(115)
Teachers	0.0	0.0	0.0	21.6	9.8	11.8	43.1	13.7	100.0	(51)
Technicians	4.3	2.1	12.8	8.5	6.4	17.0	27.7	21.3	100.0	(47)
Managers	8.1	16.3	14.0	36.6	8.7	9.3	2.9	4.1	100.0	(172)
Clericals	0.0	0.5	1.0	7.4	3.9	6.9	12.8	67.5	100.0	(203)
Sales	0.0	0.0	2.9	1.4	2.9	8.7	31.9	52.2	100.0	(69)
Foremen	0.0	0.0	0.0	16.7	0.0	50.0	0.0	33.3	100.0	(6)
Crafts	0.9	3.7	0.0	10.0	6.8	10.5	7.8	50.2	100.0	(219)
Operatives	0.5	0.5	3.0	5.0	0.5	4.0	4.5	81.9	100.0	(199)
Labourers	0.0	8.6	7.1	4.3	0.0	5.7	2.9	71.4	100.0	(70)
Skilled services	2.4	0.0	0.0	17.1	2.4	14.6	17.1	46.3	100.0	(41)
Unskilled services	0.0	0.0	0.9	1.8	0.0	8.8	10.6	77.9	100.0	(113)
Farmers	0.0	50.0	50.0	0.0	0.0	0.0	0.0	0.0	100.0	(10)

continued overleaf

Table 3.3 (cont.)

(b) Distribution of classes within occupations (% by column)

Occupational categories	Class[1]							
	B	SE	PB	M	AM	S	SAE	W
Professionals	23.1	15.3	7.6	14.7	15.3	16.1	11.8	3.5
Teachers	0.0	0.0	0.0	6.7	8.5	4.8	14.4	1.1
Technicians	7.7	1.7	7.6	2.5	5.1	6.5	8.5	1.5
Managers	53.8	47.5	30.4	38.7	25.4	12.9	3.3	1.1
Clericals	0.0	1.7	2.5	9.2	13.6	11.3	17.0	21.0
Sales	0.0	0.0	2.5	0.6	3.4	4.8	14.4	5.5
Foremen	0.0	0.0	0.0	0.6	0.0	2.4	0.0	0.3
Crafts	7.7	13.6	27.8	13.5	25.4	18.5	11.1	16.9
Operatives	3.8	1.7	7.6	6.1	1.7	6.5	5.9	15.0
Labourers	0.0	10.2	6.3	1.8	0.0	3.2	1.3	7.7
Skilled services	3.8	0.0	0.0	4.3	1.7	4.8	4.6	2.9
Unskilled services	0.0	0.0	1.3	1.2	0.0	8.1	7.8	13.5
Farmers	0.0	8.5	6.3	0.0	0.0	0.0	0.0	0.0
Total	100.0	100.0	100.0	100.0	100.0	100.0	100.0	100.0
(N)	(26)	(59)	(79)	(163)	(59)	(124)	(153)	(652)

[1] Key to Wright class categories: B = bourgeoisie; SE = small employers; PB = petite bourgeoisie; M = managers; AM = advisory managers; S = supervisors; SAE = semi-autonomous employees; W = workers.

in terms of abstract principles deriving from the formal (and highly unrealistic) propositions of earlier and more crude versions of Marxist class theory? Classes, as he puts it,

> are not merely analytical abstractions in Marxist theory; they are real social forces and they have real consequences. It matters a great deal for our understanding of class struggle and social change exactly how classes are conceptualized and which categories of social positions are placed in which classes. Above all, it matters for developing a viable socialist politics how narrow or broad the working class is seen to be and how its relationship to other classes is understood. (1979: 30–1)

So how 'realistic' is Wright's working class in terms of his socialist objectives? In other words does, his particular conception of the proletariat possess any *external* validity, in that it reflects a meaningful grouping of class actors in society?

One way of addressing the problem is to examine Wright's model of the class structure alongside an alternative. The official, and most commonly used, measure of social class in Britain today is that devised by the Registrar-General for the analysis of census and related statistics. This schema rests on the assumption that society is a graded hierarchy of occupations ranked according to skill. Occupations are allocated to five basic social classes (with the armed forces classified separately), according to the degree of expertise involved in carrying out their associated tasks, and the resulting categories are assumed to be homogeneous in these terms. Since occupations are placed in social classes on the basis of judgements made by the staff at the Office of Population Censuses and Surveys, and not in accordance with any coherent body of social theory, the classification has rightly been described as an intuitive or *a priori* scale. Since 1921, when it was first used in the analysis of official statistics, a number of changes have been implemented both in the method of classifying occupations and in the allocation of particular occupations to social classes. In practice, however, the overall shape of the model has changed very little during the past 50 years.[3]

Superimposing the Registrar-General's class map of Britain on that drawn by Wright (as in Table 3.4) confirms that fully one-quarter of the respondents classified by Wright as proletarians are redistributed to the skilled nonmanual category. In large part these are the same routine clerical and secretarial workers who, in Wright's terms, lack workplace autonomy and so are indistinguishable in class terms from the manual working class. Now, it may well be the case (as Wright claims) that these particular white-collar workers perform largely routinized tasks under externally imposed terms and conditions, and it may even be true that the material rewards extracted for such labour are no greater than those typically earned by skilled or even unskilled manual labourers. But, considered from Wright's point of view, a problem soon emerges in that the socio-political proclivities of the two groups are somewhat different. As we shall see, analysis of the British data suggests that the 'real consequence' of even routine or

Table 3.4 Distribution of Wright classes within Registrar-General's classes, Great Britain (% by column)

| | | | | Wright classes[1] | | | | |
Registrar-General's classes	B	SE	PB	M	AM	S	SAE	W
1 Professional	19.2	8.5	3.8	8.0	6.8	8.1	2.6	0.6
2 Intermediate	69.2	44.1	36.7	55.2	44.1	33.9	34.6	6.6
3N Skilled nonmanual	0.0	15.3	12.7	12.3	27.1	18.5	34.0	25.2
3M Skilled manual	11.5	23.7	34.2	19.0	22.0	34.7	14.4	31.4
4 Partly skilled	0.0	6.8	10.1	1.2	0.0	3.2	13.7	26.5
5 Unskilled	0.0	1.7	2.5	0.0	0.0	0.8	0.7	9.5
6 Armed forces	0.0	0.0	0.0	4.3	0.0	0.8	0.0	0.2
Total	100.0	100.0	100.0	100.0	100.0	100.0	100.0	100.0
(N)	(26)	(59)	(79)	(163)	(59)	(124)	(153)	(652)

[1] For Wright class categories see Table 3.3.

Table 3.5 *Aspects of socio-political class formation, Great Britain: Registrar-General's classes (% by column)*

	Registrar-General's classes						
	1	2	3N	3M	4	5	6
Self-assigned class							
Middle (incl. upper)	83.7	65.4	52.5	26.1	26.8	23.1	66.7
Working	16.3	34.6	47.5	73.9	73.2	76.9	33.3
Total	100.0	100.0	100.0	100.0	100.0	100.0	100.0
(*N*)	(43)	(292)	(276)	(329)	(198)	(65)	(9)
Voting intention							
Conservative	42.9	45.6	48.6	28.1	28.1	22.4	88.9
Labour	14.3	21.9	23.5	49.5	44.9	53.4	0.0
SDP/Liberal	35.7	23.3	19.0	16.1	15.2	17.2	0.0
Would not vote	7.1	9.2	8.9	6.3	11.8	6.9	11.1
Total	100.0	100.0	100.0	100.0	100.0	100.0	100.0
(*N*)	(42)	(283)	(247)	(317)	(178)	(58)	(9)

'deskilled' nonmanual work is to shape class identities in this country in such a way as to give those involved a socio-political profile that has more in common with that for the middle classes than that for the proletariat. This casts considerable doubt on the viability of the socialist politics informed by Wright's definition of its working-class constituency. Two sorts of data in particular tell against Wright's account: those on self-assigned class and on voting.

Table 3.5 reports the data in question. The top half of this table shows self-assigned class according to the Registrar-General's class categories for respondents to the British survey. It will be seen that there are very clear differences between manual and nonmanual workers. In particular, the distribution of responses for routine nonmanual workers (class 3N) is rather similar to that for other nonmanual employees, with a majority in each class category identifying themselves as middle (or upper) class. This is very different from the situation that prevails among manual employees where, irrespective of skill, well over 70 per cent in each category place themselves in the working class. The bottom half of the table raises similar sorts of questions about Wright's classification of routine clerical workers as part of the proletariat rather than as a separate class grouping. In terms of their voting intentions, class 3N (routine clerical) employees are again more akin to other nonmanual workers than to manual workers at any skill level. In fact, they are (if anything) rather more likely to vote for the (bourgeois) Conservative Party than those in the professional or intermediate class groupings, and are only marginally more likely to vote Labour (socialist). Here too there is a definite break at the manual/ nonmanual line. Somewhere between 45 per cent and 53 per cent of those in each manual class category intend to vote for the Labour Party while less than 30 per cent will vote Conservative. Among nonmanual workers – including those involved in routine clerical tasks – these proportions are neatly reversed.

In so far as class locations offer a clue for mapping class consciousness, as Wright suggests they should, then there are good grounds in these data for placing routine clerical employees, if not in with, then closely alongside other nonmanual workers of a more obviously middle-class tenor. There is no evidence here that clerical and administrative employees, no matter how routinized their particular work tasks, are uniformly 'proletarianized' and therefore part of a large undifferentiated working class.

Why then does Wright's scheme fail to capture the class socio-political characteristics of routine clerical as compared with manual employees? One answer must be that his resolutely structuralist approach to class analysis leads him to the conclusion that class location – defined as a relationship to the means of production – provides the mainspring for class consciousness. But class is a process as well as a structure. As research elsewhere has shown, if we distinguish locations in the structure from the individual incumbents of these, we see that for many people routinized clerical work constitutes a moment in a career trajectory through the structure. Highly qualified managerial trainees, for example, are often initiated into large bureaucracies via a spell on the clerical 'shopfloor' – but they are, from the outset, destined to move on to unambiguously 'middle-class' managerial and professional class locations. Of course, at the initial routine clerical level, they are often working alongside other groups whose typical career trajectories are quite different. On the one hand there will be those former manual employees (mostly unqualified males, and by now rather elderly) who have been promoted into the company office, and for whom clerical work represents the pinnacle of a life-long career in hitherto proletarian positions. On the other hand, there are those (mostly unqualified young women) who start their short paid-working lives performing routine tasks in clerical occupations, but also finish their careers in the same class location when they suspend formal employment on marriage or in order to raise children.

Clearly, therefore, any account of the class relationships embodied in clerical work must take cognizance of the very different mobility trajectories of the individuals who may at any one time find themselves in that particular class location. It was for this reason that my colleagues and I on the British team collected sufficient occupational data, in the British survey, as would permit a replication of the Oxford Social Mobility Study of the early 1970s. This well-known study uses the class categories devised by John Goldthorpe, which are based on a neo-Weberian conception of class as defined by the market and work situations of particular occupations, to examine patterns of class formation in modern Britain. Like Goldthorpe we addressed ourselves to the problem of exploring the relationship between demographic class formation (patterns of class mobility and immobility) and socio-political class formation (the emergence of distinctive styles of life, patterns of association and political demands among specific social collectivities so identified). The results of our analysis are rather too extensive and complicated to report here. (For a full account see Marshall et al., 1988.) However, with regard to routine clerical workers in particular, it is worth recording briefly our finding that, for somewhere between a quarter and a third of those involved in performing such tasks, routine clerical work is merely the starting point for a secure career in management or the professions; for others (perhaps 5 to 10 per cent of all working-class employees) it is the culmination of an unambiguously proletarian work history; while for large numbers of young females it offers a temporary employment status (without career prospects) in the transition from adolescence to young motherhood (and these comprise about half of all clerical workers in the British sample).[4]

Because Wright's class framework, in common with those proffered by most other structural Marxists, is static and devoid of human agency, he cannot conceptualize the problems associated with this distinction between class positions and the individuals situated in them, and in particular must ignore the issues raised for socio-political class formation by the rather widespread experience of social mobility. In the case of routine clerical employees these complications raise serious doubts about the claim that such workers commonly constitute part of the proletariat. The class analysis reported above confirms that these doubts are well founded – despite its merely precursory nature, being conducted both in terms of the sociologically unsophisticated class scheme used by the Registrar-General, and without the benefit of the dynamic element introduced by the study of mobility trajectories.

The marginal working classes

If the pattern of socio-political preferences among Wright's proletarians tends to suggest that this class grouping is in fact rather heterogeneous, then those for the so-called marginal working classes imply even greater disparities within class categories. It should be remembered that Wright's objective is to map the class structure in order to formulate a realistic political strategy for socialists. The political rationale of his work, in common with that of other neo-Marxist theorists such as Poulantzas and Carchedi, is 'to find, beneath the bewildering and partly depressing appearances of the present, the bases of strategies for the future, an inventory of forces and allies available in coming struggles for the overthrow of capitalism' (Therborn, 1985: 142). Ahrne and Wright's analysis suggests that supervisors in the United States, and those in semi-autonomous and lower management positions in Sweden, are available to the working class as potential allies in its struggle for socialism. Given appropriate organizational and political strategies, the bourgeois ideological hegemony in which these marginal groups are implicated can be undermined, and a broad cross-class coalition in favour of radical egalitarian policies substituted. Of course, because class is more salient and the unions have a broader base in Sweden than in the United States, that coalition is potentially a much larger force in the former country than in the latter.

This may or may not be an accurate interpretation of the American and Swedish data. That is not an issue here. What is clear, however, is that the basic socio-political data from the British survey suggest that any *generalized* imputation of embryonic socialist preferences to those in putatively marginal working-class locations is highly implausible. Identification of these groups as the realistic allies of the British proletariat would therefore be quite mistaken. For example, of the eight class categories identified in Wright's model, only proletarians and supervisors comprise a majority of individuals who are prepared to attribute a working-class identity to themselves (see Table 3.6). Managers, semi-autonomous employees, and of course the self-employed as a whole are more likely to identify themselves as middle class. But the bottom half of the table, which shows the pattern of voting intentions for the various class groupings, is even more damning. It is hardly surprising that the majority of supervisors describe themselves as working class: most have been promoted to the exercise of supervisory functions from proletarian positions and, in many other respects, are indistinguishable from their working-class former peers. Voting intentions are probably a better indication of the propensity for collective action and only among proletarians does the Labour Party collect the largest single share of the votes. Managers, both at the policy-making and merely advisory levels, are more than twice as likely to vote Conservative than Labour; semi-autonomous employees are about one-third more likely to do so; while supervisors are quite as likely to vote for the right-wing as the left-wing political party. (About a quarter of the respondents in each of these class locations vote for the Liberal/Social Democratic Alliance or political centre.) These data tend to underline the rather problematic nature of Wright's argument that a 'realistic' socialist strategy could be based on a class alliance that incorporated either semi-autonomous employees or those in lower-level management. In Britain, at least, neither group offers much promise as a candidate for such an alliance.

In fact the origins of this rather hostile ideological environment for Wright's 'broad left' alliance are not difficult to uncover. Further analysis reveals that the 'marginal working-class' categories in his model are no more homogeneous in class terms than are the alleged 'proletarians'. Brevity dictates that a comprehensive account of the problem cannot be given here but, in any case, a single illustration – that provided by the semi-autonomous employees – serves sufficiently to make the general point. Looking back at Table 3.4 it will be seen that, in terms of the Registrar-General's class categories, approximately two-thirds of Wright's semi-autonomous employees are redistributed into the nonmanual classes while one-third are placed in the manual groupings. In fact semi-autonomous employees appear in almost every Registrar-General's social class – as

Table 3.6 Aspects of socio-political class formation, Great Britain: Wright classes (% by column)

	Wright classes[1]							
	B	SE	PB	M	AM	S	SAE	W
Self-assigned class								
Middle (incl. upper)	82.6	66.7	54.1	61.2	64.9	42.0	55.4	30.9
Working	17.4	33.3	45.9	38.8	35.1	58.0	44.6	69.1
Total	100.0	100.0	100.0	100.0	100.0	100.0	100.0	100.0
(N)	(23)	(51)	(74)	(147)	(57)	(112)	(139)	(609)
Voting intention								
Conservative	66.7	66.0	47.9	49.0	49.1	34.3	38.6	28.7
Labour	12.5	11.3	15.5	21.1	22.6	34.3	29.1	46.6
SDP/Liberal	8.3	15.1	23.9	20.4	24.5	25.0	26.0	15.6
Would not vote	12.5	7.5	12.7	9.5	3.8	6.5	6.3	9.1
Total	100.0	100.0	100.0	100.0	100.0	100.0	100.0	100.0
(N)	(24)	(53)	(71)	(147)	(53)	(108)	(127)	(551)

[1]For Wright class categories see Table 3.3.

indeed do Wright's workers and his managers/supervisors. The two class schemes are simply incommensurable.

If we then identify the 153 semi-autonomous workers in question, and record for each individual his or her particular occupation, we can see why it is not difficult to challenge the integrity of Wright's categories. The listed occupations include those of teachers, computer programmers and social workers, but also of motor mechanics, assembly workers and even coal-miners. In Wright's terms, these individuals appear in the same (semi-autonomous) category because they are non-owners of capital and non-managers, yet claim to have high autonomy in carrying out their work. However, because of respondents' differing perceptions as to what constitutes 'autonomy of conception and execution in the work task', this particular class category embraces everyone from lawyers, draughtsmen, surveyors and doctors on the one hand, to hospital orderlies, van rounds-men, caretakers and fork-lift truck drivers on the other. A school cleaner, answering Wright's questionnaire, can fairly claim to plan his or her own work, to determine its specific tasks, and to labour at a chosen pace: he or she can start on one floor of the building or on another, can decide to vacuum today and polish tomorrow, to break for coffee at any time, and even (within reason) when to start and finish work itself. Prima facie, therefore, this person is a semi-autonomous employee. Conversely, our survey also contains many examples of professionals and technicians who report a (to them) low job autonomy, and so are classified as proletarians. For example, there are several teachers, draughtsmen, financial brokers and senior administrators (in principle all archetypal semi-autonomous employees) who, perhaps disillusioned with their particular jobs at the time of interview, claimed that they could not design aspects of their own work and that they laboured at tasks and at a pace that were externally imposed.

So, because of the problems raised by the indeterminate context of the answers to questions on job autonomy, we have 'proletarian' chartered accountants and 'semi-autonomous' school janitors. There are, therefore, good grounds for questioning the coherence of the class categories them-selves. Indeed the demographic problems of the semi-autonomous location are reflected in the divergent socio-political inclinations of its incumbents as shown above. They are, quite simply, a heterogeneous group of people whose particular Wright class location provides no clues as to the collective likelihood of their joining in a class alliance in pursuit of broadly socialist objectives.

The revised Wright schema

Wright himself states that 'all other things being equal, all units . . . within a given class should be more like each other than like units in other classes *with respect to whatever it is that class is meant to explain*' (1985:

137). In particular, the theoretical formulation of class categories in terms of relationships of exploitation and domination at the point of production (yielding the basic and contradictory class categories of the Wright schema) supposedly illuminates the study not only of the processes of production themselves (including those of so-called deskilling), but also of socio-political orientations and therefore likely collective action. In fact, as we have shown, Wright's schema is not robust in these – his own – terms. The classification has little external validity. It fails, from the evidence of the British survey at least, to provide a suitable measure of its supposed object.

Of course, as was previously noted, it might be objected that this rather negative conclusion is unwarranted given that Wright has revised his class framework and provided for an entirely different conceptualization of class relationships. Principal among his reasons for doing so was the worry that the concept of contradictory class locations embraced by the original model was insufficiently economistic. It rested, according to Wright, on a theory of domination rather than of exploitation. So, in a lengthy autocritique (Wright, 1985), he has adapted the game-theoretic view of exploitation developed by Roemer (1982) for the purposes of returning exploitation to centre-stage.

The new class model that results is rather more complicated than the original and requires some explanation. The pivotal idea of exploitation is, for Wright, a combination of economic oppression with appropriation. Participants in the 'production game' are defined by their assets since those holding particular assets are, to varying degrees, able to deprive others of equal access to them. According to Wright's interpretation of history, feudal exploitation is situated in the unequal distribution of assets in labour power, and leads to the class relation between lords and serfs; capitalist exploitation is based on the unequal distribution of alienable assets and produces the class relation between bourgeoisie and proletariat; and socialist exploitation derives from the unequal distribution of inalienable assets (skills) and results in the class relation between experts and workers. However, as in the earlier model, the principal asset which is unequally distributed within any particular mode of production is not the only asset so distributed: it is merely the primary basis of exploitation. For example, in capitalism the principal asset exploited by capitalists is ownership of the means of production, and this is the defining feature of the system. However, capitalists can also exploit workers through their control of organization assets. Thus, in order to cope with the 'variability of the concrete', Wright produces a class typology which incorporates all of the assets which are unequally distributed in different modes of production (Table 3.7).

The new twelve-class model is in two segments – one comprising owners of the means of production and the other consisting of non-owners. Class locations in the latter segment are further differentiated according to organization assets and skill (or credential) assets – the two subordinate relations of exploitation characteristic of capitalist society. Thus has Wright

Table 3.7 *The revised Wright class categories*

Owners of means of production	Non-owners of means of production (wage-labourers)			
1 Bourgeoisie	4 Expert managers	7 Semi-credentialled managers	10 Uncredentialled managers	
2 Small employers	5 Expert supervisors	8 Semi-credentialled supervisors	11 Uncredentialled supervisors	Organization assets
3 *Petite bourgeoisie*	6 Expert non-managers	9 Semi-credentialled workers	12 Proletarians	
		Skill/credential assets		

reconceptualized the basis of the various contradictory locations within class relations. There are now no fewer than eight such locations (cells 4 to 11). Cells 9 and 11 are 'marginal working-class' positions, since their incumbents have very limited control over organization or skill assets, while those in other contradictory locations are more obviously of the 'new middle class'.

This new schema is operationalized somewhat differently to the original. Organization assets are defined in terms of an individual's relation to supervision and decision making in his or her organization. Three categories emerge from this: managers, defined as people who have direct involvement in decision making, and real authority over subordinates; supervisors, who lack decision-making powers, but do have real authority over others; and non-managers, who have neither supervisory nor decision-making powers. Skill assets are more difficult, since a credential means nothing unless it is exploited: as Wright notes, a PhD in chemistry is not exploiting his or her credentials if employed on an assembly line. So, in order to match credentials to jobs, Wright includes job traits in the operationalization of this asset. This is done in terms of both the aggregated occupational variable used in Table 3.3 and, for certain occupations, a measure of job autonomy. The three categories of skills which result are those for 'experts', 'skilled employees', and the non-skilled. The experts include all professionals, together with managers and technicians holding a college degree; skilled employees embrace teachers, craftworkers, managers and technicians without degrees, and sales and clerical workers with both degrees and high autonomy; and the non-skilled are all other sales and clerical workers and all manual and service workers. Production assets, on the other hand, raise no new problems of operationalization since, as in the previous schema, these involve a simple distinction between owners and non-owners. The former are then differentiated according to the numbers they employ: capitalists are owners with ten or more employees; small employers have from two to ten employees; and the *petite bourgeoisie* have one employee or none.

This is a lengthy exercise in theoretical and operational reasoning and I cannot do justice to the complexities of Wright's argument here. However, there are a number of serious problems in the analysis which David Rose and I have discussed at length elsewhere (Rose and Marshall, 1986). Our most fundamental theoretical objection concerns the introduction of *occupational* titles into the algorithms for generating *social classes*. After all, Wright's whole intellectual enterprise was launched on a critique of precisely this practice, and on the claim that occupations map 'only' the technical relations of production while social classes are defined by 'more fundamental' social relations of production (see Wright, 1980b). Since the object of the exercise is to demonstrate the analytical superiority of the latter over the former, it is surely problematic to incorporate occupational codings into the definition of class itself.

But this and other principled objections have been pursued elsewhere. My concern here is simply to show that Wright's reformulation of his class framework fails to solve the problem of heterogeneity identified above in respect of the original model. Table 3.8 confirms this suspicion. It gives the distribution of Wright's proletarians within the Registrar-General's class categories, and can be compared with Table 3.4, for the original Wright model. In fact, as the comparison shows clearly, Wright's reworking of his class framework has heightened rather than solved the problem of routine clerical employees within the working class. Almost none of these clerical workers have been redistributed to other non-proletarian positions and, since the overall numbers in working-class locations now constitute a proportionately smaller percentage of the workforce as a whole, they now comprise over one-third (rather than, as hitherto, one-quarter) of all so-called proletarians. But of course, as we have seen, their basic socio-political proclivities – class identity and voting intention – show a quite different pattern to that found among the manual workers with whom they share an allegedly proletarianized class position.

In fact this table suggests strongly that similar sorts of problems are encountered elsewhere in Wright's revised scheme. For example, semi-credentialled employees are spread across several nonmanual and manual Registrar-General's categories, as are (to a lesser extent) uncredentialled managers and supervisors. The nature of these divergences is explored at length elsewhere (see Marshall et al., 1988). In this short exposition I have attempted simply to raise the general issue of the lack of homogeneity in Wright's class categories and illustrate one source of the problem. It is for this and other theoretical, operational, and substantive reasons that the British research team as a whole, while saluting our colleague's resourcefulness in organizing the comparative enterprise, nevertheless harbour serious doubts about the utility of his approach to class analysis.

Table 3.8 Distribution of revised Wright classes within Registrar-General's classes, Great Britain (% by row)

Wright classes	Registrar-General's classes								
	1	2	3N	3M	4	5	6	Total	(N)
Bourgeoisie	19.2	69.2	0.0	11.5	0.0	0.0	0.0	2.0	(26)
Small employers	8.5	44.1	15.3	23.7	6.8	1.7	0.0	4.5	(59)
Petite bourgeoisie	3.8	36.7	12.7	34.2	10.1	2.5	0.0	6.0	(79)
Expert managers	23.0	73.0	1.4	2.7	0.0	0.0	0.0	5.6	(74)
Expert supervisors	27.6	72.4	0.0	0.0	0.0	0.0	0.0	2.2	(29)
Expert non-managers	14.8	85.2	0.0	0.0	0.0	0.0	0.0	4.1	(54)
Semi-credentialled managers	0.0	58.7	13.5	20.2	1.0	0.0	6.7	7.9	(104)
Semi-credentialled supervisors	4.0	38.0	12.0	42.0	2.0	0.0	2.0	3.8	(50)
Semi-credentialled workers	0.0	25.4	7.4	63.0	3.7	0.0	0.5	14.4	(189)
Uncredentialled managers	0.0	0.0	52.4	45.2	2.4	0.0	0.0	3.2	(42)
Uncredentialled supervisors	0.0	4.4	35.6	51.1	6.7	2.2	0.0	3.4	(45)
Proletarians	0.0	0.5	35.8	19.3	33.2	11.2	0.0	42.9	(564)

Notes

I am grateful to Håkon Leiulfsrud, a member of the Swedish research team, who provided useful comments on an early draft of this chapter.

1 The participating countries include Australia, Canada, Denmark, Finland, Japan, New Zealand, Norway, the Soviet Union, Sweden, the United Kingdom, the United States of America, and West Germany.

2 The questions are as follows:

   (a) Is yours a job which allows you to design and plan important aspects of your own work or is your work largely defined for you?

   (b) Would you say yours was a job which required you to design or plan important aspects of your own work or is this something you have done on your own initiative?

   (c) Do you decide the specific tasks or jobs you carry out from day to day or does someone else?

   (d) Does someone else decide how much work you do or how fast you work during the day?

   (e) Can you decide, officially or unofficially, the time you arrive and leave work?

   (f) Can you considerably slow down your pace of work for a day when you want to?

   (g) Can you decide on your own to introduce a new task or work assignment that you will do on your job?

3 The class categories are given the following labels: 1, professional occupations; 2, intermediate occupations; 3N, skilled occupations, nonmanual; 3M, skilled occupations, manual; 4, partly skilled occupations; 5, unskilled occupations; 6, armed forces. Individuals are assigned to a Registrar-General's social class by a threefold process. First, they are allocated to an occupational group, according to 'the kind of work' they do and 'the nature of the operation performed'. Each occupational category is then assigned 'as a whole to one or other social class and no account is taken of differences between individuals in the same occupation group e.g. differences of education or level of remuneration'. Finally, persons of particular employment statuses within occupational groups are removed to social classes different to that allocated the occupation as a whole, so that (for example) individuals of foreman status whose basic social class is 4 or 5 are reallocated to class 3, and those of managerial status are almost all reallocated to social class 2 (OPCS, 1980: vi, xi). On the origins of this class framework see Szreter (1984) and for a cogent commentary see Marsh (1986b).

4 A similar account of clerical work will be found in Stewart et al. (1980), Goldthorpe and Payne (1986) and Llewellyn (1981).

4

Social Class and Underclass in Britain and the USA*

Class analysis has been subject to mounting criticism on the grounds that large and growing numbers within any population are routinely omitted from its inquiries. Almost all forms of class analysis are rooted firmly in the sphere of production. Class positions are allocated on the basis of occupational titles, location within the organizational hierarchies of paid work, or some other such attribute pertaining to employment. In practice, therefore, groups such as the retired, welfare dependants, and domestic housekeepers are effectively – and, it is now claimed, unwarrantably – excluded from the research agenda.[1]

A variety of pragmatic solutions to this problem of exclusion might be adopted at the operational level. For example, one could refer to the last job of those unemployed or retired; or, for cohabiting but non-employed respondents, the job of their employed partners. There are good (and well-rehearsed) arguments both for and against these research strategies. The period of time that may have elapsed since a person last held a job might be a few months or many years; some people do not have cohabiting partners; and, for those who do, it remains a controversial research issue as to whether class standing is most appropriately assigned to households or individuals within households.

We will address the last of these problems – that of identifying the unit of class composition – at some length elsewhere and so do not intend to pursue this matter here (see Marshall et al., Chapter 5 in this volume). But the more general question remains unanswered. Is class analysis seriously undermined by its apparent neglect of large numbers of people who do not form part of the analysis, but are affected by class processes, and surely therefore an important component of the class structure?

Class analysis: the missing millions

There is a sizeable lobby of critics who have argued strongly to this effect. For example, in their critical review of studies of class in British sociology, Vic Duke and Stephen Edgell (1987) complain that almost all operationalizations of the central concept exclude economically inactive adults. This yields a 'restrictive and distorted view of the class structure' since it excludes something like 40 per cent of the adult population of Britain. In the view of these authors, 'generalisations about the class structure and class relationships are likely to be less than "totally" valid when they are based on such a small and unrepresentative section of the adult population', and so 'it should be routine to obtain relevant data for the economically inactive as well as the economically active.'

Duke and Edgell are not alone in voicing such criticisms. Others have insisted that welfare dependants and the retired should be questioned about their previous jobs so that these groups can be incorporated within any class analysis. Many have argued that last job serves equally to classify unwaged domestic labourers, although some maintain that this is a poorer indicator of a woman's class than is occupation held prior to the birth of her first child, while a few are in favour of treating 'housewife' as a class category in its own right. Parallel arguments are commonly made about unemployment. A number of critics make a distinction between the short-term and long-term unemployed, treating the former in terms of previously held occupations, and the latter as an underclass having their own distinct class location. Various multiple indicator approaches have also been proposed. These apply additional criteria – such as family consumption patterns, income, educational attainment, and presence of dependent children – in determining the class standing of both households and their constituent members.[2]

It is clear that critics do not agree about a preferred alternative to what they take to be the status quo of class analysis. Some maintain that the various groups hitherto excluded can satisfactorily be incorporated within existing approaches and theories. Others argue that the social classes of men and women should be classified separately. Radicals would abandon the whole enterprise of class analysis altogether. The various proposals are not easily reconciled.[3]

It is impractical in this context to review systematically such a disparate and extensive literature. In any case, it is almost certain that the great majority of the proposed amendments to the established practice of sampling only from those currently in employment would prove to be unworkable in practice, were they ever to be attempted in the field. Most have been promoted only in programmatic fashion, with little thought given to the empirical consequences of their adoption, notably that they would generate huge amounts of entirely artefactual social mobility, either between employment and non-employment of individuals, or between a great variety of household types differentiated according to no clear and consistent criteria – always assuming, that is, that the operational complications raised by the necessity of summing multiple indicators of the various social characteristics could themselves be solved.

Nevertheless, it remains the case that there is widespread agreement among a large number of otherwise diverse commentators that exclusion of non-employed individuals from contemporary class analysis greatly restricts its usefulness, because it is allegedly misleading to generalize about the class characteristics of populations on the basis only of a sample of those in employment. Not everyone has an occupation. Class theories which are rooted in the sphere of employment are likely therefore, according to their critics, to give a partial or distorted picture of the processes of class formation. In this chapter we wish simply to explore whether or not this accusation is well founded.

Operationalizing social class

There are of course a number of distinct traditions in class analysis. However, although (for example) the Marxist, status attainment, and Weberian approaches start from quite different conceptions of class, their operational logic is similar, in so far as social class is determined in each case by reference to the characteristics of an individual's occupation. Thus, to mention only some leading exponents, Erik Wright (1979) explores class in terms of ownership, autonomy, and authority in the workplace; Donald Treiman (1977) examines the perceived prestige scores pertaining to occupations; and John Goldthorpe (1980) highlights relations and conditions of employment. For the sake of brevity we will here refer only to the last of these, but our arguments are intended to apply equally to class analyses which rest on any of the competing schemes, since all are grounded in the world of paid employment.

Details of the now familiar eleven-category Goldthorpe class scheme are shown in Table 4.1. In their report of the findings from the Comparative Analysis of Social Mobility in Industrial Nations (CASMIN) Project, Erikson and Goldthorpe (1992a: 37) describe the aim of this schema as being 'to differentiate positions within *labour markets* and *production units* or, more specifically . . . to differentiate such positions in terms of the employment relations they entail'. For this reason it is important to distinguish between the employment relations of the self-employed and of employees. However, within the fairly heterogeneous category of employee, it is also possible to make 'meaningful distinctions' according to differences in 'the labour contract and the conditions of employment'. According to Erikson and Goldthorpe (1992a: 42), 'it is the distinction between employees involved in a service relationship with their employer and those whose employment relationships are essentially regulated by a labour contract that underlies the way in which, within our class schema, different employee classes have been delineated.' So-called service-class (or salariat) occupations offer incremental advancement, employment security, and the possibility of exchanging commitment to the job for a high level of trust on the part of employers. Working-class occupations, on the other hand, tend to have closely regulated payment arrangements and give employees much less control over their jobs.

How then is this scheme operationalized? Typically, a social class distribution is obtained by eliciting information about both occupational title (for example electrician or nurse) and employment status (self-

Table 4.1   *The Goldthorpe class categories*

Full version		Collapsed version	
I	Higher-grade professionals, administrators and officials: managers in large industrial establishments: large proprietors	I+II	Service class: professionals, administrators and managers: higher-grade technicians: supervisors of nonmanual workers
II	Lower-grade professionals, administrators and officials: higher-grade technicians: managers in small industrial establishments: supervisors of nonmanual employees		
IIIa	Routine nonmanual employees, higher grade (administration and commerce)	III	Routine nonmanual workers: routine nonmanual employees in administration and commerce: sales personnel: other rank-and-file service workers
IIIb	Routine nonmanual employees, lower grade (sales and services)		
IVa	Small proprietors, artisans, etc., with employees	IVa+IVb	*Petite bourgeoisie*: small proprietors and artisans, etc., with and without employees
IVb	Small proprietors, artisans, etc., without employees		
IVc	Farmers and smallholders; other self-employed workers in primary production	IVc	Farmers: farmers and smallholders and other self-employed workers in primary production
V	Lower-grade technicians; supervisors of manual workers	V+VI	Skilled workers: lower-grade technicians: supervisors of manual workers: skilled manual workers
VI	Skilled manual workers		
VIIa	Semi- and unskilled manual workers (not in agriculture, etc.)	VIIa	Non-skilled workers: semi- and unskilled manual workers (not in agriculture, etc.)
VIIb	Agricultural and other workers in primary production	VIIb	Agricultural labourers: agricultural and other workers in primary production

Source: Erikson and Goldthorpe, 1992a.

employed with employees, manager in large establishment, and so forth). In the British case, the categories and definitions most commonly used are those found in the *Classification of Occupations*, published by the Office of Population Censuses and Surveys. A class position is obtained for each respondent by cross-classifying his or her occupational title and employment status, all combinations having previously been allocated a place within one of the eleven Goldthorpe class categories, according to the different conditions and relations of employment experienced by typical individuals so described.

A particular strength of the Goldthorpe scheme is that it can meaningfully be collapsed according to circumstances and sizes of sample. The seven-category collapse shown in Table 4.1 is that used most often by Goldthorpe and his colleagues in the CASMIN Project. It is apparently well suited to the crossnational analysis of mobility regimes using relatively large data-sets. But further simplification is legitimate where, for example, one is dealing with specific sorts of occupational structures. In countries such as Britain, where the agricultural sector is relatively small, it is sensible to use a five-category version of the scheme which does not identify farmers and their employees separately within (respectively) the *petite bourgeoisie* and the working class as whole. Small sample sizes may require further merging of categories. A three-class version of the scheme is also widely used. In this particular chapter, however, we shall be using a five-category collapse that is appropriate to the sample sizes and countries under discussion, distinguishing between the salariat, routine clerical employees, *petite bourgeoisie* (including farmers), skilled manual and non-skilled workers (including agricultural labourers).

Employment and non-employment

As will by now be evident, the procedure by which a Goldthorpe class distribution is created for a population routinely omits the various non-employed individuals earlier identified, and said by critics to undermine class analysis by their absence; namely, the retired, domestic housekeepers, unemployed and other welfare dependants. How, if at all, do these omissions limit the utility of this form of investigation?

In fact it is not at all clear to us that they do. We have reached this conclusion by considering evidence generated by the International Social Justice Project (ISJP).[4] We draw only on the British and American data. The choice of these two countries is not arbitrary, but was made in the light of recent arguments about the so-called underclass, as will be explained shortly. Class positions were generated for all employed respondents in each of the two countries by using Goldthorpe class algorithms following the logic described above. A social class was then assigned to non-employed respondents, according to either their last main job or, in the few cases where there was no previous employment, the job of their parent or guardian at the time the respondent was aged 15.[5] In this way, all but a handful of British and American interviewees were distributed to Goldthorpe classes, and the various non-employed groups usually excluded from the analysis (the retired or disabled, unemployed, single and partnered housekeepers, and adult students in the samples) were incorporated for study.

The class socio-political characteristics of the two types of respondents – those currently in employment and those non-employed – were then examined. Table 4.2 shows the results of this exercise separately for each country. It will be seen from the table that the overall pattern of voting and class identities among employed and non-employed respondents is not appreciably different in either country. Thus, for example, in the case of the United States, those currently in jobs within the service class were equally

Table 4.2 *Class identity and party preference by Goldthorpe class, comparing currently employed and non-employed respondents, GB and USA (%)*

(a) GB

Class[1]		(N)	Voting intention[2]				Class identity[4]	
			C	L	LD	WNV	Working	Middle
S	Employed	(235)	38	20	15	6	32	53
	Non-employed	(120)	31	21	24	5	29	62
PB	Employed	(78)	46	13	18	12	42	46
	Non-employed	(42)	43	21	17	12	43	36
RC	Employed	(128)	28	18	16	13	53	35
	Non-employed	(101)	41	20	6	8	42	44
SM	Employed	(107)	32	25	12	14	63	24
	Non-employed	(110)	15	56	6	11	74	18
NS	Employed	(182)	25	39	10	9	74	20
	Non-employed	(192)	20	42	9	9	71	21

(b) USA

Class[1]		(N)	Party preference[3]		Class identity[4]	
			Rep	Dem	Working	Middle
S	Employed	(410)	44	44	20	79
	Non-employed	(119)	49	42	16	82
PB	Employed	(76)	53	33	21	78
	Non-employed	(14)	43	29	14	79
RC	Employed	(116)	53	36	36	64
	Non-employed	(83)	47	34	18	78
SM	Employed	(126)	37	44	51	48
	Non-employed	(66)	27	56	44	53
NS	Employed	(228)	40	46	53	47
	Non-employed	(131)	36	50	35	57

[1] Classes: S = salariat (Goldthorpe classes I and II); PB = *petite bourgeoisie* (IV); RC = routine clerical (IIIa); SM = skilled manual (V and VI); NS = non-skilled manual (IIIb and VII).
[2] Voting intention (GB): C = Conservative; L = Labour; LD = Liberal Democrat; WNV = would not vote; excludes others.
[3] Party preference (USA): Rep = Republican; Dem = Democratic; excludes no stated preference.
[4] Class identity: working, includes lower; middle, includes upper; excludes none or refused class concept.

divided in terms of party-political preferences (the Republican and Democratic Parties each attracting 44 per cent support), and attributed class self-identities in the ratio of 20 per cent (working) to 79 per cent (middle). Among non-employed respondents who were formerly in service-class jobs, or who grew up having service-class parents, the corresponding figures were 49:42 (party preference) and 16:82 (class identity).

The results suggest that, at least in terms of these particular class characteristics, the non-employed respondents who are excluded from a

Table 4.3 *Loglinear analysis of party preference, class identity, Goldthorpe social class and economic activity, GB and USA*

(a) GB

Model	G^2	d.f.	P	rG^2	delta
Class identity					
1 C+E+I	187.72	13	0.000	–	16.8
2 CE+I	160.78	9	0.000	14.4	16.5
3 CE+CI	5.77	5	0.329	96.9	2.8
4 CE+EI	159.51	8	0.000	15.0	16.6
5 CE+CI+EI	5.27	4	0.261	97.2	2.4
Voting intention					
1 C+E+V	146.63	22	0.000	–	17.4
2 CE+V	124.48	18	0.000	15.1	15.9
3 CE+CV	35.74	10	0.000	75.6	7.2
4 CE+EV	107.49	16	0.000	26.7	14.2
5 CE+CV+EV	26.45	8	0.001	82.0	6.3

(b) USA

Model	G^2	d.f.	P	rG^2	delta
Class identity					
1 C+E+I	169.10	13	0.000	–	15.6
2 CE+I	127.63	9	0.000	24.5	13.4
3 CE+CI	16.35	5	0.006	90.3	4.0
4 CE+EI	122.75	8	0.000	27.4	13.4
5 CE+CI+EI	2.95	4	0.566	98.3	1.7
Party preference					
1 C+E+P	58.90	13	0.000	–	8.3
2 CE+P	12.35	9	0.011	63.8	4.9
3 CE+CP	3.82	5	0.575	93.5	2.0
4 CE+EP	20.37	8	0.009	65.4	5.2
5 CE+CP+EP	3.27	4	0.513	94.4	1.9

C = class (salariat, *petite bourgeoisie*, routine clerical, skilled manual, non-skilled manual).
E = employment (currently employed, currently non-employed).
I = class identity (middle, working).
V – voting intention (GB: Conservative, Labour, Liberal Democrat).
P = party preference (USA: Republican, Democrat).
G^2 = log likelihood ratio.
rG^2 = % reduction in G^2 achieved by each model treating the main effects as a baseline.
delta = % misclassified cases.

conventional class analysis are, if considered as a whole, not dissimilar to their currently employed peers. Having included the former in the analysis one is not led to conclusions different from those that would be reached on the basis of data pertaining to employed respondents alone.[6]

This interpretation of the data is vindicated if one then fits a loglinear model separately for each country (see Table 4.3). The aim here is to assess the pattern of association between our socio-political class indicators (class identity and party preference) on the one hand, and class or employment (currently employed versus currently non-employed) on the other. In the British case, class identity is shown to be very strongly related to class position, but has no relationship to employment as such (compare models 3 and 4). As regards voting intention, the best-fitting model shows associations with both class and employment, and it is also necessary to include the three-way interaction term (*CVE*) in order to provide a satisfactory fit to the data. Clearly, the fact that model 5 does not fit means that the effect of class on voting intention does differ by employment; however, as will be seen from a comparison of models 3 and 4, employment as such is a *relatively* minor determinant of vote. A calculation of the relevant odds ratios also shows that it exerts an uneven influence as well, so that there is (for example) significantly more differentiation in voting intention between employed and non-employed skilled manual workers, than among their semi-skilled and unskilled counterparts. Similarly, in the United States, although both class and employment influence class identities, whether or not an individual is currently employed is of much less (and indeed little substantive) importance. Class but not employment is associated with political preference.

Our conclusion is therefore that it is entirely reasonable, in a class analysis, to treat the various categories of non-employed merely as displaced class actors. As far as we can see, there is little to be gained by incorporating into the research programme of class analysis those individuals without employment, since they are not very different from their matching (employed) class counterparts. It seems that the shortcomings of social class research on this particular issue may well have been greatly exaggerated.

The underclass

Of course critics might reasonably claim that our analysis thus far is too crude, since the non-employed are not a homogeneous group, but a diverse category which encompasses privileged and unprivileged alike. Respondents who retire from the more privileged class positions are likely to see their relative advantages perpetuated into old age. Similarly, unemployment (especially long-term unemployment) and welfare dependency are also class-related, affecting the working classes disproportionately. It is therefore hardly surprising that the employed and non-employed elements of each class are rather similar. Perhaps a more specific objection is warranted. Might it not be the case, as is increasingly suggested, that the really serious problem for social class research is created by the large numbers of impoverished welfare dependants who are not in employment, at least not on a regular basis, and have therefore fallen through or dropped out of the class structure entirely? Are there not growing numbers of people who are so irregularly in work, and therefore so marginal to civil society, that the constitute a discrete group, whose existence is simply overlooked in the conventional class literature, and whose class-related attributes are so distinct that they require separate treatment in a class analysis?

Reasoning along these lines, W.G. Runciman (1990: 381, 388) has argued that there are seven classes in British society: an upper class, three middle classes (upper, middle and lower), two working classes (skilled and unskilled) – and an underclass. The latter embraces 'those who are excluded from the labour market entirely, whether through debt, disability or a lack of any minimal skill in consequence of which they are permanently consigned to the category of the long-term unemployed'. Note that this is not a group of workers disadvantaged within the labour market. It is, rather, those members of society 'whose roles place them more or less permanently at the economic level where benefits are paid by the state to those unable to participate in the labour market at all'. Many of these individuals are members of ethnic minorities, and many are women (particularly single mothers), but it is their long-term unemployment and therefore welfare dependency (rather than ethnicity or gender as such) that defines their membership of the underclass. Runciman – like many others (for example, Rex, 1986: 75–6) – believes that the class characteristics (including the class identities and voting behaviour) of these people are distinct from those of the working classes. Is this in fact the case? To what extent is the class analysis programme compromised by its failure to deal with the contemporary underclass?

The now extensive debate about the underclass stems from a predominantly American literature which addresses two phenomena that are argued to be related; namely, high levels of youth unemployment, and an increasing proportion of single-parent households. The black population is disproportionately affected by both joblessness and single parenthood. The term 'underclass' itself suggests a group which is in some sense outside the mainstream of society – but there is little or no agreement about the nature and source of the exclusion. One interpretation, advanced by writers such as Charles Murray (1984), is that overly generous welfare provision promotes dependency, the breakup of the nuclear family household, and socialization into a counter-culture which devalues work and encourages criminality. An alternative view, proffered by Douglas Glasgow (1980) and others, emphasizes the failure of the economy to provide equal opportunities for secure employment, and the consequent destabilization of the male-breadwinner role. Murray locates the source of exclusion in the attitudes and behaviour of the underclass itself whereas Glasgow points to the structured inequality that disadvantages particular groups in society.

The precise natures of both the structural disadvantages and the cultural attributes in question are themselves a matter of dispute. One disagreement is about whether the problems of the disadvantaged black population originate in their colour or their class position. Early in his work, William Julius Wilson (1978: 1) makes reference to 'a vast underclass of black proletarians – that massive population at the very bottom of the social class ladder, plagued by poor education and low-paying, unstable jobs'. This depicts the underclass as a black phenomenon, defined in terms of vulnerability in the labour market, and without reference to behavioural or attitudinal factors. However, in a later study he writes about 'individuals who lack training and skills and either experience long-term unemployment or are not members of the labour force, individuals who are engaged in street crime and other forms of aberrant behaviour, and families that experience long term spells of poverty and/or welfare dependency' (Wilson, 1987: 8). In other words, unstable unemployment has become absence of employment; there is now no explicit reference to race; and, furthermore, the definition has been expanded to include criminality and welfare dependence – thus acknowledging that the socially undesirable attributes of underclass life that are central causes in Murray's account can in fact follow as consequences in Wilson's essentially structural approach.

Although discussion about the nature and extent of underclass membership has been most fully developed in the United States, the issues have also been debated at length in Britain, and no less acrimoniously. For example, in a more recent work, Murray (1990) has argued that the difference between the USA and Britain is simply that the former 'reached the future first'. Using metaphors of social pathology, he suggests that an underclass defined by illegitimacy, violent crime and dropout from the labour force is growing, and will continue to do so because there is a generation of children being brought up to live in the same way. By contrast, Duncan Gallie (1988) has explored the potential for cultural cohesion and collective self-awareness as defining characteristics of the underclass, and concluded that the non-standard employment patterns and long-term unemployment of the 1980s may have provided a structural basis for a distinctive underclass, but that there is no real evidence for its cultural underpinning.

It is not our purpose here either to review the extensive literature on the underclass or to attempt an authoritative definition of this seemingly elusive sociological subject. However, in order to facilitate our investigation of the socio-political characteristics of those normally included within and conventionally excluded from class analysis, the following observations must perforce be recorded.

First – and leaving aside the (many) studies of the underclass which simply fail to define the term precisely – current research reflects two basic approaches to the phenomenon. Either the underclass is characterized as being excluded from civil society on account of its extreme deprivation (due to poverty or lack of employment); or, alternatively, it is seen as being at variance with mainstream behaviour and attitudes (as testified to by the prevalence of voluntary joblessness, welfare dependency, unwed parenting, juvenile delinquency and crime generally). Possible links to ethnicity and residence in 'extreme poverty areas' are merely variations on this basic theme. Dispute then turns on the causality that is deemed to prevail between social structure, poverty, behaviour and attitudes (see Auletta, 1982: 50, 253, 265–8; Gans, 1993).

Second, in practice most commentators associate the underclass with either extreme poverty or long-term unemployment, although there is no consensus about how these circumstances arise. As Robert Aponte (1990: 132) puts it, 'on the one hand, there are those that see self-defeating attitudes and behaviour – as in the long-discredited "culture of poverty" thesis – as the primary cause of poverty. On the other, there are those that argue that we must look to the structure of opportunities for the explanation of poverty and the often accompanying pathologies.'

Finally, these unresolved disputes about causality notwithstanding, it is widely (though not universally) held that the underclass shares in a distinctive subculture of cynicism, resignation and despair. As Aponte suggests, some have drawn parallels between this particular 'culture of fatalism' and earlier apparently similar sociological constructs, such as the 'culture of poverty' (much discussed in the United States during the 1960s) and the 'dependency culture' transmitted by so-called cycles of deprivation (a focus of controversy in Britain in the 1970s). Others argue that the debate about the underclass is distinguished by its explicit concern with the relationship between racism and poverty. In both cases, however, the overwhelming impression conveyed by the literature is of an underclass culture comprising largely negative traits which include apathy, indifference towards authority, and defeatism.[7]

It may well be, as some have suggested, that at this level the debate is as much about the politics of social policy – about the need for privileged classes to justify their place in society by pointing to the individual failings of the poor and unemployed – as it is about reasoned sociological analysis (see, for example, Bagguley and Mann, 1992; Morris, 1993; Westergaard, 1992). Nevertheless, while recognizing the obvious limitations of our own cross-sectional data, we think it is possible to explore empirically some of the issues surrounding the concept of the underclass – specifically from the point of view of determining whether or not the poorest and most persistently unemployed people in the American and British samples are culturally distinct from the wider population in the terms implied by the thesis of the underclass 'culture of fatalism'. Is there a distinctive underclass subculture or do the processes of socio-political class formation transcend the alleged boundaries imposed by poverty and unemployment?

Poverty and unemployment

In addressing this problem we first pursued the questions of poverty and unemployment separately. Household income was taken as the best available proxy for the former. This was recoded into twenty (5 percentile) income bands for each country. The bottom 5 per cent was taken as a poverty threshold. This corresponded to annual household income of not more than £3,200 in Britain or $7,000 in the United States. Household size, a mediator of poverty, was considered by means of the (British) Department of Social Security equivalence scale. A weighting was therefore attached to household income according to the composition of the household; namely, unity for a partnered couple, 0.61 for a single or additional adult, and 0.23 for each child aged under 18 (see Coulter et al., 1992). Using this weighted-income criterion, a 'poverty' group of some 216 individuals was identified in Britain, compared with a 'non-poverty' group of 836 respondents (and another 237 interviewees who withheld income details). In the United States, the corresponding groups comprised 169, 1,080 and 129 respondents, respectively. Full-time students were excluded from these and subsequent calculations.

How do those in greatest poverty compare with the rest of the population in terms of the allegedly distinctive cultural attributes of the underclass? Six questions relating to such attitudes as fatalism and political disillusionment were considered.[8] Table 4.4 shows the percentage of each of the two groups expressing the various responses to these questions in both Britain and the United States. If the arguments about underclass culture were indeed sound, one would expect the poor in each country to be significantly more likely to view personal wealth as due to rich people having 'the right connections', and to their taking unfair advantage of the opportunities provided within the economic system. Those in poverty would also tend to be dismissive of rewards for effort, skill and intelligence, doubtful of real choice prevailing in elections, and sceptical of the motives of public officials. Presumably, also, they would be consistently less inclined to take the opposite views. But what Table 4.4 in fact reveals is that there is no such pattern to the responses in either country. It is true that those in poverty are consistently more likely to express 'the underclass view' – although rarely by more than a few per cent. In general terms, however, the differences between the two groups are not marked and can seldom be described as more than minor. It should also be noted that, in this respect, the results are remarkably similar for Britain and the United States.

But what if the underclass is characterized instead as those who compete least effectively (and sometimes not at all) in the labour market? This shifts the focus from the poorest households in our sample to those comprising the long-term unemployed. In pursuing this approach we identified among our non-employed respondents a sub-group comprising single, working-age individuals, who had not been in regular employment for in excess of the previous twelve months, and partnered individuals for whom this was true not only of themselves but also of their spouses. This amounted to 74 individuals in Britain and 41 in the United States. The numbers are admittedly small, but these comprise a core of chronically welfare-dependent individuals, among whom the culture of fatalism ought surely to be evident if theories of the underclass are at all empirically sound in this respect. These long-term economically inactive respondents were then

Table 4.4 *Fatalistic attitudes by poverty, GB and USA (% by row, excludes 'don't know')*

(a)

		Very often	Often	Sometimes	Rarely	Never
(i) Rich people are rich as a result of the economic system allowing them to take unfair advantages						
GB	Poverty	24	26	26	10	2
	Non-poverty	15	29	36	14	2
USA	Poverty	23	27	26	15	2
	Non-poverty	13	25	38	21	2
(ii) Rich people are rich as a result of their having the right connections						
GB	Poverty	45	36	12	4	2
	Non-poverty	32	45	20	1	0
USA	Poverty	44	34	18	3	0
	Non-poverty	31	44	22	3	0

(b)

		Strongly agree	Somewhat agree	Neither	Somewhat disagree	Strongly disagree
(iii) People get rewarded for their effort						
GB	Poverty	6	37	14	29	12
	Non-poverty	3	45	16	31	6
USA	Poverty	21	46	1	16	12
	Non-poverty	13	58	7	17	5
(iv) People get rewarded for their intelligence and skill						
GB	Poverty	9	46	12	24	7
	Non-poverty	5	51	13	26	6
USA	Poverty	23	57	2	11	5
	Non-poverty	15	59	6	15	3
(v) Public officials don't care much what people like me think						
GB	Poverty	33	33	13	14	2
	Non-poverty	18	47	12	20	2
USA	Poverty	25	33	7	20	12
	Non-poverty	21	44	8	20	6
(vi) In elections in this country, voters have a real choice						
GB	Poverty	25	39	7	17	9
	Non-poverty	21	39	8	22	10
USA	Poverty	34	31	3	14	17
	Non-poverty	23	38	4	19	16

compared with the 748 and 936 individuals in the British and American samples who were in employment at the time of the study. The responses of the two sorts of groups to the same six attitudinal questions are shown in Table 4.5. Perhaps curiously, among both the British and the Americans, it is the economically inactive who are the more likely to agree strongly that

Table 4.5 *Fatalistic attitudes by long-term unemployment, GB and USA (% by row, excludes 'don't know')*

(a)

		Very often	Often	Sometimes	Rarely	Never
(i) Rich people are rich as a result of the economic system allowing them to take unfair advantages						
GB	Employed	16	29	35	15	2
	Unemployed	19	22	31	12	3
USA	Employed	12	25	39	20	3
	Unemployed	17	22	49	12	0
(ii) Rich people are rich as a result of their having the right connections						
GB	Employed	33	42	21	7	0
	Unemployed	39	39	16	1	0
USA	Employed	30	45	22	3	0
	Unemployed	49	27	24	0	0

(b)

		Strongly agree	Somewhat agree	Neither	Somewhat disagree	Strongly disagree
(iii) People get rewarded for their effort						
GB	Employed	3	41	16	35	55
	Unemployed	7	49	8	22	14
USA	Employed	13	57	1	16	12
	Unemployed	17	46	7	17	5
(iv) People get rewarded for their intelligence and skill						
GB	Employed	5	48	13	26	6
	Unemployed	11	50	10	20	8
USA	Employed	16	59	7	15	4
	Unemployed	24	56	5	12	0
(v) Public officials don't care much what people like me think						
GB	Employed	19	46	13	20	1
	Unemployed	30	27	19	15	4
USA	Employed	20	43	10	20	7
	Unemployed	22	49	2	12	15
(vi) In elections in this country, voters have a real choice						
GB	Employed	19	36	10	25	10
	Unemployed	20	37	4	26	8
USA	Employed	23	39	3	18	15
	Unemployed	32	29	2	20	17

effort, intelligence and skill are rewarded. They are also more inclined to give strong endorsement to the view that real choice is a feature of elections, and to disagree strongly with the statement that public officials don't much care about people like themselves. In general, however, the patterns of responses within the two groups are not markedly different.

These results would seem to offer little support for the view that the chronically economically inactive are somehow more prone to attitudes of defeatism and mistrust than are their employed peers.

There is therefore little to suggest that, at least in terms of those attitudes here considered, the most financially deprived and the least economically active (of a working age) are radically different from the remainder of the population. On some items they are slightly more likely to express sentiments said to characterize the underclass, but the differences are not large, nor are they systematic. On other items, they are more prone to extreme views, but at either ends of scale. However, the main issue here is whether or not these people more often endorse 'the underclass view', and systematically they do not.

We should emphasize perhaps, that we are in no way suggesting our poor and unemployed respondents actually constitute an underclass, albeit that many previous commentators might include such individuals under this heading. It is not our purpose here to offer yet another definition of the so-called underclass. Our claim is merely that, in so far as arguments about the culture of such an underclass can be tested in this way, then appropriately fatalistic attitudes ought to be fairly widespread among the poorest and most seriously welfare-dependent individuals in our study; yet, as we have seen, evidence to this effect is hard to uncover.

Contrasting interpretations of fatalism

Our results thus far would tend to support the view of those critics who have denied that the poorest members of society constitute an underclass. But, as Alan Walker (1990: 55) points out, the essence of the argument about the underclass is that the latter consists not necessarily of the poorest people, but of people who *act* differently, and not just from the middle class but from other poor people as well. The underclass is defined, not only by its poverty, but additionally by its propensity for deviant parental, educational, and labour-market behaviour. To what extent do our data support this version of the underclass thesis? In other words, does belonging to these sorts of allegedly underclass groups significantly influence attitudes towards political and economic processes in society, over and above any effects attributable merely to poverty itself? Ultimately, it is the answer to this question that separates those (such as Murray) who favour a behavioural version of underclass theory, from those (such as Walker) who offer a structural interpretation.

One influential (and entirely typical) behavioural definition of the underclass is advanced by Erol Ricketts and Isabel Sawhill (1988), who argue that 'underclass areas' in the United States are those with relatively high proportions of high school dropouts, prime-aged males not working regularly, households with children headed by females, and those receiving public assistance.[9] We therefore considered, for our American and British data, the attitudinal characteristics of single females with children; individuals in households receiving welfare benefits or social security; respondents in the lowest standard age-group (aged less than 25) with no formal educational qualifications; and those who claimed to have been unemployed in the long term (for more than the previous twelve months) or, separately, out of work for at least two years of the previous ten. Afro-Caribbean and Asian interviewees were also identified in order to address the issue of race. Is it the case that any of these characteristics have a further influence on the attitudes that we take to be indicative of the underclass culture of fatalism, once the limited effects of poverty itself are controlled for, again using weighted household income as a proxy for the latter? If this were in fact true, one might be led to conclude that fatalistic attitudes would then have to be viewed as, to some degree, particular to the various groups said by Ricketts and Sawhill to constitute an underclass.

The results of the relevant logistic regression are shown in Table 4.6. As will be seen, weighted household income among British respondents is associated with three of the six underclass attitudes; namely, those regarding wealthy individuals as having been afforded unfair advantages through the economic system or possessing the right connections, and concerning the motives of public officials. Among the Americans this is the case for four of the items, where we found that the greater the household income, the less the propensity of the respondent to adopt the underclass view. It should be noted, however, that in no case did income account for more than 4 per cent of the variation in the respondents' attitudes – and generally it accounted for much less.

Further to these income effects, there were relatively few additional associations with the supposedly underclass characteristics, and (more importantly) no systematic evidence of a generalized fatalistic attitude. In the United States, Afro-Caribbean respondents were more likely to disagree strongly that effort and skill are rewarded, indeed were over three times more likely to do so than their white and Asian counterparts. Single females with children and those aged under 25 with no formal educational qualifications were also cynical of effort being rewarded. Six such instances were identified in the British data, involving Afro-Caribbean and young respondents without educational qualifications (on two occasions each), and (on one occasion each) households receiving state benefits and single females with children.

There are, of course, many interesting points of detail that might be considered here. One could speculate as to why membership of particular sub-groups or access to certain levels of household income are associated with some of the attitudes in the two countries. Why is it, for example, that black and young respondents with no educational qualifications in Britain express a degree of cynicism towards real choice in elections which is in excess of that shown by their counterparts in the United States? But it is not necessary to debate such issues here. What is important to the argument of this chapter is the *pattern* of the findings as a whole. This shows

Table 4.6 *Logistic regression of income and 'underclass effects' on fatalistic attitudes, GB and USA*

Underclass attitudinal question[1]	Income effect	Further behavioural effects
Great Britain		
(i)	Yes ($p < 0.001$)	Households receiving benefits ($p = 0.047$) (OR = 1.43)
(ii)	Yes ($p < 0.001$)	Single females with children ($p = 0.038$) (OR = 1.76)
(iii)	No	Afro-Caribbeans ($p = 0.015$) (OR = 3.68) Aged under 25 with no educational qualifications ($p = 0.018$) (OR = 5.07)
(iv)	No	–
(v)	Yes ($p < 0.001$)	–
(vi)	No	Afro-Caribbeans ($p = 0.011$) (OR = 3.62) Aged under 25 with no educational qualifications ($p = 0.038$) (OR = 4.05)
United States		
(i)	Yes ($p = 0.005$)	–
(ii)	Yes ($p = 0.025$)	–
(iii)	Yes ($p < 0.001$)	Single females with children ($p = 0.037$) (OR = 2.31) Afro-Caribbeans ($p < 0.001$) (OR = 3.22) Aged under 25 with no educational qualifications ($p < 0.001$) (OR = 5.23)
(iv)	Yes ($p < 0.001$)	Afro-Caribbeans ($p < 0.001$) (OR = 3.22)
(v)	No	–
(vi)	No	–

[1] Attitudinal questions (i) to (vi) as in Tables 4.4 and 4.5. Response categories dichotomized according to whether or not the 'underclass view' is endorsed: (i), (ii) very often + often versus other responses; (iii), (iv), (vi) strongly disagree + somewhat disagree versus other responses; (v) strongly agree + somewhat agree versus other responses. OR = odds ratio.

that there is evidence of household income having a limited association with attitudes. Beyond this, however, the groups that most commonly are said to comprise the underclass tend not to be systematically distinct from the rest of the population – at least in terms of the allegedly underclass attitudes here under investigation. In so far as there is a pattern to our findings, it can better be explained by poverty itself than by any of the other frequently cited attributes that might identify members of an emerging and distinctive underclass.

Conclusion

In this chapter we have argued that, within the limitations imposed by our cross-sectional data, we can find no evidence to suggest that the non-employed respondents who are invariably omitted from an orthodox class analysis display class-related characteristics that are so distinctive that they undermine the logic of the class analysis research programme. We are therefore inclined to be sceptical about the charge that class analysis is fatally flawed because typically it rests only on the employed respondents in any population.

Why is this charge so often reiterated? In our view, the problem probably lies in the widespread tendency among critics to think of class in static rather than dynamic terms, or as a structure rather than a process. The metaphor of class that lies behind much of the recent criticism is that of the layer-cake – with the rich at the top and the working class at the bottom. This pushes critics to complain about those at the extremes – the 'icing' and the 'base' as it were – who are seemingly not accorded sufficient attention. Runciman's critique, for example, takes precisely this form.

The layer-cake metaphor is misleading. As we have seen, the fact that individuals are not in employment at any particular time (and therefore likely to be omitted from a class analysis) does not mean that they have dropped out of the class structure, and are no longer affected by their earlier class experiences. This is surely an empirical issue. How does unemployment (or a change of status which takes one into the category of the non-employed) affect values, behaviour, or whatever? Our results show that, at least in the case of voting and in attributing class identities, the non-employed seem to carry much of the baggage of class with them when they leave the labour market.

Finally, as regards the so-called underclass in particular, we would argue that a subculture of fatalism is not a feature by which such a group can easily be recognized. In this respect, our results are consistent with those obtained by other researchers, who have been unable to identify an underclass in terms of its particular attitudes to work, job search behaviour, or degree of social marginalization (see also, for example, Heath, 1992; Gallie, 1994b). Against this background, the concept itself looks increasingly flawed, and certainly fails to provide a platform from which to launch a convincing critique of class analysis because of its 'missing millions'.

Notes

* Gordon Marshall, Stephen Roberts and Carole Burgoyne. The authors wish to thank Rosemary Crompton, Anthony Heath, Colin Mills, David Routh, Stefan Svallfors and Adam Swift for helpful comments on an earlier draft of this chapter.

1 See, for example, the criticisms of Abercrombie and Warde (1988: 126), Saunders (1990a: 30, 118), Delphy and Leonard (1986: 66, 73) and Allen (1982: 138).

2 See, for example, Dex (1985: 150-1), Murgatroyd (1982), Hagan and Albonetti (1982), Heath and Britten (1984), Dale et al. (1985), Harris and Morris (1986), Walby (1986) and Roberts and Barker (1986).

3 Compare, for example, Acker (1973), Garnsey (1978), Haller (1981), Murgatroyd (1984), Pahl (1984) and Wright (1989a).

4 Fieldwork for the surveys was conducted in 1991. The British study comprises 1,319 personal interviews obtained by Research Surveys of Great Britain. It uses the Postal Address File as a sampling frame and is representative of the adult population of Great Britain. The American survey organization (the Survey Research Center of the Institute for Social Research at the University of Michigan) drew an equal probability sample of households in the United States (yielding a total of 1,414 interviews) and conducted telephone interviews. These figures represent response rates of 71 per cent and 72 per cent respectively for each country. Full technical details of the surveys are given in Kluegel et al. (1995).

5 Another obvious possibility would have been to give partnered respondents the class of their cohabitee – where he or she had paid work. Arguably, this makes more sense than allocating class on the basis of previous employment. However, we wanted in this chapter to avoid the 'unit of analysis' controversy that has been discussed elsewhere at length (see Marshall et al., Chapter 5 in this volume). Our principal concern here is with the claim that class analysis is compromised by the exclusion of a large proportion of the population who are not employed. This implicitly assumes an approach to class analysis which takes the individual as the unit of class composition. We recognize this is a controversial stance. For example, the so-called conventional approach (favoured by Erikson and Goldthorpe, among others) does not – strictly speaking – exclude non-employed but partnered women, since their class standing is seen as being determined by that of their employed male partners (see Erikson and Goldthorpe, 1992b). In other words the unit of class composition is taken to be the household. By contrast, when critics such as Stephen Edgell (1993: 39) argue that the 'traditional class analytic framework' which focuses 'solely on economically active males' is likely to lead to erroneous conclusions about class processes because it excludes 'women, the retired, students, the unemployed and the underemployed', this presupposes that the relevant unit of analysis is the (male) individual. It is this wider claim that is the focus of the present chapter.

6 Of course, the analysis in Table 4.2 shows that there are *some* differences between certain of the classes and their non-employed counterparts, and indeed it would have been surprising if employment had *no* effect whatsoever on these sorts of dependent variables. However, from the point of view of the dispute about class analysis, the most important finding to emerge from the table is that it shows no clear *pattern* to these differences. The non-employed groups are not systematically different from their employed (class) peers. Moreover, such differences as do exist are relatively minor, in comparison with those that distinguish the classes themselves – as is evident from the models shown in Table 4.3.

7 See, for example, Saunders (1990a: 122–4) and Stafford and Ladner (1990: 138–40). On the earlier debates about the culture of poverty and transmitted deprivation see, respectively, Valentine (1968) and Rutter and Madge (1976).

8 We are of course aware that the concept of fatalism itself is not unproblematic. In the strict sense, the term refers to a system of beliefs which holds that everything has its appointed outcome, and that this cannot be avoided by effort or foreknowledge and must merely be accepted as an unavoidable fact of life. In his elaboration of Durkheim's (1952: 276) famous footnote, David Lockwood (1992) suggests that fatalism is a matter of degree, and can result from either 'physical or moral despotism'; that is, from force of circumstances such as the condition of slavery, or from the constraints imposed by a system of explicitly fatalistic beliefs such as those embraced by the Hindu doctrine of reincarnation. More loosely, the phenomenon has been associated with poverty, chronic illness, and unemployment. Thus, for example, Oscar Lewis (1964) maintains that a sense of resignation and fatalism is a characteristic of those sharing in the culture of poverty. Similarly, in her discussion of the passive worker thesis (the idea that female employees are generally more acquiescent than are males), Kate Purcell (1982) argues that women's behaviour at work is informed by a fatalistic approach to life, fostered by gender socialization, and reinforced by manual working women's class

circumstances. In these more diffuse usages, as in the debate about the underclass, the concept of fatalism carries rather imprecise connotations. It is not clear which specific attitudinal characteristics would constitute the phenomenon in question – or how salient these are for behaviour. The questions that we have selected from the ISJP as indicators of a fatalistic attitude would seem nevertheless to be consistent with previous references to individuals being cynical towards established values of work and order, or feeling they are at the mercy of 'the system' rather than being presented with opportunities to exploit, although we accept that they are an imprecise operationalization which is far from ideal and does not exhaust the concept. Reliability analysis of the items yields a Cronbach's alpha of 0.54: this is not very high, but since this is a large data-set and alpha gives the lower bound of reliability for a range of such indicators, it is probably acceptable (see Cortina, 1993).

9 For methodological criticisms of this work see Aponte (1990: 126–30).

5

Class, Gender, and the Asymmetry Hypothesis*

Is orthodox class analysis sexist? During the past decade this issue has come to dominate sociological discussion of social inequality in advanced societies. Early in the 1970s, feminists began to mount a sustained challenge against the orthodox view that social classes comprised households centred on a male 'head', whose formal employment (whether conceptualized in terms of occupational prestige, socio-economic standing, or labour-market situation) was a valid indicator of the class location of all household members. These critics argued that the conventional approach to class analysis was naive, at a time when large numbers of married women were not only in full-time jobs but also concentrated in particular parts of the occupational structure, so that the male and female class distributions for any society were invariably rather different. Official statistics also showed that households were quite commonly headed by single females.

Moreover, sociological research seemed to suggest both that the division of resources within households favoured men over women, and that the occupational classifications which formed the basis of most class analyses were sex-specific – since they displayed a high degree of differentiation between occupations dominated by males but were relatively insensitive to distinctions between occupations in which women were in a majority. Against this background, orthodox class analysis stood accused of (at worst) intellectual sexism, or (at best) the only marginally less damaging charge of tunnel vision.

During the 1980s these criticisms were the subject of vigorous discussion and they generated a substantial literature which has already been reviewed on several occasions. It is not our intention (and it would, in any case, be quite impracticable) to pursue all of the questions raised by previous contributors to the debate.[1] Rather, attention here will be concentrated on three conceptually distinct though empirically interwoven issues, since it seems to us that these emerge repeatedly in earlier attempts to describe the relationship between class and gender. First, there is the matter of taxonomy itself, and whether or not extant class schemes are at all suitable for the study of women's employment. Second, there is the question of how sex segregation in the occupational structure relates to regimes of class inequality and class mobility; or, more specifically, of the connections between absolute mobility rates and relative mobility chances. Finally, we must consider the so-called asymmetry hypothesis, concerning the pattern of relationships among the class positions of spouses and the various attitudinal and behavioural attributes that are said to be (at least in part) a function of social class standing. The last of these, in particular, addresses the problem which is central to the whole debate; namely, that of identifying the appropriate unit of class composition.

Discussion about the first of these issues remains largely programmatic. It is clearly the case that, because of such processes as sex typing and patriarchal exclusion, there is a marked vertical and horizontal segregation of occupations in the labour markets of most advanced industrial societies. However, it is then a moot point as to whether the subsequent crowding of women into a relatively small number of occupational categories and statuses is an artefact of supposedly sexist class taxonomies, or merely a reflection of the realities of male power over the world of paid work. On this point, critics of the conventional view seem to want to argue both that sex discrimination in employment constrains women into lower-level jobs and grades, and that any classificatory device that reflects this oppression is somehow inadequate or sexist. Attempts to devise non-sexist class taxonomies that supposedly obviate this difficulty have proved singularly unsuccessful. These have foundered on the rocks of ad hocery, since the categories that have been devised for women typically embrace such characteristics as the presence of dependent children, stage in family life-cycle, educational attainment, and lifestyle – although it is by no means clear how (if at all) these may be said to be criteria that define class membership.[2] Until an operational classificatory scheme is devised which not only includes more women on a more finely differentiated basis, but also does so in a manner that is consistent with a recognizable theory of the delineation of the structure of class positions within modern society, then there is probably little to be gained by pursuing this particular line of criticism.

Similarly, dispute about the connections between sex segregation in the occupational structure and underlying regimes of class inequality seems to us to centre on the prior choice of conceptual context, rather than the plausibility of the empirical materials introduced as evidence by the various protagonists. On the one hand, advocates of the conventional view acknowledge that absolute mobility rates confirm the relationship between women's class origins and their employment chances as being system-atically less favourable than that for men, but they also insist that this is primarily the result of the less favourable opportunity structure within the labour market for women – rather than of sex differences in class fluidity patterns. In support of this conclusion they cite recent large-scale surveys which have compared typical occupational histories for both sexes (attributing a social class location to each individual by reference to his or her own employment) and which show that the pattern of relative mobility rates (or social fluidity) underlying women's intergenerational mobility is virtually the same as that which characterizes mobility among men. In other words, while the standard origin-to-destination mobility matrices do indeed confirm that the position of women within the class structure is different from (and less favourable than) that of men, these differences in absolute rates are almost entirely attributable to differences in the marginal (destination) distributions. *Sex* segregation in the occupational structure means that men and women are likely to end up in different destinations – but class inequalities scarcely vary by sex. This suggests that class background and sex do not 'interact', as critics of the conventional view often claim, since the forces that shape the association between origins and destinations among men would seem to be 'sex blind' – operating in much the same way among women. Women are distributed to different destinations because they are women – because of the status attribute of gender – and not because *class* processes operate differently for each sex. The social practices that generate sex segregation in employment (hence women's restricted opportunities) are therefore of a different order from those that form the subject matter of class analysis.[3]

In reply, critics have complained that this interpretation takes the occupational division of labour for granted, or at least as being the product merely of 'capitalist relations of production' or 'market forces', whereas in fact the impact of these processes on the structure of occupations is mediated by a number of additional factors – the most important of which is sex. The occupational categories that form the basis for class analysis are said to reflect the phenomenon of 'gendering', since men are concentrated into 'men's occupations', women into 'women's occupations'. Critics acknowledge that it is the position of the occupation, rather than the sex of the individual, that determines the status of the incumbent – but insist that the labour-market characteristics and status of the occupation itself will often have been decisively shaped by gender. Since social class is investigated using criteria that have been socially constructed in this way, it is not possible empirically to study classes in isolation from the several factors that structure the occupational division of labour, including not only gender but also (for example) ethnicity and type of political regime.[4]

This seemingly unresolved issue has attracted much attention. However, a good deal of this seems to us entirely unwarranted, since the evidence of similar relative class mobility chances among men and women is not (and never has been) in dispute. The controversy is only about the extent to which sex segregation in the labour force (itself the result of patriarchal processes which are widely recognized even by conventionalists) should be brought within the scope of class analysis. Our summary of the argument should have made it clear that the principal protagonists seem to be separated by the – again programmatic – issue of defining their respective fields of inquiry, in particular the research agenda of class analysis, since the substantive arguments of one side in no way preclude (indeed are wholly consistent with) those of the other. One of us has previously explicated this observation at some length. Its accuracy is testified to by Rosemary Crompton's recent appeal to 'bring status back in' to the research programme of 'class analysis'. By contrast, the most ardent defenders of the conventional position (John H. Goldthorpe and Robert Erikson) argue that class and status are not only conceptually distinct, but also empirically separable aspects of the stratification order. Perusal of these and other contributions confirms, however, the existence of near consensus about the actual facts of class mobility among women and men.[5]

Finally, conventionalists have claimed that empirical studies of class composition processes tend to reveal an asymmetric pattern of association by sex between class self-identity and a respondent's social class on the one hand, and the class position of his or her partner on the other. More specifically, where both respondent and spouse in a dual-earner conjugal family are assigned a class position individually (by reference to their own employment), there is (as one would expect) a tendency to class homogamy, and a strong association between the husband's class position and his own (subjective) class identification. When both associations are controlled for, there is typically little or no association between the latter and the wife's class position, although the obverse is not also true. Thus, not only is a woman's class identification weakly associated with the class position indicated by her own employment, but it is invariably also the case that a further significant (and usually stronger) association exists between a wife's class identification and the social class standing of her husband or partner. This pattern is also found when political partisanship, rather than class identity, is investigated. In short, as Goldthorpe puts it, not only 'sexist' sociologists but also married women themselves seem to view their class position as one which, at least in its socio-political aspects, is derived largely from the employment of their husbands.

The most controversial strand in the debate about class and gender would, therefore, seem also to be the most obviously empirical; namely, that of determining the relative merits of different approaches, from the point of view of explaining observed patterns of socio-political class formation. On the one hand, advocates of the orthodox approach claim that married women continue to see their class interests and affiliations as being more importantly determined by their husbands' employment than by their own. They argue further that this is a rational and realistic perception, when set against the differences that still persist between spouses, especially in terms of workforce attachment, worklife continuity, and contribution to family income. On the other hand, critics insist that patterns in class affiliation in the household division of labour and in socio-cultural perspectives are generally different in cross-class and class-homogamous families, and that the conventional approach will increasingly be at odds with the empirical reality of a class structure that is differentiated by sex, comprises a large number of families headed by females, and embraces a growing proportion of unambiguously 'cross-class' households in which partners hold quite dissimilar positions in the labour market. Against this background, it is argued, individuals rather than households are a more appropriate unit in terms of which to analyse class socio-political pro-cesses.[6] The issue here, therefore, is mercifully clear-cut. Which of these competing accounts of class composition in late-twentieth-century industrial societies is empirically the more sound?

Data and methods

In addressing this question we should investigate a range of advanced industrial societies. In the first place, the debate has already been conducted (if only implicitly) in comparative terms, and it is at least possible that the contradictory results reported by earlier researchers are to be attributed to differences of national context (for example between the United States and Britain). Moreover, there are prima facie grounds for supposing that societies with dissimilar employment profiles will display distinct patterns of socio-political class formation, even considered in the narrow terms within which the debate has been construed. It would indeed be surprising if (say) British women, many of whom choose not to take paid employment or are able to work only part-time, identified with their jobs in precisely the same way as did their Czechoslovak sisters – the majority of whom will of necessity have been employed full-time for most of their adult lives.

Our data are therefore taken from the International Social Justice Project (ISJP). This recent crossnational survey would seem to be particularly suited to empirical investigation of the asymmetry hypothesis, since it records strictly comparable details of the employment situations of male and female partners, and the class identification and voting behaviour of all respondents. These allow us to model the relationships between class identification or voting and the social class standing of marital partners, attributing class (where both partners are employed) on an individualistic basis, thus investigating the force of conventionalist claims that married (or cohabiting) women themselves view their class position as one which, at least in these limited respects, is derived primarily from the employment of their husbands (or male partners).[7]

At this juncture, it is worth noting that there is one strand in the recent literature on this subject that we will not be pursuing, although data are in principle available within the ISJP; namely, the issue of whether or not wives' *other* 'social characteristics' are relevant to the explanation of their class identities. Studies which have addressed this issue, at least by way of supposedly resolving the dispute about conventional versus alternative approaches to class analysis, seem to us to be entirely misconceived. Orthodox class analysts have never claimed that social class membership alone explained class identity – far less that it constituted a key to the full range of socio-cultural preferences. Their argument is simply that, in so far as class standing explains these phenomena, there are less satisfactory and more satisfactory ways of defining the unit of the class analysis itself. The addition of variables that are (conceptually if not always empirically) independent of class – such as trades union membership, educational qualifications, years of post-compulsory schooling, race, or (for that matter) a preference for opera rather than country music – will almost certainly explain variance over and above that attributable to class as such (and for men as well as women).[8]

The class categories used throughout our analysis are those devised by John Goldthorpe and his colleagues for use in the Comparative Analysis of Social Mobility in Industrial Nations Project. These have been validated, refined for comparative analysis, and would seem to be particularly well suited to crossnational research.[9] The ISJP researchers collected occupational information in a standardized fashion, and coded this to the German employment status (*Berufstellungen*) and 1968 ISCO (International Standard Classification of Occupations) categories, to which specially designed algorithms were then applied in order to generate Goldthorpe class variables that we believe to be crossnationally comparable. The relatively small numbers in the samples require a collapsed version of the scheme which distinguishes three categories: the salariat or service class (including large proprietors, managers, professionals, and administrators); the intermediate classes of routine clerical employees, *petite bourgeoisie* (including farmers and smallholders), technicians, and supervisors of manual workers; and the working class of skilled and non-skilled manual workers (including agricultural labourers and those involved in personal service).

The countries included in the project were chosen across the range of capitalist and communist (now post-communist) types of industrial societies. There is considerable variation, within as well as between these broad types, from the point of view of class and sexual inequalities. For example, among the capitalist states, Britain is characterized by a long history of liberal individualism, exemplified most recently in the *laissez-faire* policies pursued by successive radically pro-market governments. Legislation supporting women's rights has been relatively slow to develop in this country, with equal social citizenship being enacted only gradually during the past two decades, and in some important respects still subject to test in the courts. By 1985 women comprised 45 per cent of the total British workforce and the economic activity rate among women of working age had reached 60 per cent, although some 43 per cent of women working were employed part-time.

The former West Germany is an example of a 'semi-corporatist' society. The key interest groups of employers, trades unions, and the government itself have successfully managed a consensus about wages and prices that has sustained the post-war economic miracle. In formal terms, equality between the sexes has long been a plank of government policy. (The equal rights clause of the constitution has been in force for over four decades.) During the long post-war boom, special measures were implemented by the German state and German management to improve the situation of women in the labour force, notably by means of expanding opportunities for vocational training and further education, by an affirmative action programme to open up career hierarchies, and by a number of measures which recognized and attempted to relieve the 'double burden' of family and employment commitments among females (such as the extension of flexitime, job-sharing, maternity leave, and childcare facilities). However, there is evidence that the recession of the 1980s undermined many of these policies, as women's employment came to be defined as a problem rather than an opportunity. Correspondingly, the relevant statistics show a rise in female part-time employment, and an increasing segmentation of labour markets by sex. By 1985, 40 per cent of all employees were women, representing a participation rate among eligible women of some 50 per cent. Approximately one-third of women in the Federal Republic worked part-time.

The former state socialist societies are no less diverse in these respects. For example, Slovenia has a post-war history of 'market socialism', as a relatively wealthy part of (what was) Yugoslavia. This is exemplified in the mixed nature of the systems of industrial reward and control. These featured pay schedules that incorporated a basic wage plus an incentive bonus for fulfilling quotas or norms, and workers' councils that maintained the appearance of a proletarian state, although in practice the cleavage between management and workers was as salient as in many Western capitalist societies. Slovenia also belongs to the countries with a Catholic tradition, where paternalistic patterns of life and work have historically been emphasized, although changes in favour of women during recent decades have resulted in rather similar economic activity rates for the sexes. In 1991 the economic activity rate was 54 per cent among adult women, as against 68 per cent among adult men. Among married women the rate was 74 per cent – as compared with 79 per cent of married men. Part-time employment is exceptional for both sexes. Although there has not been special legislation aimed at the improvement of the position of women (except for general rules claiming equal rights for both sexes), one can find particular social policy measures that have achieved this effect, notably in the areas of parental leave, child benefits, prevention of night work for women, and public investment in childcare facilities.

By comparison, East Germany was an authoritarian state socialist society of a relatively orthodox kind, based on a highly centralized command economy and rigid bureaucratic state apparatus and Party hierarchy. Skilled manual workers were relatively less disadvantaged vis-à-vis routine clerical employees than in most Western societies. As in Slovenia the state proclaimed an ideology of egalitarianism in which sex equality was explicitly acknowledged as a central principle of socialism. However, although this was not made explicit at the level of ideology, the East German political elites also made a systematic attempt to translate rhetoric into policy by implementing a strategy of positive discrimination in favour of women, notably in the areas of education and employment. For example, special training provision was made for older female workers, to help compensate for missed opportunities in their youth; the state provided extensive childcare facilities for working mothers (over 60 per cent of children aged 1 to 3 were in crèches in 1981); and the facility to take time off work to tend a sick child was extended to both parents. These and similar policy measures did not eliminate the familiar inequalities between the sexes, but they did make the former GDR more advanced in this respect than were most of the other state socialist societies, and indeed more so than many of its Western capitalist neighbours. The suggestion is often made that this development owed less to socialism than it did to East German labour shortages and to the German tradition of encouraging vocational skills to create a skilled workforce. Nevertheless, for whatever reason, by the early 1980s women in the GDR constituted 50 per cent of the labour force: 87 per cent of eligible females were in paid employment, and although some 29 per cent worked part-time, this generally consisted only of a slight shortening of the working day from eight to six hours.

In short, these are four industrial societies which have had significantly different historical trajectories, and (at the time of our surveys) rather diverse formal economic and political regimes. The other capitalist and post-communist states for which we have data could be ranged in similar fashion across dimensions mapping (for example) formal and *de facto* equality or inequality between the sexes; the proportion of women employed and on what basis; or, perhaps, the extent of sex segregation in labour markets. However, since the evidence regarding socio-political class formation in households is either contradictory or simply unavailable, we have no clear basis on which to construct *a priori* a typology of societies to which expectations of symmetry or asymmetry in patterns of class composition can be attached. At this stage we can simply observe that the countries included in the analysis embrace a broad range of institutional arrangements for managing the social inequalities associated with class and sex. The selection is not exhaustive; for example, the southern European industrial states (such as Italy and Spain) are a conspicuous omission. However, if (as critics claim) the 'participation revolution' among women has indeed undermined the logic of the conventional approach to class analysis, then this should be evident somewhere in the range of societies under consideration.

Findings

What then do our data suggest about patterns of class composition? The results of modelling the relationships between respondent's class, partner's class, and respondent's class identification are shown for each of the countries and both sexes in Table 5.1. In setting out the table, we have followed the format introduced by Erikson and Goldthorpe (1992b) in their most recent article on the subject, since this offers a concise means of conveying the results for several countries. Four models are fitted to each data-set. The first of these (model 1) states that there is some degree of class homogamy, but no further associations exist, so that the respondent's class

Table 5.1 Results of fitting loglinear models to three-way tables relating Goldthorpe class of respondent (R) and class of spouse (S), as determined by the 'individual' approach, to respondent's class identity (I), in ten countries

		N	G^2R	G^2S	d.f.	ΔR	ΔS	G^2pa	d.f.
Britain	Men	370	28.8	26.1	6	23.9*	27.7*	9.3	4
	Women	405	69.9	17.5	6	5.0	51.9*	11.9	4
USA	Men	367	19.2	48.9	6	75.1*	36.6*	4.5	4
	Women	402	36.9	15.9	6	45.6*	76.6*	3.4	4
W. Germany	Men	388	13.5	54.6	6	56.7*	12.5*	2.0	4
	Women	370	25.2	31.3	6	37.1*	29.2*	2.7	4
E. Germany	Men	332	8.2	85.9	6	82.8*	5.4	2.8	4
	Women	316	23.8	29.8	6	39.8*	31.1*	2.3	4
Slovenia	Men	318	29.0	36.0	6	36.3*	28.3*	4.4	4
	Women	413	14.6	56.1	6	53.5*	10.9*	4.0	4
Hungary	Men	270	15.3	21.0	6	43.8*	26.5*	6.4	4
	Women	281	8.0	9.0	6	28.6*	24.7*	1.6	4
Bulgaria	Men	473	30.4	64.8	6	42.0*	17.1*	6.8	4
	Women	439	28.7	91.2	6	51.5*	13.5*	6.6	4
Czechoslovakia	Men	373	3.4	15.9	6	67.3*	4.5	2.5	4
	Women	349	9.4	10.5	6	32.3*	27.9*	2.9	4
Poland	Men	465	29.2	29.5	6	30.6*	30.0*	10.7	4
	Women	450	13.7	49.9	6	64.8*	9.2*	7.7	4
Estonia	Men	253	13.3	52.0	6	58.8*	11.4*	4.0	4
	Women	238	32.8	50.4	6	46.6*	28.2*	5.9	4

Models: 1 RS+I; 2 RS+RI; 3 RS+SI; 4 RS+SI+RI.
G^2R = fit of model 2 (RS+RI).
G^2S = fit of model 3 (RS+SI).
ΔR = improvement in G^2 when RI is added to model 3, expressed as % of baseline model 1.
ΔS = improvement in G^2 when SI is added to model 2, expressed as % of baseline model 1.
Statistically significant improvements in fit (at 5% level or better) are marked by an asterisk.
G^2pa,d.f. = fit of model 4 (all pairwise associations).

identity is unrelated to the class of either partner. This model is unrealistic but acts as a convenient baseline against which to judge models 2 and 3, which then postulate further associations between respondent's class and respondent's class identification, and spouse's class and respondent's class identification, respectively. The final model (model 4) proposes that both of these class associations are present together.

The first of the numerical columns in the table indicates the numbers of male and female respondents on which the analyses rest in each country. The second column reports the fit of model 2, and the third column the fit of model 3, with the degrees of freedom (which are the same for each model) shown in the fourth column. The fifth and sixth columns then report the improvement in fit that is obtained when the RI (respondent-class/respondent-identity) and SI (spouse-class/respondent-identity) associations are added into models 3 and 2 respectively – expressed as a percentage of the baseline model. The last two columns show the log likelihood ratio and degrees of freedom for the fit of model 4. This way of presenting the results means that the relative strengths of the RI and SI associations are in each case easily compared. The larger the values in the fifth column (ΔR) compared with those in the sixth column (ΔS), the more strongly is the respondent's class identity associated with his or her own class, relative to its association with the class of the spouse. In other words, we can compare directly the improvement in fit that is obtained by introducing the RI and SI associations, taking into account the RS association included in the baseline model. (Table 5.2 follows the same format but with class identity having been replaced by 'vote in last election'.)[10]

If we consider first the case of married or cohabiting men, in all but one country the association between men's class identities and their own class positions is stronger than that between their class identities and the class locations of their wives. East German and Czechoslovakian men apparently do not take their partners' employment into account when making judgements about their own class identities. However, in most other countries, men apparently do take their partners' employment into account when making judgements about their own class identities – although the association between a man's class identity and his own class is generally by far the stronger of the two relationships. Britain, Poland, and Slovenia are the exceptions. Here, comparison of the fits for models 2 and 3 suggests (surprisingly) that a married man is about as likely to assess his class identity in relation to his wife's occupation as he is in relation to his own, and in Britain indeed appears to be (slightly) more likely to do so.

But it is the results for women that are perhaps more damaging from an orthodox point of view. Only those for Britain and the United States support the conventionalist claim that employed females identify more strongly with their partner's class (model 3) than their own (model 2) – although the latter association is significant and should be included to obtain a satisfactory fit to the data. At the other extreme are Slovenia,

Poland, Bulgaria, and Estonia. In these countries, employed women are substantially more likely to nominate a class identity appropriate to their own jobs than they are to derive this from the occupations of their partners, although in each case the best-fitting model (model 4) again includes associations with both their own class position and that of their male partner. In East and West Germany, Hungary, and Czechoslovakia, the situation is more complex, since cohabiting women identify with both their own and their partners' jobs, and to about the same degree. (Although it is perhaps worth noting that, in each case, the association between the women's class identities and their own jobs is marginally stronger than that between their class identities and the jobs of their partners.)

In short, while the findings for class identification among men might be said to be of limited value in settling the dispute about the unit of class composition (since both the individual and conventional approaches would treat men similarly), those for women tend to undermine the conventionalist claim that there is a clear asymmetry in patterns of socio-political class formation. A wife's class identification is not as a rule more strongly associated with her spouse's class than with a class position assigned to her on the basis of her own employment. In certain countries, the class identities of women are more strongly governed by their own occupational experiences, so that the results for the sexes can fairly be said to be (more or less) symmetrical.

The data on voting behaviour provide stronger support for the conventionalist position – although on a much smaller sample of countries (see Table 5.2). The proliferation of electoral parties in most Central and Eastern European states is such that political preferences could not reliably be examined in this way. (For example, no fewer than 32 Czechoslovakian political parties contested the national elections prior to the survey, and these cannot meaningfully be collapsed into a small number of homogeneous groupings.) However, the rival claims were assessed in respect of voting behaviour in the Western democracies and in the former East Germany (a special case in which post-communist politics were constituted along existing West German lines), and the findings are generally in line with conventionalist predictions. British women are much more likely to vote in accordance with the class of their partner's job than in accordance with their own. For women in the German countries, though not statistically significant, the class position of husbands is also the more important. Among the men, on the other hand, voting is associated with the respondent's class alone. In the United States, there is no clear association between a woman's vote and the class indicated by her own employment, although there is a small but significant association between a man's class and his vote.

Taken as a whole, these findings provide some, but by no means unequivocal, support for a conventional approach to class analysis. Proponents of the orthodoxy have argued that the class socio-political preferences of married or cohabiting women are less strongly associated

Table 5.2 Results of fitting loglinear models to three-way tables relating Goldthorpe class of respondent (R) and class of spouse (S), as determined by the 'individual' approach, to respondent's voting behaviour (V), in four countries

		N	G^2R	G^2S	d.f.	ΔR	ΔS	G^2pa	d.f.
Britain	Men	308	11.3	22.9	12	50.0*	16.6	5.5	8
	Women	358	43.1	25.4	12	25.2*	51.8*	8.6	8
USA	Men	266	8.8	21.2	6	59.8*	2.7	8.7	4
	Women	262	7.3	7.6	6	21.8	18.6	4.3	4
W. Germany	Men	318	14.3	21.8	12	37.3*	15.6	8.9	8
	Women	292	20.1	15.5	12	14.2	33.0	12.0	8
E. Germany	Men	235	14.7	26.3	12	45.2*	9.5	11.7	8
	Women	224	11.2	6.2	12	8.8	43.2	4.9	8

Models and parameters as for Table 5.1 with V replacing I.

with their own employment than with that of their male partners; while, conversely, there is little or no association between the class standing of working women and the class socio-political preferences of their male partners. Both propositions seem to hold true in the case of voting behaviour. However, where class identity is concerned, neither can stand without qualification. In Slovenia, Poland, Bulgaria, and Estonia, the class identities of women are substantially more likely to be associated with their own employment than they are with that of their male partners. German, Hungarian, and Czechoslovakian women show a similar (if less pronounced) independent-mindedness. In the case of married or cohabiting men, Britons, Poles, and Slovenians are about as likely to hold class identities that reflect the employment of their wives or female partners, as they are to situate themselves according to their own class standing.

Of course, it is necessary in all cases to include the spouse-class/ respondent-identity association when considering the class identities of females, and in Britain this association is indeed much stronger than that between the respondent's own class standing and her class identity. It is also true that in (almost all) the countries considered here, the association between a man's class standing and his class identity is greater than that between the latter and the class of his employed female partner, although the findings for Poland and Slovenia scarcely offer compelling evidence of this proposition – while those for Britain actually refute it (though only just). In short, while some of our results conform to conventionalist expectations, others would seem to raise clear doubts about assumptions of asymmetry in processes of socio-political class formation.

Conclusions

In this chapter we have argued that the treatment of gender differences has provoked most controversy in the recent literature on social class; that this is principally a disagreement about the unit of class composition; and that the debate therefore turns on the empirical evidence concerning patterns of socio-political class formation. On this last point our investigation of the data from the International Social Justice Project may be said to be inconclusive. Some of the evidence is clearly contrary to conventionalist expectations that the unit of class composition is the household and that class membership is most appropriately assigned via the husband's occupation.[11] However, the alternative view, which takes the individual as the unit of class composition and attributes class socio-political characteristics to individuals within households on the basis of their own employment, finds no less partial vindication.

There is, of course, a third possible strategy for assigning class positions which we have not yet addressed; namely, to adopt some kind of joint classification of husbands and wives. A few contributors to the debate have suggested that this is in fact the approach best suited to deal with the increasingly complex structure of households generated by the increase in female employment. In this way, it is argued, one might distinguish single-earner and dual-earner households, and, within the latter, differentiate the various types of class-homogamous and cross-class families. Advocates of this strategy claim that, across a variety of attributes which include voting behaviour, more of the variance within and between conjugal families can be accounted for using a joint classification than if households are indexed simply according to the employment of husbands alone. In other words, the unit of class composition remains the household, but class membership is assigned via joint classification of the husband's and wife's occupations or employment statuses.[12]

It should be observed, however, that this attempted solution to the problem generates rates of class mobility that are spuriously high (since every movement in or out of the labour market by the wife alters the class standing of the family), and also confounds class effects with those of household composition. Indeed, joint classification so accentuates problems of identifying class boundaries that the whole rationale of class analysis is undermined, which is presumably not what its proponents intended. In any case, conventionalists have never denied that 'women's jobs make a differ-ence' in terms of the explained variance in relevant dependent variables, but have merely insisted that any such differences are demonstrably insufficient to warrant the abandonment of the conventionalist approach. They have also rightly objected that the issue is not explained variance as such, but rather how the pattern of association between the respondent's class, spouse's class, and dependent variables is to be understood. Perhaps in recognition of these criticisms, the joint classification approach to the problem has attracted only limited support, and appears now to have been abandoned by its most noted advocate.[13]

One interpretation of our results might be that the data are somehow unreliable. While this possibility can never be ruled out, we find it hard to identify likely sources of error, since we are working with nationally rep-resentative samples and thoroughly piloted questions on class identity and voting behaviour. It could also be argued that any attempt to test a thesis about socio-political class formation using data taken from the post-communist societies of Eastern and Central Europe is misconceived. The usual class identity question may be thought inappropriate in this context. For example, if identities were to be only weakly correlated with class, the asymmetry effect (which is, after all, a class effect) would either be negligible or be harder to detect in the data (or both). However, com-parison of the results for the Western capitalist and state socialist societies shows that the association between objective class and professed identity is as strong in the latter as in the former, and that the percentages of respondents who refuse the class concept or say that they 'don't know' to which class they belong are generally no higher.[14] On that basis, we can see no good grounds on which to discount our results for Central and Eastern Europe, as if they were somehow less reliable than those for the West.

It might then be argued that our rather crude three-category collapse of the Goldthorpe classes sacrifices discriminatory power at the expense of conventionalist claims. However, having repeated the analysis using a more nuanced five-category version of the class scheme, we can confirm that the results are substantially unaffected by this change.[15] It is perhaps also worth noting that part-time as well as full-time female employees have been included in the analysis. To that extent, our data are constructed in such a way as might favour asymmetry and the conventional view, since it can plausibly be argued that women who work only a few hours each week will be more inclined to take the class characteristics of their fully employed partners. This makes our results with respect to class identity all the more surprising. It is hard to see how they might be dismissed as merely artefactual.[16]

Other explanations seem more plausible. One is that the process of socio-political class formation has been subtly different in East and West. The communist ideology of egalitarianism, with its strong emphasis on equality between the sexes, may have encouraged married women (most of whom have been in full-time employment for a large part of their adult lives) to construct class identities in terms of their own occupations rather than those of their partners. In this context, it is noteworthy that the most striking refutations of the asymmetry thesis are to be found among women in the Central and Eastern European countries, where the class identities of females are in all cases more strongly associated with their own employment.[17] By contrast, the conventionalist case looks stronger in the West, where the results for British and American women clearly confirm conventionalist expectations, and those for West German women are only marginally contrary. One possible explanation for this last finding, however, may lie in the observation that West Germans generally, and cohabiting or married women in particular, attribute predominantly middle-class identities to themselves. No less than three-quarters of all West German respondents, and four-fifths of married and cohabiting women, describe themselves as middle class. This is likely to override any effect on class identity from the male partner's class. Our finding for class identities among British men is simply counter to the run of results obtained from recent similar studies and to that extent may be regarded by conventionalists as unconvincing.[18]

A further possibility is that the two dependent variables which we have considered relate to processes of socio-political class formation in rather different ways. It seems to us worthy of note that it is the data for voting behaviour, rather than those for class self-placement, which provide strongest support for conventional claims. On the face of it, this would seem problematic for the conventional position: one might expect class identification to be a better indicator of class formation than political preference, yet the conventional position is arguably weaker with regard to the former than the latter. But this, we would suggest, is not a substantial challenge to the conventionalist, who might very well assert the counter-claim that it is the extent to which the orthodox position is supported by our data on voting behaviour that really matters – simply because it is the way a person votes that is the best and most significant indicator of that action which class analysis seeks to explain.

It is not surprising, the conventionalist might argue, that individuals should consider household rather than personal interest when thinking about political partisanship, and it seems reasonable to suppose that voting is likely to involve a prior exchange of views between cohabiting partners. By contrast, it is plausible to argue that husbands and wives – whether employed or not – are rather unlikely to be involved in periodic negotiations about class identities (either their own or that of the household as a whole), and are thus less likely to answer questions about class affiliation in terms of an articulated household interest. These intuitively appealing considerations are supported by our data, and the defender of the conventional position may simply argue that however much people think as individuals about their class identities, the way they act politically is on the basis of their household and not their individual class position.

In this regard it is unfortunate that we do not yet have suitable voting data for the former state socialist countries, and it will be intriguing to see how the pattern of associations in which we are interested emerges, if these societies develop forms of class politics. At present, on the evidence reported here, it seems that women in the post-communist states are inclined to think as individuals in adopting identities appropriate to the class positions implied by their own jobs. Western women are more likely to identify with the employment of their husbands. Might this not be precisely because men and women in the West have long had the opportunity to express an explicit household interest by voting for political parties which tend to formulate their electoral programmes along class lines? If this is the case then the situation in the East is unlikely to be sustainable indefinitely and the Western pattern can in due course be expected to emerge. We await the results of future research with interest.

Meanwhile, we accept of course that our own findings pertain to only a limited number of countries, and we do not wish to be guilty of reading too much into these particular data. In any case, it would be difficult to construct a precise causal narrative to explain our results without conducting a great deal of additional research, and of a type quite different from that reported here. It is clear that mere labour-force participation alone cannot be the whole story, since the asymmetry effects predicted by conventionalists persist, even when the analysis of class identities is restricted to full-time employees in those countries (such as Britain) where part-time employment is relatively common. However, it may be that women's participation in employment has an indirect effect, in that wives who live in societies in which most other women are employed for most of the time come to define their roles in somewhat different terms from women in societies in which a majority (or even a substantial minority) of females take the role of housewife. Communist ideology, with its emphasis on *de jure* (if not *de facto*) equality between the (more or less fully employed) sexes, will then have reinforced this process. But we offer these merely as suggestions which might account for our findings and as a starting point for additional study. Future research might profitably concentrate on identifying factors which explain the relationship between gender and class formation. This is one area of research where systematic and rigorously comparative crossnational analysis is still in its early stages, and until such time as work is undertaken on larger samples and a wider range of societies, we will simply be unable to pursue Adam Przeworski and Henry Teune's (1970) celebrated programme of 'replacing the names of nations with the names of variables'.

For the moment, the issues are only partly empirical, since – as we hope to have shown – the debate thus far has been characterized as much by conceptual confusion as by factual dispute. Feminist critics have tended to muddy the empirical water, since there is simply no justification for their claim that a conventional approach to class analysis is self-evidently sexist, merely because it seems to privilege the study of men. This critique overlooks the fact that the arguments in favour of the orthodoxy are explicitly premised on a recognition of the consequences of labour-market segmentation and the resulting economic dependence of the majority of women within conjugal families. But women are disadvantaged because they are women, not because they form a particular social class, or are somehow exposed to a unique combination of the forces that help shape the intergenerational transmission of class privileges. On the other hand, if our evidence from the post-communist societies of the East is to be believed, then proponents of the conventional view should not be tempted to extend their claims about asymmetric processes of socio-political class formation beyond the immediate confines of the capitalist West.

Notes

* Gordon Marshall, Stephen Roberts, Carole Burgoyne, Adam Swift and David Routh. The authors wish to thank Göran Ahrne, Rosemary Crompton, Jon Ivar Elstad, Robert Erikson, Geoff Evans, John H. Goldthorpe, Håkon Leiulfsrud, and Tore Lindbekk for their helpful comments on an earlier draft of the argument, and Goldthorpe and Erikson for their patience in dealing with what must have seemed like endless requests for information. Our data are taken from the ISJP, which was supported in whole or in part by the National Council for Soviet and East European Research, National Science Foundation, and Institute for Social Research, University of Michigan (USA); National Scientific Research Fund (Hungary); Economic and Social Research Council and British Academy/Leverhulme Trust (UK); Deutsche Forschungsgemeinschaft (Germany); Institute of Social Science, Chuo University (Japan); the Dutch Ministry of Social Affairs; the Bulgarian Academy of Sciences; the Grant Agency of the Czechoslovak Academy of Sciences; Saar Poll Limited (Estonia); the Ministry of Science and Technology of the Republic of Slovenia; the State Committee for Scientific Research (Poland); and the Russian Federation Ministry of Labour.

1 For overviews see, for example, Bonney (1988), Duke and Edgell (1987), the papers collected in Payne and Abbot (1990a) or Crompton and Mann (1986), and (perhaps most

usefully) the exchange between Susan McRae and Shirley Dex on 'Class and Gender' in Clark et al. (1990).

   2 See, for example, Dale et al. (1985), Murgatroyd (1984) and Roberts and Barker (1986). Martin and Wallace (1984: 24, 35) state that 'the customary classifications of social class and socio-economic group are not very satisfactory bases for classifying women's jobs because most of the more common women's jobs fall into a limited number of categories', and offer instead a typology of women's occupations 'constructed inductively . . . on the basis of type of occupation', grouping together 'occupations sharing certain characteristics'. Unfortunately the characteristics in question are never made clear, nor indeed is the relationship between the occupational categories so identified and either the concept of social class itself or the (allegedly 'malestream') scales of occupational prestige that are used elsewhere throughout the analysis.

   3 See Goldthorpe (1987: ch. 10) and Erikson and Goldthorpe (1992a: ch. 7).

   4 See, for example, Crompton and Sanderson (1990: 3–15) and Crompton (1993: 93–7).

   5 Compare Marshall et al. (1988: 81–5), Crompton (1993: 126–34) and Erikson and Goldthorpe (1992a: 252–3).

   6 In defence of the conventional view of the household as the unit of class composition see Jackman and Jackman (1983: 140–52), Felson and Knoke (1974), Rossi et al. (1974), Hodge and Treiman (1968) and Erikson and Goldthorpe (1988; 1992b). Revisionists on this issue include McRae (1986), Leiulfsrud and Woodward (1987), Ritter and Hargens (1975), Hiller and Philliber (1978), Van Velsor and Beeghley (1979) and Abbott and Sapsford (1987).

   7 The ISJP is primarily a survey of popular beliefs about distributive justice. Based on a common research design and interview schedule, developed and fielded by colleagues working in a number of democratic capitalist and former state socialist societies, the study investigates attitudes towards a range of justice issues among nationally representative samples of men and women. Some of the preliminary findings for Britain have been reported elsewhere (see, for example, Swift et al., 1992; Burgoyne et al., 1993). The countries involved in the project are Bulgaria, Czechoslovakia, Estonia, East and West Germany, Holland, Hungary, Japan, Poland, Russia, Slovenia, Great Britain, and the United States. National sample surveys are representative of adults, with fieldwork carried out in the summer of 1991, and an average sample size of approximately 1,500. The analysis reported here omits the Dutch, Japanese, and Russian cases. The first of these studies lacks sufficient information to create a class variable that is comparable crossnationally. The Japanese sample is too small to be included in this particular investigation. The percentage of Russian respondents expressing a positive preference is too low to permit a reliable analysis of class identities.

   8 Recent examples of studies in this genre include Abbott and Sapsford (1986), Baxter (1991) and Hayes and Jones (1992a). Hayes and Jones (1992b) also commit this fallacy in a parallel analysis of political party identification among married men and women.

   9 An extensive exposition of the theoretical rationale, categories, and operationalization of the Goldthorpe class schema is given in Erikson and Goldthorpe (1992a: 29–47). For a validation see Evans (1992).

   10 Respondents were asked a two-part question on class identities: first, whether or not they thought of themselves as belonging to any particular social class; then a supplementary, asking them to suppose they were asked to say to which class they belonged, and indicate which that would most likely be. They also provided information on their own employment, on their vote at the last national election, and on their spouse or partner's employment only.

   11 Erikson and Goldthorpe have more recently proposed an alternative means for operationalizing the conventional approach. This involves the principle of 'dominance' in attributing heads to households. Here, the class of the household is determined by giving priority to the conjugal partner whose labour-market participation may be regarded as dominant, in terms of employment status and level of economic activity. In practice, this means that employment takes priority over non-employment, full-time employment over part-time, and higher-level employment (judged according to the criterion of an appropriate class schema) over lower-level employment. Typically, most heads of household continue to be males in the terms of these criteria (indeed, in our samples, this is true for all countries), so

that this refinement has limited implications for the analysis reported in this chapter. See Erikson (1984) and Erikson and Goldthorpe (1992a: ch. 7).

12 Examples of the joint approach include Britten and Heath (1983), Heath and Britten (1984) and Graetz (1991). A complex variation on the theme of joint classification is also proposed by Osborn and Morris (1979), whose 'composite index of social class' attempts to treat economically active and inactive members of the population together, by generating an index score for each family using summed and weighted scores for seven different variables: father's occupational class; parents' education; social rating of neighbourhood of residence; type of tenure; bathroom availability; type of accommodation; and a 'crowding' variable based on the ratio of persons to rooms in households. It is hard to conceive of any theory of class which could justify operationalization of the concept in terms of this particular combination of indicators. Nor is it surprising (or damaging to the case in favour of a conventional approach to class analysis) to learn that all seven variables together achieve greater discriminatory power than does social class alone, in predicting language and general developmental indices for young children.

13 Anthony Heath has recently revised his position, on the basis of an investigation of the impact of respondent's and spouse's class on voting behaviour in Britain over the period 1974–87, and now maintains that 'the search for a single simple rule for the classification of families, such as the conventional procedure or the individual procedure, may be fruitless.' His analysis suggests complex interaction effects, which result in women in service-class and blue-collar occupations taking more account of their own class than of their partner's, whereas women in the *petite bourgeoisie* and routine nonmanual class take relatively little account of their own class position (see De Graaf and Heath, 1992). It is not clear what kind of classification strategy this implies – although the unit of class composition would still seem to be the household.

14 Only in Russia and Estonia did this figure exceed 10 per cent (and in Estonia only marginally so). A filtering error in the Russian questionnaire resulted in there being too few cases to model the data reliably. For this reason we have not included the Russian data in the analysis, although on the limited numbers available (246 males, 176 females) the results are consistent with those for the other post-communist states, with ΔR and ΔS being 53.8 per cent and 14.3 per cent respectively for married and cohabiting women. (The corresponding figures for men are 72.6 per cent and 9.7 per cent.)

15 The loglinear analysis using five class categories – by further distinguishing between the *petite bourgeoisie*, routine clerical workers, and skilled manual working class (including technicians and supervisors) – is at the margins of acceptability as regards cell sizes. This is why our primary investigation employs the (seemingly conservative) three-class collapse. However, there are only minor differences between the two sets of results, and the weight of the evidence is not shifted one way or the other.

16 Unfortunately, in all countries, there are too few respondents working part-time (less than 30 hours per week) to permit separate analyses according to full-time or part-time employment. In the case of the post-communist states, part-time employees (of both sexes) form a relatively small proportion (usually 5 per cent and never more than 10 per cent) of those in employment, in any of the samples. In the British case, part-time employees constitute approximately one-third of all employees in the sample, a significantly higher proportion than in West Germany or the United States (18 per cent and 17 per cent respectively). Since the results for class identity among British and American women vindicate the conventionalist approach, we have therefore replicated the analysis on full-time employees alone, and find that the pattern of associations is unaltered. Our operationalization of the Goldthorpe class variable is also somewhat unusual in that individuals who have been out of the labour market for several years (for example through retirement or unemployment) have been allocated a class position on the basis of their last occupation. It is of course more usual to restrict analyses of this sort to those currently in employment. A more inclusive strategy is pursued here simply to increase the number of available cases. However, presumably this too should in principle yield outcomes which favour the conventional approach, since women who have left the labour market upon marriage or childbirth might reasonably be expected to define their

class interests in terms of the jobs held by their currently employed male partners. In any case, we have repeated the analysis for only those respondents currently in employment, and can confirm that our findings are substantially unaffected by this restriction. The sole exception to this generalization is Britain. If the analysis is restricted to those currently in employment, then the (otherwise curious) finding for British men is reversed, with the association between a man's class identity and his own job becoming stronger (although not by much).

17 It is also worth noting here that the results recently reported by Erikson and Goldthorpe (1992b: 98) included only one for a country outside the West (Hungary) – although the pattern of class identities among Hungarian women observed tends in fact to support conventionalist claims. This is an especially curious anomaly since our data and theirs appear to have been produced by the same Hungarian research agency.

18 See, for example, the data for British men reported in Erikson and Goldthorpe (1992b), and note 16 above. We are also grateful to John Goldthorpe for kindly making available results obtained from his analysis of the British General Election Survey for 1992. Those for British men (as well as women) further support conventionalist arguments. In the former case, the ΔR and ΔS are 55 per cent and 8 per cent respectively, while the corresponding figures for women are 1 per cent and 70 per cent (n = 399 and 431).

Part III
SOCIAL MOBILITY

6

Proletarianization in the British Class Structure?*

Just as the thesis of embourgeoisement formed the linchpin for debates in class analysis during the affluent years of the early 1960s so has the argument about proletarianization of the class structure come to hold centre-stage during the recessionary 1980s. Although one process is prima facie the inverse of the other there are several close similarities in the arguments themselves. Both were taken up seriously by sociologists after first having been popularized by non-academics or by academics writing in semi-popular format for a non-specialist audience. Both, indeed, were already public issues by the time they entered the arena of sociological discussion. In the former case the various folk-theories were organized about the commonly held belief that Western societies were witnessing the demise of the class system and emergence of a mass consumer society. Similarly, the harbinger of sociological debates about proletarianization was a popular belief that economic problems in the advanced industrial societies had created a newly impoverished class of subemployed and unemployed marginal workers and welfare dependants, and a working class whose traditional skills and work practices had been undermined by the organizational imperatives of standardized and automated production.

Because they were rooted in such diffuse and often polemical origins, subsequent sociological discussions of embourgeoisement and proletarianization were generally multifarious and mostly confused, more or less from the outset. It was not until the late 1960s, and the publication of the Affluent Worker Study, that the theoretical foundations of the embourgeoisement thesis were clarified and its core propositions subjected to systematic empirical scrutiny. A similar adjudication in the ongoing debate about proletarianization has yet to be attempted. The present analysis offers a modest contribution towards that end. It reports some of the findings from a national survey of class processes in Britain. These seem to the authors to bear directly on the issue of proletarianization and so help to clarify the parameters of the debate. They also suggest that, while there are many matters yet to be resolved, the central premise of the thesis is clearly flawed: the changing British class structure does *not* reflect a process of so-called proletarianization.

The concept of proletarianization

In order to substantiate this conclusion we must deal perforce with certain theoretical preliminaries. We would wish to distinguish at the outset four rather different usages of the principal concept itself. These refer to the proletarianization of the class *structure* as a whole; of *individuals* within that structure; of particular types of *jobs*; and of the social *consciousness* of individuals and groups in society.

The first of these perspectives has most obviously been shared by the various neo-Marxist proponents of a structural class analysis. The argument here concerns the distribution of class places within class structures. Advocates of proletarianization maintain that the historical tendency is for the numbers occupying working-class positions to expand in relation to other social classes. Thus Erik Wright (1985) has argued that proletarians constitute a growing proportion of the American labour force; indeed, by the 1980s, they are purportedly the largest single class grouping in most advanced capitalist societies. A second and closely related interpretation is that proffered by Rosemary Crompton and others who have documented the so-called deskilling of particular jobs (see, for example, Crompton and Jones, 1984). In this version of the thesis, some of the seemingly non-proletarian places in the structure (notably those occupied by routine clerical and administrative employees) are deemed in fact to involve the execution of tasks that have been entirely routinized, and for this reason offer jobs which are largely indistinguishable in content from those performed by unskilled manual workers. Note that in both of these versions of the argument it is the characteristics of class locations themselves which are at issue. However, a somewhat different perspective is adopted by authors such as John Goldthorpe, who see the thesis of proletarianization as applying primarily to trajectories through the structure, and so to the likelihood of persons from particular class backgrounds arriving at working-class destinations, by means of either intergenerational or career mobility. For these commentators (see, for example, Goldthorpe and Payne, 1986) it is people rather than places in the structure that constitute the focus of theoretical interest. Finally, such proponents of the thesis as Richard Edwards (1979) have adopted a socio-political interpretation of its central tenet, and explored the degree to which particular sectors of the nonmanual labour force sympathize with the political aspirations of the working class and so constitute its likely allies in class struggles.

It will be obvious that these diverse interpretations of the argument imply very different sorts of analytical enterprises. The first suggests that the central task is one of 'mapping' any given class structure so as to determine the size of the working class in relation to other class locations. Of course, an unambiguous criterion of 'working-classness' is a precondition of these cartographic enterprises, and it is this criterion itself which is the focus of interest for those who take proletarianization to be a reference to the deskilling of erstwhile 'middle-class' jobs. Consequently, instead of surveying whole class structures (so as to document the distribution of classes within them), these commentators concentrate their research efforts on case-studies in the organization of occupations and control of production (and seek to demonstrate that the distribution of occupational classes itself may be misleading since many nominally middle-class jobs have in fact been 'proletarianized'). Nevertheless, whether one is interested primarily in the class structure as a whole or in particular positions within it, the common concern is with the characteristics of class locations. It is class places that are the centre of research interest. By contrast, those who view the thesis of proletarianization as a statement about class processes within the structure (or what John Goldthorpe calls 'demographic class formation') are drawn logically to the investigation of social mobility, and to the movement of individuals into or out of the working class. Attention is here shifted from the attributes of class places themselves to the class trajectories of individuals moving between these places – or not moving between them as the case may be. Finally, of course, interest in the objective features of class structure and processes gives way to the investigation of subjective elements, if proletarianization is viewed as primarily a socio-political process. The issues of class identity, shared values, and probable voting behaviour come to the fore and displace questions about occupational trajectories and the organization of production.

Naturally, we accept that this fourfold schema is simply a heuristic device for organizing the relevant literature, since in practice most commentators seem to move easily to and fro between these rather different views of the problem. In one text, for example, Stewart Clegg and his colleagues commence their coverage of the issue by observing that Harry Braverman's (1974) seminal discussion of proletarianization is centrally concerned with 'the twin processes of deskilling and increased control developed through technological innovation . . . of formerly skilled working-class positions'; that is, with how 'the capitalist labour process withdraws the last vestiges of skill and control over work from the working class'. They then move on to consider the 'increasing activism of the majority of other professional and technical workers whose tasks are becoming increasingly proletarianized', and speculate that the 'proletarianization of the new middle class' which has led to 'increased white-collar union militancy' offers a 'framework for the new middle class to form defensive coalitions with highly unionized working-class groups'. It is duly noted that professionals and managers under threat of proletarianization create 'insurmountable problems for any theoretical determination concerning their class formation'. Additional difficulties in mapping the class structure are also created by gender and by social mobility: on the one hand, the 'proletarianization' of routine white-collar labour has often involved its 'feminization', while on the other the variable work histories of individuals mean that 'the young articled clerk whose position is subjectively defined merely as a status passage *en route* to a credentialled position, is a different type of "proletarianized" worker from one who has had, and still expects to have, a lifetime in the lower-status position' (Clegg et al., 1986: 156ff.). Clearly, in this particular discussion, the process of proletarianization is variously identified with each of the four developments noted above: the deskilling of particular jobs; socio-political radicalism among the working class and its allies; changes in the composition of the class structure; and career trajectories through that structure.

Clegg and his colleagues are not exceptional in this regard. Most proponents of the thesis link the routinization of tasks *per se* either explicitly or implicitly to the proportionate expansion of *de facto* working-class places in the structure and to the increased likelihood of militancy directed against the ruling classes. In some cases the association of proletarian 'class consciousness' with deskilled labour is (rightly) held to be contingent and a matter for empirical investigation. Elsewhere a crudely deterministic version of sociological reductionism seems to prevail, whereby radicalized labour provides evidence for the degradation of working-class skills; or, conversely, it is assumed that putative processes of occupational deskilling will lead inexorably to 'proletarian' protest against capitalist forms of production (compare, for example, Wright, 1985: ch. 7; Crompton, 1979). It is not necessary to pursue the details of the different accounts here. Rather, our fourfold distinction of the central tendencies in the relevant literature allows us to make two important observations by way of situating the present chapter in the context of the debate about proletarianization, and so helps clarify the basis of our critique and its conclusions.

First, it is clear that in much of the earlier discussion disputes about alleged proletarianization have often reached an impasse because participants in the various controversies have rooted their conclusions in different interpretations of the argument itself, and so have tended to talk past each other. The exchanges between Goldthorpe and Crompton offer a case in point. The former maintains that the post-war periods of affluence and recession alike have seen the continuous expansion of a relatively privileged 'service class' of professionals, administrators, managers and other skilled white-collar workers. Moreover, in mapping the class structure beyond this stratum, Goldthorpe places routine white-collar employees in an 'intermediate-class' position, on the grounds that the market situation, work situation, and typical socio-political proclivities of lower-level clerical and administrative personnel are observably different from those of manual workers generally. Crompton, by contrast, argues that the expansion of administrative and professional occupations is probably more apparent than real because many of these involve the performance of increasingly routinized and therefore degraded labour. Moreover, and contra Goldthorpe, routine clerical work has certainly been deskilled because such employees commonly experience the same limited autonomy in the workplace as do unskilled manual workers. Since clerks often perform routine tasks under close supervision they are effectively proletarians. Goldthorpe, in reply, can find no systematic evidence in favour of either of these claims.

In his view, particular case-studies of occupational deskilling (such as the study of local authority, life assurance, and banking clerks in which Crompton herself was involved) can readily be offset against others reporting an upgrading of occupational skills and tasks, and in any case are themselves not inconsistent with his own claim that the *net* result of organizational and technical changes over the whole economy is one of increasing both skill levels and the proportion of the workforce benefiting from service-class conditions of employment (compare Crompton, 1980; Crompton and Jones, 1984; Goldthorpe, 1980; Goldthorpe and Payne, 1986).

The most striking feature of this particular disagreement is that it (like many others in the debate as a whole) is rooted in rather different interpretations of the thesis at issue. Goldthorpe's contention is that the argument about proletarianization is a statement about class structures as a whole – the proportionate class positions that comprise this structure and the patterned mobility of individuals between these positions. Since, in his view, macro-sociological issues of this kind can be resolved only on the basis of macro-sociological data, then particular case-studies that report degrading or upgrading of labour are of little value for or against the thesis of proletarianization *per se*. Of course Crompton takes such case-studies to be the very means by which key issues can be decided. She is unconvinced by Goldthorpe's social survey approach since only close observation and intensive interviewing can establish whether or not the *content* of particular jobs (as opposed to their associated *occupational titles*) has changed over time. Given this fundamental disagreement about what constitutes evidence for or against the thesis it is scarcely surprising that the issue of proletarianization remains a matter of unresolved controversy.

This brings us to our second point and to the matter of the evidence available from our own study. It is axiomatic that, however one constructs a causal scenario for the proletarianization process, all versions of the argument necessarily apply to the condition of class structures as a whole. On this point Goldthorpe seems unassailable. One has only to imagine an extreme counterfactual instance to see why. It is entirely feasible (though admittedly unlikely) that one hitherto middle-class occupation might be deskilled while all previously working-class occupations are upgraded. A case-study of the former can hardly then be taken as sufficient evidence for the proletarianization of the employed population. Rather, an adequate test of the thesis requires aggregate data pertaining to the workforce as a whole (or a representative sample thereof), in order to chart any changes in the distribution of class places available together with the movements of individuals across these. Individual case-studies can tell us nothing about these net effects. For this reason the following analysis concentrates on the social mobility data from our national survey. These permit one to draw at least tentative conclusions about both changes in the class structure (hence the relative size of the different classes) and the mobility chances of individuals within that structure (hence the comparative likelihood of their arriving at proletarian class destinations). For technical reasons, it is most appropriate to analyse these data using the 'shift-share' technique earlier employed by Erik Wright, one of the principal advocates of the proletarianization position. Both the mobility data themselves, and the shift-share technique that we shall use in analysing them, require further comment.

Social mobility

The use of mobility data as a means of inspecting changes in the class structure immediately raises a series of practical research problems. First, there is the question of choosing the relevant unit of class analysis, since both individuals and families constitute possible subjects for investigation. A separate problem is that of selecting the most appropriate cross-sectional data to address a longitudinal issue (parental class at respondent's age 14 and parental class now are only two of the many options available to researchers). Finally, and most obviously, one must operationalize the notion of social class itself. Here too there are several alternative measures available.

This is not the place to enter into a prolonged discussion of the relative merits of alternative units for class analysis. The exchange between Goldthorpe and his critics has aired the salient theoretical and practical issues at some length. In principle the options are threefold: individuals can be assigned a class position appropriate to their own employment (if any); according to the class of a putative 'head of household'; or in terms of some composite measure which takes into account the possibly differing class situations of the respondent and his or her partner. In practice, a satisfactory composite measure has yet to be devised, and since gender is explicitly an issue in the debate about proletarianization, it seems appropriate, in the present context, to look at the class distributions and mobility of men and women separately. To that extent we adopt an individual (rather than a family-based) approach to the problem. This solves the problem of class destinations. However the measurement of class origins raises additional difficulties. Should one take father's employment as the only datum on the grounds that, for most respondents, it is his labour-market participation which will have been the major determinant of life-chances? Or, since for at least a minority it will have been mothers who were 'heads of household', is it perhaps more satisfactory to have respondents nominate a 'chief childhood supporter' who might be either parent or, indeed, some other guardian? In practice, as we shall see shortly, it makes little difference to the results whichever strategy one elects to pursue.[1]

A further problem is that of selecting cross-sectional data appropriate for investigating the relationship between class background and class destination. Mobility researchers must of necessity equate the latter with present class position (while recognizing that, for some people, additional career mobility will subsequently ensue). Class of origin is rather more problematic. One convention is to ask respondents about their parents' occupations when the respondents themselves were aged 14. The rationale behind this strategy is that it is around this age 'at which most . . . respondents would be making decisions important for their own occupational futures (whether concerning their actual entry into work or their continuation in full-time education) while still within the sphere of influence of their families of origin' (Goldthorpe, 1980: 64). Alternatively, one might ask about parental occupation when the parent or guardian was the same age as the respondent is now, the underlying logic here being that such an approach somehow helps to control for life-cycle effects. Our own national survey collected both sorts of data and again, as we shall see, the differences to be observed are not significant from the point of view of the mobility analysis itself.[2]

Finally, since alternative conceptions of 'social class' operationalize the notion in quite different ways, one is pushed (usually by prior theoretical considerations) to select one particular measure from the various neo-Marxist and neo-Weberian options that are available. In fact our own survey employed two quite different measures of social class. One, devised by Erik Wright for an international comparative analysis of class structures and rooted in the Marxist tradition, maps social relations at the point of production in terms of ownership of productive means, the degree of autonomy exercised by individuals at work, and their involvement in decision making and the supervision of other employees. The other, constructed by John Goldthorpe for the Oxford Social Mobility Study of England and Wales and resting more on Weberian premises, equates class with particular combinations of occupational title and employment status. The present analysis relies on Goldthorpe rather than Wright class categories for the simple reason that the latter prohibit analysis of social mobility. Long and detailed questioning is required in order to allocate respondents to appropriate Wright classes. This renders impractical the attempt to collect the information necessary to determine Wright class backgrounds. Few individuals possess sufficiently detailed knowledge about the specific decision-making and supervisory responsibilities and degree of autonomy at work of their parents – always assuming they are prepared to spend in interview the not inconsiderable time required to divulge this. The best one can hope for in such retrospective exercises is an occupational title, perhaps with a short description of the sort of work involved, and an indication of employment status (whether the parent was a manager, self-employed, or whatever). In fact this sort of information, which can be collected fairly concisely, is sufficient to code to occupational titles, employment statuses, and hence Goldthorpe classes. For this reason these offer the more suitable measure of class in so far as the issue of class trajectories and social mobility is concerned.[3]

Taking these difficulties into account we can examine changes in the class structure by comparing the distribution of origins with that of destinations.

Table 6.1 *Goldthorpe class origins and destinations, with origins determined by (i) respondent's father at respondent's age 14 and (ii) respondent's chief childhood supporter at same age as respondent, Great Britain (%)*

Goldthorpe class	(i)		(ii)	
	Origin	Destination	Origin	Destination
I	8.9	9.8	7.2	10.6
II	9.5	18.1	7.7	18.8
III	3.6	19.2	5.3	18.9
IV	13.5	8.7	13.7	9.1
V	17.5	7.9	18.1	7.7
VI	22.0	12.6	23.6	12.3
VII	25.0	23.7	24.4	22.6
Total	100.0	100.0	100.0	100.0

(i) $N = 1,156$ (ii) $N = 1,057$

Goldthorpe classes:

Service
I   Higher-grade professionals, administrators, and officials; managers in large industrial establishments; large proprietors.
II   Lower-grade professionals, administrators, and officials; higher-grade technicians; managers in small business and industrial establishments; supervisors of nonmanual employees.

Intermediate
III   Routine nonmanual employees in administration and commerce; personal service workers.
IV   Small proprietors, artisans, etc.; farmers and smallholders; self-employed fishermen.
V   Lower-grade technicians; supervisors of manual workers.

Working
VI   Skilled manual workers.
VII   Semi-skilled and unskilled manual workers.

Table 6.1 gives the relevant figures for employed respondents in our sample using alternative measures of class background. Matrix (i) compares the class destinations of men and women with their class origins as determined by the class of their fathers only, at the time when respondents were aged 14. Matrix (ii) shows class of origin as determined by the respondent's 'chief childhood supporter' when he or she was the same age as the respondent is now (and, therefore, a slightly different distribution of class destinations).[4] Taking these two strategies for determining class background to be extreme cases – since the former automatically nominates a male head of household and ignores the influence of life-cycle whereas the latter standardizes for life-cycle effects and permits the head of household to be either sex – we see that, in both cases, the evidence militates against the thesis that the British class structure has been subject to a process of proletarianization. The proportions in classes I, II and III have increased, while those in classes V, VI and VII have correspondingly decreased. In other words there has been a clear shift away from manual labour towards both routine and specialized white-collar work. This conclusion holds true across both measures of class background; that is, no matter whether one samples fathers at respondent's age 14, or chief childhood supporters at respondent's age now. In most cases the difference in the marginal distributions is less than 1 per cent and nowhere is it greater than 2 per cent. These changes suggest that, comparing origins and destinations for a representative sample of employed adults in Britain, the working class (classes VI and VII) has shrunk from approximately 48 per cent to 35 per cent of the total workforce while the service class (classes I and II) has expanded from around 15 per cent to 29 per cent.

Of course, it is possible that, within this net movement, certain sub-sections of the total population have been subject to systematic downward mobility, and in that sense proletarianized. Indeed it has commonly been argued by proponents of the argument that one group in particular – women – are especially subject to this process. For this reason it is important to look, not only at the proportionate size of class locations themselves, but also at the trajectories of individuals between places of class origin and those of class destination. Table 6.2 does precisely this, by showing the mobility matrix from which the figures in matrix (i) of Table 6.1 were derived, in this case in the form of a class composition table. These data show the class origins of respondents within each social class. Again they provide scant comfort to those who would argue that certain hitherto middle-class sections of the working population have experienced systematic proletarianization. It is true that there are observable differences between the sexes. For example, of those men presently in top service-class (I) locations, 35 per cent are from service-class origins, 35 per cent are from intermediate-class origins, while the remaining 30 per cent have been recruited from working-class backgrounds. The corresponding percentages for women are 55, 25, and 20. In other words proportionately more men than women are likely to be upwardly mobile into the service class from other class locations. On the other hand, however, proportionately more men than women have been downwardly mobile from service-class to class III (routine white-collar) destinations. (Twenty-seven per cent of male class III employees hail from service-class backgrounds as compared with 18 per cent of females in this class position.) In other words, comparing the figures for men with those for women, there is no evidence that women as a whole are peculiarly exposed to systematic downward mobility into the working class. Indeed, among respondents presently to be found in proletarian class locations, proportionately more men than women have arrived there from non-proletarian backgrounds. Similarly, almost as many female as male routine clerical (class III) employees have working-class backgrounds, some 42 per cent in the former case as compared with 49 per cent of the latter.

Table 6.2 *Goldthorpe class composition by sex and class of father at respondent's age 14, Great Britain (%)*

Class of origin	Class of destination						
	I	II	III	IV	V	VI	VII
Males							
I	19.4	15.7	14.6	3.9	1.4	5.0	3.7
II	15.1	21.5	12.2	7.8	8.2	8.3	3.7
III	3.2	5.8	0.0	1.3	2.7	7.5	0.6
IV	12.9	11.6	12.2	36.4	12.3	11.7	9.3
V	19.4	14.9	12.2	13.0	20.5	13.3	16.7
VI	12.9	12.4	31.7	14.3	28.8	25.0	26.5
VII	17.2	18.2	17.1	23.4	26.0	29.2	39.5
Total	100.0	100.0	100.0	100.0	100.0	100.0	100.0
(*N*=687)	(93)	(121)	(41)	(77)	(73)	(120)	(162)
Females							
I	20.0	12.5	11.0	12.5	0.0	0.0	5.4
II	35.0	13.6	6.6	0.0	0.0	3.8	4.5
III	0.0	9.1	3.9	0.0	5.6	3.8	1.8
IV	20.0	15.9	12.7	16.7	11.1	3.8	9.8
V	5.0	26.1	23.8	20.8	5.6	19.2	13.4
VI	20.0	13.6	24.3	16.7	44.4	38.5	24.1
VII	0.0	9.1	17.7	33.3	33.3	30.8	41.1
Total	100.0	100.0	100.0	100.0	100.0	100.0	100.0
(*N*=469)	(20)	(88)	(181)	(24)	(18)	(26)	(112)

We are not here suggesting that the class distributions of men and women are somehow similar. The marginals to Table 6.2 make it patently clear that this is far from being the case. From those respondents in our sample who are presently in employment (N = 1,315) the following statistics can be obtained: 82 per cent of class I are males while 82 per cent of class III are females; 82 per cent of class V (supervisors) and almost 82 per cent of class VI (skilled manual workers) are men; less than 6 per cent of all men are to be found in class III locations whereas almost 40 per cent of all women are so located; and, finally, 13 per cent of men are to be found in class I as against 4 per cent of women. In fact, this degree of class segmentation by sex is not surprising, given what is known about the differential structuring of occupational opportunities and operation of labour markets for men and women. However it does not alter the conclusion that follows clearly from the mobility data reported in Tables 6.1 and 6.2. Macro-sociological evidence suggests that, far from the class structure of Britain showing signs of systematic proletarianization, there is in fact considerable upward mobility into professional, administrative and managerial as well as routine clerical positions. Indeed, there has been a net expansion in non-proletarian rather than proletarian places, and women as well as men have benefited from this.[5]

Shift effects in the class structure

Unfortunately the argument about proletarianization – even in the straightforward sense of increasing the relative size of the working class – is rather more complex than this and cannot be resolved simply on the basis of mobility matrices alone. It is quite possible, for example, that the observed expansion in service-class places is an artefact of Britain's changing industrial structure. The post-war growth in the public sector – particularly in the National Health Service, education, social welfare services and local government – has generated a disproportionate rise in professional and administrative employment, since a high percentage of public sector occupations involve mostly white-collar work. It is similarly possible that this sectorally based development masks ongoing processes of proletarianization within other sectors of the economy, and that as the growth in state employment is halted by economic recession, the underlying tendency towards proletarianization of the class structure elsewhere will become increasingly apparent (and will soon embrace the public sector itself). Indeed some proponents of the thesis have argued precisely this. Erik Wright, for example, maintains that there has been a marked growth of working-class locations within economic sectors, though this has been more than offset (temporarily) by the relatively more rapid expansion of those sectors that were proportionately less proletarianized to begin with. Wright speculates that, as far as the United States is concerned, this shift in the composition of classes within sectors (and effective proletarianization of the class structure) will become obvious as the worsening fiscal crisis adds a decline in state employment to that induced in the transformative industries by competition from abroad.[6]

This particular defence of the proletarianization argument introduces the distinction between 'industry shift effects' and 'class composition shift effects' in the class structure. Wright's own argument rests on such a shift-share analysis of US census data for the period 1960 to 1970. Since this technique is relatively unfamiliar within sociology some preliminary clarification is probably in order.

Industry shift effects refer to that part of the overall change in the class structure which is due to shifts in the labour force from industrial sectors with one distribution of classes into sectors with a different distribution of classes. In other words they are a measure of changes in the class structure which can be attributed to differences in the relative growth of industries. Between different industries the actual proportions in each class vary widely. For example, within agriculture there is a very high proportion of employers and semi-skilled manual workers; in finance there is a very high proportion of clerks; while in most manufacturing industries there is a high proportion of skilled manual workers. One can see, therefore, how different rates of growth in different industrial sectors will affect the overall class composition of the labour force. Rapid deindustrialization and the growth of the public and service sectors may, by themselves, have been sufficient to effect the observed transformation in the British class structure during the period since 1945. Other things being equal, a decline of manufacturing and an expansion of the state should decrease the number of employees in 'working-class' jobs and increase the numbers in 'middle-class' jobs, since proportionately more of those involved in manufacturing are blue-collar workers whereas state employment is largely white-collar.

Of course Wright (and others) want to argue that all other things are *not* equal since, within industrial sectors, the transformation of class relations can create (and has created) proportionately more working-class jobs over time. In other words, the expansion of professional/managerial jobs and decline in the numbers in proletarian positions has been generated entirely by industrial and sectoral changes in employment, since the (hidden) effect of technological and organizational changes determining the occupational mix within industrial sectors has been to increase the proportionate size of the working class. These are class composition shift effects: the proletarianization (or, in theory, the embourgeoisement) of class structures within industrial sectors.

Some analysts (Wright included) also separate out 'interaction shift effects', which are the result of simultaneous shifts in employment across industrial sectors with different class structures, and shifts in the internal class structures of these sectors themselves. Mathematically these are simply a residual term comprising the difference between the combined industry shift and class composition shifts and the net change in the workforce. Invariably they form a small proportion of aggregate changes in the class structure and most commentators simply ignore them in any subsequent analysis.[7]

In fact a decomposition by shift-shares of the appropriate mobility data from our survey provides further evidence against the proletarianization thesis. The results are reported in Table 6.3. This shows, separately for men and women in each Goldthorpe class, how much of the total difference in the change between the distribution of parents and that of their offspring is due to changes in Britain's industrial structure, and how much is attributable to different class distributions within industrial sectors. The figures are obtained by applying the shift-share technique to two sets of cross-tabulations. The class distribution of fathers within each of twelve industrial sectors is compared with that of their sons, while the sectoral and class distribution of mothers is compared with that of their daughters.[8] Column 1 in the table shows the total difference in the class distributions of mothers as against daughters and fathers as against sons. Thus, taking the figure for males at the top of the column, we see that in our sample there are proportionately more sons in class I than fathers – indeed the former is greater than the latter by 5.3 per cent. (Class I fathers are 7.8 per cent of all fathers having employed sons while the sons themselves are 13.1 per cent of all male employees having fathers whose class positions can reliably be ascertained.) Continuing down column 1 we can see that, simply put, and for both sexes alike, the proportions in classes I to III tend to have grown,

Table 6.3 *Decomposition of changes in the British class structure by sex (%)*

	1	2	3	4
Class	Total difference	Industry effect	Class effect	Interaction effect
Males				
I	5.3	3.8	2.1	−0.6
II	7.3	5.5	3.1	−1.3
III	3.3	1.3	0.6	1.2
IV	−3.3	−2.1	−0.8	−0.4
V	−4.5	−4.9	−0.3	0.7
VI	−4.4	−1.6	−2.4	−0.4
VII	−3.4	−1.9	−2.3	−0.8
Females				
I	3.1	3.1	0.5	−0.5
II	7.2	5.7	2.3	−0.8
III	15.8	11.2	3.2	1.4
IV	−4.4	−2.9	−0.1	−1.4
V	0.2	−0.4	−0.8	1.0
VI	−3.5	−2.3	−1.6	0.4
VII	−17.7	−14.4	−3.3	0.0

while those in classes IV to VII have fallen. Comparing fathers with sons and mothers with daughters, proportionately more sons and daughters are involved in skilled (professional or managerial) and routine white-collar work, while proportionately fewer are in self-employment or in manual work at any level.

The question then arises of whether this general pattern can be attributed to changes in the industrial structure itself, or to differences in the class structure within sectors and at the level of production units. Columns 2 and 3 of Table 6.3 decompose the relevant industry shifts and class composition shifts for each class and sex by means of a counterfactual analysis. The industry shift column tells us what the total difference would have looked like had the distribution of classes within industrial sectors remained constant while the relative sizes of industrial sectors themselves had changed. (In other words, we hypothesize the fathers' distribution of class within industrial sectors but the sons' distribution of class across industrial sectors.) Thus, for class I males, we see that changes in the industrial structure alone would have increased the proportion of sons over fathers in class I by 3.8 per cent. However, column 3 poses the complementary counterfactual by holding sectoral distribution constant over the years, and so showing what the total difference between the class distributions of fathers and sons in column 1 would have looked like had the industrial structure remained unchanged while the class distributions within each sector changed. (This matches the sons' distribution of employment within industrial sectors to the fathers' distribution of employment across industrial sectors.) In the case of class I males, this class composition shift would also have increased the proportion of sons over fathers, by an estimated 2.1 per cent. In short, upgrading into class I persists, even when inter-industry shifts are allowed for. (The interaction effect, in column 4, is simply the difference between the total difference in class distributions for fathers and sons, and the sum of the industry shift and class composition shift components, in this case a negligible −0.6 per cent.)

Looking at the table for males as a whole, there are both class effects and industry effects to be observed for each social class, with no clear pattern underlying the analysis. Industry effects are slightly larger than class effects in the case of skilled and routine nonmanual employees (classes I, II and III), while the opposite is true for the working class (classes VI and VII). That is, the increase in professionals, managers, administrators and routine clerical workers is not simply the consequence of a growth in the service sector (within which these sorts of occupations have been relatively more numerous) and decline in the manufacturing sector (in which manual occupations are more typical), since such upgrading persists when inter-industry shifts are excluded. The proportion in working-class positions declines while that in the service class increases, and not simply (as Wright and other advocates of proletarianization would have it) because of fairly transient shifts induced by changes in the industrial structure, but also because of class composition shifts – the actual occupational mix occurring at the level of production units. In broad terms the two sources of change each account for about half of the total difference in class locations of fathers as compared with sons. On the basis of these data at least there is scant evidence to support the claim that males in the labour force are subject to some long-term process of class proletarianization.

The findings in respect of the females in our study are perhaps less clear-cut. Again, both class and industry shifts can be observed, though here the latter are in each case significantly larger than the former. Most obviously, there has been a massive decrease in the proportion of female employees involved in semi-skilled and unskilled manual work (class VII), and a corresponding increase in the relative size of the routine clerical category (class III). Industry shifts account for between 70 and 80 per cent of the difference in each case. It is possible to see this pattern as evidence that the obvious upgrading in the class structure is but a temporary phenomenon which obscures some underlying logic of proletarianization among women. However advocates of this thesis would be well advised to bear in mind two of our corollary findings before proposing such a conclusion. The first is that industry shifts do not explain the total differences at issue. Unambiguous class upgrading occurs (though to a relatively small extent) even when all changes in the industrial structure are allowed for. Second, and more importantly, this upgrading in the class structure persists when class mobility among the female respondents to our survey is analysed by cohort. (In fact, it is more pronounced among 16–31 year olds than among 32–47 year olds, and among the latter than among 48–64 year olds.) This suggests that the growth of service-class and routine white-collar occupations among women is not simply the result of the increased importance of the service and public sectors within the economy, since class shift effects persist among even the youngest employed respondents, who arrived in the labour force during the period which saw an accelerated relative decline in manufacturing. Despite this, it is still the case that professional, managerial, and administrative occupational classes continue to expand, and manual ones to shrink, even when all inter-industry shifts are allowed for.

Conclusion

In this chapter we have argued that the literature about the process of so-called proletarianization is rather confused but that, at least according to the data available from our own national sample survey of the class structure in Britain, there is little or no evidence to support the irreducible propositions relating to the central argument. Whether the thesis is seen as pertaining to the proportion of working-class locations within class structures, or to the mobility of individuals towards proletarian locations within these structures, the material from our study suggests that a net upgrading (rather than a degrading) has actually occurred. Proletarians now form a smaller proportion of the class structure than hitherto, and there has been significant upward social mobility into skilled and routine nonmanual work, with no counterbalancing downward movement. These tendencies persist even when the overall changes in the class structure are decomposed so as to allow for (perhaps temporary) inter-industry shifts. Crucially, class composition changes do not substantiate the proposition that the proportionate size of the working class is increasing at the level of individual production units, since these changes show a decline in Goldthorpe classes VI and VII and an increase in classes I to III.

Of course it is always open to proponents of the thesis to concede this point and shift the ground of the argument by claiming that the upgrading in the class structure is more apparent than real because most of the new managerial, professional, and administrative jobs involve routinized and therefore degraded labour. In reply one can only say that those who advance this interpretation of the thesis of proletarianization have yet to provide the necessary corroborating evidence. Most of the relevant studies of putative changes in occupational skills, in levels of job autonomy, or in the organization of tasks at the point of production have proven simply to be inconclusive. The most systematic of these studies to date, that of office workers by Crompton and Jones, concludes that the 'vast majority' of clerical places involve routine wage-work. The authors take this to be strong evidence in support of Braverman's contention that clerical work has been proletarianized. However, their case is somewhat undermined by their own findings, which show also that the 'office proletariat' is not a homogeneous mass but is differentiated by, for example, age, credentials, and gender. There is also a great deal of movement in and out of clerical work. Crompton and Jones themselves acknowledge that the majority of men who start their working lives as clerks will have been promoted by the age of 35. Research elsewhere shows that the bulk of clerical work is performed by women whose career trajectories embrace routine nonmanual and manual jobs alike. A significant minority of clerical workers are male ex-manual workers who have been promoted from the shopfloor late in life.[9]

It is difficult, given this information, to see how clerical work has been in any sense proletarianized, since even if the associated tasks themselves are highly routinized, they are done by young credentialled employees (mostly men) *en route* to promoted service-class destinations; older men who are by past (as well as current) experience proletarian; and women of all ages whose occupational careers embrace 'proletarian' nonmanual and manual work alike. There is actually no group of individuals here who have been proletarianized. Moreover, there are in fact good grounds for arguing that clerical work has always involved routine and often trivial tasks, and that the introduction of automated office machinery is likely to be perceived by clerical workers themselves as involving an extension (rather than a diminution) of autonomy and skill in the office.[10] At best, therefore, the argument that routine clerical and administrative employees are *de facto* proletarian because they perform rather routine nonmanual tasks is unproven. At worse, this trivializes the thesis of proletarianization itself, by reducing an argument about conditions of employment across the class structure as a whole to a largely futile dispute about whether or not microprocessor technology involves more or less 'skill' on the part of the operator than does keeping a handwritten ledger.

Naturally there are other legitimate objections which can be raised against our analysis. Perhaps the most forceful of these would point to the many individuals who, during the course of the economic recession, have lost their jobs and are therefore entirely omitted from the above analysis. One could argue that there are 3 million to 5 million unemployed who today find themselves 'proletarianized' by recent changes in the British class structure. In fact, however, our own data simply confirm the findings of all previous studies of the unemployed and subemployed in this country; namely, that the individuals so 'proletarianized' through being excluded from the workforce are overwhelmingly drawn from the working class itself, and therefore have previous as well as present proletarian experience. For example, taking the narrow definition of unemployment as including only those presently out of a job who are registered with a Job Centre or Employment Office and are available immediately for paid labour were they to be offered it, our evidence suggests (see Table 6.4) that around two-thirds of those presently jobless were hitherto already to be found in working-class locations. Another 8 per cent were supervisors of manual workers in their last full-time jobs; 12 per cent were engaged in routine clerical and sales work; while fewer than 12 per cent held service-class

Table 6.4   *Unemployment and Goldthorpe class experience among unemployed respondents, Great Britain (%)*

	I	II	III	IV	V	VI	VII	Total	(N)
Class of last full-time job	3.1	8.5	12.4	2.3	7.8	21.7	44.2	100.0	(129)
Class of origin	3.0	7.0	8.0	10.0	17.0	23.0	32.0	100.0	(100)

positions. Broadly the same pattern can be seen if class origins, rather than class of last job, are inspected.[11]

All of these findings tell against the central proposition of the proletarianization scenario. Proportionately fewer individuals are to be found in the working class now than was the case a generation ago; there is a net upward mobility out of this class into routine and skilled nonmanual work; and this remains true when inter-industry shifts are allowed for. Moreover, there is no evidence to suggest that routine clerical and administrative work is subject to some secular trend towards occupational deskilling, since the experiences of different groups of clerical workers are obviously different: some are upwardly mobile into professional and managerial positions, some have in any case arrived at clerical work from proletarian backgrounds, and others are performing routine administrative tasks on a long-term basis but are as likely to view recent changes in the organization of these as skills acquired rather than as occupational deskilling. In view of these findings we are strongly inclined to return a provisional verdict of 'not proven' in the case of the thesis of class proletarianization in Britain.

Notes

* Gordon Marshall and David Rose.

1 For a lengthy discussion of these issues see Marshall et al. (1988: ch. 4). The principal issues are covered in the celebrated exchange about the Oxford Social Mobility Study in the journal *Sociology*: see Goldthorpe (1983; 1984b); Heath and Britten (1984); Stanworth (1984); Erikson (1984); and Dale et al. (1985).

2 It must be conceded here that the strategy of constructing a 'class of origin' variable by determining the class of the 'chief childhood supporter' when he or she was the same age as the respondent is now provides only a limited control for life-cycle effects. Birth-cohort analysis offers an alternative means to the same end. However, even this approach does not fully separate out the confounding effects of history, age, and cohort itself. On the technical issues involved here see Goldthorpe (1980: 68).

3 The original class categories devised by Wright are described in Wright (1979). A revised scheme was introduced in Wright (1985: ch. 3). The Goldthorpe class categories are outlined in Goldthorpe (1980: 39–42). A detailed assessment of all three approaches is given in Marshall et al. (1988: chs 2 and 3). The national sample survey from which the data for this chapter were drawn forms part of Erik Wright's International Project on Class Structure and Class Consciousness. Most research teams in the project have explored their results using the class scheme devised by Wright himself, though many (including the British group) also

incorporated alternative conceptions of class into their research designs. See also Wright (1980a).

4 The construction of the 'chief childhood supporter (CCS) class of origin' variable is rather complex. Full occupational and employment status data were collected for both parents. Each respondent was then asked to nominate the person who provided most of the financial support for their family, throughout his or her childhood, up to the time they left school. Among the 1,770 respondents to the study (sampling men aged 16–64 and women aged 16–59, who were not in full-time education, mid 1984), 86 per cent nominated their fathers, 7 per cent their mothers, 5 per cent both parents equally, and the remaining 2 per cent some other relative or guardian. The 'CCS class of origin' variable was constructed from these data, privileging the occupational class of the nominated person, but that of fathers over mothers where both contributed equally to family financial support.

5 None of this implies either that Britain is an 'open' society or that men and women have the same occupational opportunities. The distinction between absolute mobility rates and relative mobility chances is crucial here. Our evidence shows both that the (considerable) degree of class inequality in Britain (or 'social fluidity') has remained unchanged throughout most of the twentieth century and that women are generally disadvantaged when compared with men. For a full discussion of these issues see Marshall et al. (1988: chs 4 and 5).

6 See Wright and Singelmann (1982). Wright published a supplementary analysis in which he retracted many of his original claims. He admits that his predictions of intensified proletarianization within economic sectors are not supported by the data for the USA since these indicate 'a decisive acceleration of the growth of managerial class locations in the 1970s and a clear deproletarianization within and across economic sectors' (see Wright and Martin, 1987).

7 A full explanation of the shift-share technique is given in Wright and Singelmann (1982: 202–5). See also Ahrne and Wright (1983).

8 Individuals were distributed into one of twelve industrial sectors: agriculture, fishing, forestry; mining; construction; durable manufacturing; non-durable manufacturing; communications and utilities; wholesale trade; retail trade; business services; personal services; professional services; state dominated services and non-profit services. This particular classification was adopted since it is that used by Wright himself in his analyses of classes in the United States and Sweden. The figures in the shift-share analysis reported in Table 6.3 are calculated from mobility tables which compare respondents' classes now and mothers' classes when respondents were aged 14 (for women) or fathers' classes when respondents were aged 14 (for men).

9 On the heterogeneity of clerical workers see, for example, Crompton and Jones (1984: 210, 239), Marshall et al. (1988: ch. 5), Stewart et al. (1980: chs 4–7) and Llewellyn (1981).

10 See, for example, the literature reviewed by Crompton and Jones (1984: 42–8) and the research reported in Webster (1986).

11 For similar findings see Goldthorpe and Payne (1986) and, more generally, Sinfield (1981).

7

Intergenerational Social Mobility in Communist Russia*

It is a sociological commonplace that we know almost nothing about patterns of social mobility in what was the Union of Soviet Socialist Republics. For example, in his review of studies of social stratification in the state socialist societies of Central and Eastern Europe up to the mid 1970s, Connor (1979: 112) reports as a 'glaring omission' the fact that 'no nationwide study of mobility has been conducted in the USSR (or if it has, it has neither been published nor even circulated in any accessible form)'. A decade later, an exhaustive search of the literature by Strmiska (1987: 144) proved equally fruitless, yielding no representative data for the largest communist state in the Western world. To this day, the Soviet Union has remained as Strmiska found it, largely a 'blank area' as far as the issue of social mobility is concerned. Most comparative analyses of Soviet-type societies have perforce been restricted to such evidence as is available for the much smaller socialist republics of Central Europe.[1]

Despite this dearth of information, or perhaps because of it, Soviet scholars regularly argued that there were important differences in mobility patterns East and West. In the late 1960s, for example, Rutkevich and Filipov (1973: 235) concluded that, in a socialist society such as the USSR, 'as a result of fundamental changes in the social class structure, most of the real barriers to social mobility disappear.' This judgement appears to have been reached more through Marxist dogma than sociological research. No substantiating evidence is cited. Instead, the authors merely insist: 'there is no doubt that only Marxist dialectics and the materialist conception of history can provide a genuinely scientific basis for understanding the social structure of any society and all the processes of its change, including social mobility.' In the mid 1980s, Aitov (1986: 256, 270) conceded that 'socialist society does not yet enjoy full social equality', but concluded from his study of social mobility in the city of Magnitogorsk that 'socialist society is far more "open" than its capitalist counterpart.'

The rhetorical flourish with which some of the Soviet researchers substituted assertion for analysis has, of course, to be understood in the context of communist censorship. Fortunately, most Western sociologists have not had to work under these sorts of conditions, far less the threat that political incorrectness would lead to incarceration in the gulag. However, the empirical issue remains. Was the 'tremendous openness' of the

USSR, to which researchers such as Aitov repeatedly alluded, an empirical reality or an illusion of Marxist-Leninist ideology? This is the question for which we shall attempt to provide at least a provisional answer in this chapter.

Literature

A literature search will reveal that the Iron Curtain was occasionally drawn aside, during the post-war years, although only so far as to reveal a glimpse of social mobility processes in the heartland of communism itself. A few unrelated city-wide studies were conducted in the two decades following the death of Stalin. The social origins of rural employees in the Tatar Republic were investigated by Arutiunian (1973) in the mid 1960s. Shkaratan (1973a; 1973b) reported on social mobility among employees in seven machine-building enterprises in Leningrad, an engineering firm with plants in four Soviet cities (Leningrad, Pskov, Porkhov, Nevel) and three cities in the Tatar SSR (Kazan, Almetevsk, and Menzelinsk). Kenkman and his colleagues (1986) studied educational and occupational attainment among a sample of those who graduated from secondary schools in the Estonian SSR in 1966. Aitov's own study was of intergenerational social mobility and educational attainment among 3,000 employees resident in Magnitogorsk in 1976. However, nothing resembling a reliable national survey ever emerged from Soviet sociology.

This is scant fare, when set against the well-documented national surveys that were conducted under communist regimes in Poland, Hungary and Czechoslovakia. Indeed, it has proved difficult to construct a convincing general account of social mobility in the USSR, on the basis of the evidence available from the very diverse earlier studies. Crossnational researchers who have made the attempt have encountered insuperable technical problems. These are evident, for example, in Yanowitch's (1977: 100–33) comparison of three of the city studies, in Kazan, Ufa and Leningrad. The respondents to the first two of these were drawn from a sample of employees in each city. The figures for Leningrad are derived from a sample only of those employed in that city's machinery industry. In Ufa the interviewees were aged 25 or older. No age restrictions applied in the other cities. Social origins were variously indexed according to the occupational class of the father (Ufa) and the 'head of family' (Kazan and Leningrad). In any case, researchers have long been aware that city-wide studies offer an unreliable indicator of the national situation, because the confounding effects of geographical mobility tend to exaggerate social mobility rates. These and other difficulties notwithstanding, Yanowitch attempted to standardize the findings on four broad social categories (peasant, worker, lower-level nonmanual employee and specialist), although it is by no means obvious that his *ex post facto* recoding achieves comparability across the studies in question.

Such shortcomings are then magnified if one attempts further to compare the findings from Soviet studies with those obtained for industrialized societies elsewhere. The problems are well illustrated by Teckenberg's (1990) crossnational comparison of social mobility in the Soviet Union and what was the Federal Republic of Germany. Working from the tables published by Shkaratan and his colleagues, Teckenberg attempts to achieve broad comparability of data for the two societies, at a fairly high level of aggregation. However, the comparison is of limited value since (among other things) it excludes agricultural workers; equates self-employment in Germany with managerial positions in the USSR; and cannot distinguish between male and female respondents.

In so far as one can identify general patterns in the patchwork of earlier studies of intergenerational social mobility, these seem to suggest rather high rates of absolute or total mobility, although relative rates (social fluidity or mobility chances) have remained largely unexplored. For example, from his reconstructed data for the three cities, Yanowitch (1977: 108–21) notes that almost two-thirds of the current class of specialists (intelligentsia) in each locale were recruited from working-class and peasant families. 'Access to the specialists' stratum is,' as he puts it, 'obviously not the restricted prerogative of a socially exclusive group.' At the same time, however, this relatively large-scale recruitment of individuals from manual and peasant origins to fill higher-level nonmanual positions is not associated with substantial downward mobility among the children of the intelligentsia. In each case, between 60 and 80 per cent of the children of specialists were themselves distributed to specialist occupations, while the proportion downwardly mobile from the intelligentsia to the skilled working class was only about 20 per cent. Downward mobility from the intelligentsia to the unskilled working class was so infrequent as to be negligible. Conversely, although somewhere between one-fifth and one-third of working-class sons and daughters arrived at specialist occupational destinations, approximately two-thirds were retained in the working class.

Aitov's (1986: 257) study of Magnitogorsk reports similar results. More than 40 per cent of all respondents had moved out of the parental social group. Again, however, the proportion of sons and daughters distributed to the intelligentsia from different social backgrounds varied between specialists, non-specialist employees, the working class and collective farmers (the percentages were 45, 22, 15 and 12 respectively). On the basis of their cohort study of the Estonian SSR, Kenkman and his colleagues (1986: 196–7) calculated indices of the links between respondents' social positions and their types of family background, and concluded that 'mobility is rooted in a succession of social position.' Unfortunately, however, the statistical and sociological meaning of the index scores themselves is not apparent from the text.

Teckenberg (1990: 43–7) alone seems to have considered the relationship between absolute mobility rates and relative mobility chances. He reports a variety of findings for the different areas within the USSR, notably in comparison with the Federal Republic of Germany, but unfortunately does so in rather sparse terms. (Neither the mobility matrices nor the models are actually reproduced.) For example, with regard to intergenerational mobility, it is simply recorded that mobility chances are poorer for unskilled and skilled workers in Germany than in the Soviet Union; that the Soviet intelligentsia is comparatively more closed than the intellectual stratum in the Federal Republic; that the 'manual versus nonmanual' boundary is relatively more permeable in the USSR; and that there is no obvious proletarianization of Soviet unskilled white-collar workers.

A shorthand way of summarizing this material would be simply to say that it paints a fragmented and unfocused picture. It is difficult to formulate a precise image, either because of the lack of detail in relation to particular studies, or because of the impossibility of achieving comparability across the different analyses. Arbitration between competing accounts is therefore impossible. On the one hand there are those such as Kende (1987: 14) who suggest that the observed rates of intergenerational social mobility in the USSR are, 'above all else', structurally induced. In other words, they are largely a consequence of such processes as economic growth, rural depopulation and the proportionate rise in the number of skilled nonmanual jobs. Teckenberg's (1990: 47) general conclusion, on the other hand, is that 'in the Soviet Union . . . quantitative differentiations in material labour market opportunities, such as are typical of class societies, do not seem to be especially pronounced.' Soviet sociologists, as we have seen, made rather more aggressive claims for enhanced social fluidity in the USSR. How do our own data bear on these conflicting arguments?

Data

Our analysis is based on a national survey of social mobility patterns in Russia, conducted during the months of October and November 1991, as part of a wider International Social Justice Project (ISJP). Under the auspices of that larger project, occupational and employment data were collected in a standardized fashion across thirteen countries participating in the study, and it is those for Russia that form the basis for our argument.

The Russian interviews were conducted on a face-to-face basis, in respondents' homes, by professional interviewers from the All-Russia Centre for Public Opinion and Market Research. Respondents were selected from a sampling frame for present-day Russia, as against the former Soviet Union, although there is nothing in the literature to suggest (and no obvious reason to suppose) that Russian mobility patterns were substantially different from those in the USSR as a whole. Since our data deal with intergenerational social mobility, and were gathered at more or less the same time as the Soviet regime was collapsing, we are in effect charting the communist experience. The final sample was compared with census data for Russia and found to be representative of the population in terms of sex, age, region and type of (urban or rural) settlement. Respondents were aged 16 and over. The total number of completed interviews was 1,734 – representing a response rate of a little over 76 per cent.

We investigate social mobility in terms of the class schema devised by John Goldthorpe and his colleagues in the CASMIN Project. The theoretical and conceptual bases of the scheme are well known and have been explained in some detail by its authors.[2] The so-called Goldthorpe classes have of course been widely used in recent studies of class mobility. Interestingly, many earlier analyses of class and mobility in the USSR unconsciously (although crudely) mimic the Goldthorpe scheme, by distinguishing between the elite (or intelligentsia or specialist) nonmanual class of professionals, managers and administrators; routine white-collar employees; skilled and unskilled manual workers; and agricultural workers or collective farmers.

Goldthorpe classes are operationalized in the ISJP in a novel way. Anticipating problems of crossnational comparability, the various teams involved in the study agreed to collect occupational data in a standardized manner, and to code the information provided by respondents to both the International Standard Classification of Occupations for 1968 and a modified version of the German employment status (*Berufstellungen*) typology. The former was chosen because it is the one occupational taxonomy for which a standard codebook exists in all the major languages. It has also been in crossnational use for a quarter of a century, so that many national research agencies are now familiar with its principles and procedures. Unfortunately, since it tends to group occupations by industrial sector and without regard to employment status, it is particularly unsuited (if taken alone) to the task of generating Goldthorpe class categories. The German employment status codes, on the other hand, were selected precisely because they are especially sensitive to the distinction between managers, employers, self-employed and employees that is central to Goldthorpe's approach. The information from these variables was then combined in a series of specially designed algorithms which are unique to our data but preserve the integrity of the original class scheme.

In the analysis that follows, having examined the basic patterns of intergenerational social mobility, we then introduce the issue of the relationship between class mobility and educational attainment in order to investigate the claim that there was a trend towards increasing 'meritocracy' in the Soviet Union. Here too we exploit the earlier work of the CASMIN team by recoding educational credentials to the sevenfold classification devised by Konig and his colleagues (1988) for crossnational comparative analysis of this issue. As in the case of the class categories themselves, the advantage to be gained by standardizing data collection and codes in this way is that one can facilitate meaningful crossnational comparison of results, and greatly reduce the likelihood of methodological artefacts in the findings derived from comparative analyses.

Table 7.1 *Distribution of Russian respondents by Goldthorpe class of origin and destination and by sex (% by column), and delta (dissimilarity index) values for origin and destination distributions*

Class	Male		Female		All	
	Origin	Destination	Origin	Destination	Origin	Destination
I+II	23.9	36.4	30.5	48.3	27.5	42.9
IIIa	2.3	3.4	1.4.	14.2	1.8	9.3
IVa+IVb	0.2	1.1	0.0	0.2	0.1	0.6
IVc	0.4	0.0	0.6	0.0	0.5	0.0
V	3.4	2.7	3.3	1.1	3.4	1.8
VI	25.5	25.9	21.7	8.5	23.5	16.4
VIIa+IIIb	31.6	27.2	27.1	23.6	29.1	25.2
VIIb	12.6	3.3	15.3	4.1	14.1	3.7

N = 1,150 (522 males, 627 females)
Delta: male 15; female 31; all 24.
Classes: I+II salariat (service class); IIIa routine clerical workers; IVa+IVb *petite bourgeoisie*; IVc farmers, smallholders; V supervisors; VI skilled manual workers; VIIa+IIIb semi-skilled and unskilled manual workers; VIIb agricultural workers.

Intergenerational social mobility

The distributions of origin and destination classes for our Russian respondents are shown in Table 7.1. Males and females are treated separately, since it is currently a controversial issue as to which is the appropriate unit in any class analysis (individual or household); and, if it is the latter, whether class positions should then be assigned to households according to the position of the 'male head', the economically dominant partner, or some composite score embracing the employment standing of both partners.[3] We will return to this problem shortly. Here, we look at the class distributions of males and females in terms of their own employment, and in relation to that of their fathers when respondents were aged 15.[4]

Our results show the effects of the sectoral changes emphasized by commentators such as Kende, most obviously in the declining numbers involved in agriculture, and the expansion of nonmanual work generally. The table also suggests, however, that there are certain distinctive features in Russian patterns of social mobility. One is the extent to which political intervention, resulting in social upheaval, has shaped the fate of certain classes. For example, the very small numbers of farmers in our origin classes, and the reappearance of a few individuals in the *petite bourgeoisie* destination class, would seem to testify respectively to the collectivization of Soviet agriculture under Stalin, and the limited revival of small businesses effected by post-communist economic reforms.

Second, and pursuing the same general theme, we might note the relatively high proportion of respondents with service-class backgrounds – 24 per cent of all men and 31 per cent of women – and the correspondingly high proportion of respondents distributed to service-class destinations

(36 per cent and 48 per cent of males and females respectively). These proportions are somewhat larger (especially in the origin class) than those reported for other industrialized societies by Erikson and Goldthorpe (1992a: 193). It seems probable that this finding reflects the functional demands of the Russian planned economy, the need to manage the Soviet empire, and the general primacy of politics over economics. The Soviet bureaucracy offered tenure and other favourable conditions of employment, especially among the *nomenklatura*, to even relatively low-level clerical employees (who, outside the Soviet system, would certainly have been in an inferior labour-market position *vis-à-vis* their bureaucratic superiors). The boundary between those doing routine clerical work and the salariat is then especially difficult to draw in the Russian context. Indeed, the figures also show that the proportion of respondents involved in routine clerical employment is correspondingly low (among both sexes), although it too has increased in line with the general shift to white-collar work. Perhaps, therefore, uniquely among advanced industrialized societies, we may expect the proportionate size of the Russian salariat to diminish somewhat in years to come, always providing of course that the transition to a mixed market economy is eventually accomplished.

Another distinctive feature of the Russian class structure is that, unlike the other state socialist societies of Eastern and Central Europe, more people are of working-class origins than have backgrounds in farming families. Russian agriculture was early to collectivize and mechanize. These processes produced economies of scale that are already evident in our table – where 'agricultural worker' is an origin class for a relatively small proportion (15 per cent) of respondents. The proportion of the workforce to be found in agriculture in our destination classes (4 per cent) is on a par with that reported for Britain – which has a very small farming population in comparison with other Western capitalist societies. Again, it is possible that this process will be reversed by the transformation of the Russian economy, as at least some of the agricultural collectives are dismantled and returned to family-sized holdings.[5]

Next, we may note the relatively large working class in Russia, comprising some 61 per cent of class origins among males in our sample, and 56 per cent of male class destinations. (The corresponding figures among females are 52 per cent and 33 per cent.) These are rather similar to the proportions found in manual origin and destination classes in the advanced capitalist societies that were investigated during the CASMIN Study. They are, in fact, closest (and almost identical) to those reported for British males. Unlike other late-industrializing capitalist (Sweden and France) or state socialist (Hungary and Poland) countries examined by Erikson and Goldthorpe, Russia has a manual working class which is shrinking as a proportion of the total class structure, reflecting shifts in the occupational structure that appear also to be found in deindustrializing Britain.

Finally, because we are able to distinguish males and females, we can see that there are some differences in social mobility across the sexes (where individuals are treated in terms of their own employment experiences). Probably the most obvious of these is in relation to skilled manual work, where about 26 per cent of men, but barely 9 per cent of women, are to be found. In the case of routine clerical work these relative proportions are more than reversed: some 14 per cent of women but only 3 per cent of men are in this class. Given what is known about the sex composition of the Soviet bureaucratic elite and management,[6] our findings for the salariat appear to be surprising, but they are probably a consequence of the fact that we cannot reliably distinguish between its upper and lower echelons (classes I and II in the full version of the Goldthorpe scheme). It seems likely that at least part of the explanation as to why such a high proportion of women are in the salariat, and why rather similar proportions of each sex arrive there from working-class origins, is to be found in the fact that males and females are being distributed to different types of service-class jobs.

Taken together, these characteristics yield a distinctive mobility profile, apparently unique to the former Russian SSR. On the one hand, as in other European state socialist societies, our data point to a fairly rapid contraction of the agricultural classes. On the other hand, quite unlike other state socialist societies, communist Russia also has a shrinking industrial working class. In this regard it is rather similar to Britain. Lastly, and uniquely, the scale of the Soviet state apparatus resulted in a proportionately larger salariat than is to be found in even the advanced capitalist societies. The delta or dissimilarity index score for the Russian male table is in fact 15, which is in line with the CASMIN results for mature industrial societies such as Britain or West Germany; somewhat smaller than the delta for the late-industrializing societies of France and Sweden; and much smaller than that for the state socialist societies of Hungary and Poland.

This distinctiveness is further illustrated if we then decompose the total mobility rates that are derived from our 8×8 class mobility tables for Russian men and women (see Table 7.2). The ratio of vertical to non-vertical mobility is in the region of six to one.[7] This makes Russia an extreme outlier in relation to the nations studied in the CASMIN Project – where the typical male TV/TNV mobility ratio is between 2.5 and three. For even the most 'mature' of industrial societies (England) the corresponding figure is only 3.4. The Russian figure again reflects the swollen salariat, expansion of white-collar employment generally, and relatively large numbers of respondents mobile into the service class from working-class and agricultural backgrounds. Furthermore, if the vertical rate is broken down into upward and downward mobility, the ratio of the former to the latter is around two. The figure for men (1.9) is in fact identical to that obtained for English males by Erikson and Goldthorpe (1992a: 195). In other words, Russia appears (at least at this aggregate level) to be a communist society of long standing, but one in which the balance of upward as against downward mobility is similar to that found in mature capitalist countries. In this respect, it is rather unlike other (more recently

Table 7.2 *Decomposition of total mobility rates (TMR) into total vertical (TV) and total non-vertical (TNV) mobility, and of total vertical mobility into total upward (TU) and total downward (TD) mobility, by sex, Russia*

	TMR	TV	TNV	TV/TNV	TU	TD	TU/TD
Males	65	56	9	6.2	37	20	1.9
Females	66	56	10	5.6	39	17	2.3
All	66	57	9	6.3	38	18	2.1

industrialized) state socialist societies in Eastern and Central Europe, where upward mobility among males more strongly preponderates over downward (typically in the ratio of approximately four to one). The pattern of social mobility in Russia therefore appears to reflect the unique combination of a state socialist polity with a relatively advanced industrial occupational structure.

Against this general background we can now consider absolute rates in outflow and inflow perspective. Table 7.3 shows the amount and pattern of mobility experienced by men and women from the various origin classes. Because of the small numbers in some of the classes, we have (in line with established practice among the CASMIN researchers) collapsed the *petite bourgeoisie* and routine clerical employees (into an 'intermediate' class), supervisory and skilled manual workers ('skilled manual' class), and farmers or smallholders and agricultural labourers ('agricultural worker' class).

Our results confirm that intergenerational class mobility was a common experience in communist Russia. Although much of this was short-range, for example between the skilled and unskilled elements of the urban proletariat, long-range mobility from the working (and even the agricultural) classes to the salariat was relatively common. The general outflow patterns observed in the earlier studies of specific Soviet organizations, cities and regions are readily apparent on the national scale. Some 57 per cent of sons and 64 per cent of daughters from salariat backgrounds were themselves to be found in salariat destinations at the time of our study. Approximately one-third of those from unskilled working-class backgrounds were socially immobile in intergenerational terms. Fewer than 15 per cent of male and female respondents having salariat class backgrounds were downwardly mobile to the unskilled working class. Among those hailing from unskilled manual origins, 30 per cent of men and over 40 per cent of women had arrived at salariat destinations, as indeed had slightly higher proportions of those with skilled manual backgrounds. Only 13 per cent of those having agricultural workers as parents actually stayed on the land: 40 per cent were intergenerationally mobile to white-collar work while the rest (not much short of one-half) moved into manual employment. Women from every origin class were much more likely than corresponding men to arrive at intermediate – in fact routine clerical – destinations.

Table 7.3 *Goldthorpe class distribution in Russia by sex (% by row)*

Origins	S	IN	SM	UM	AW	Total	(N)
			Destinations				
Males (N=522)							
S	57	6	22	14	0	100	(125)
IN	46	0	31	23	0	100	(13)
SM	32	3	36	27	3	100	(151)
UM	30	4	27	36	3	100	(165)
AW	22	9	26	31	12	100	(68)
Females (N=627)							
S	64	15	5	14	2	100	(191)
IN	44	11	11	33	0	100	(9)
SM	48	14	15	21	3	100	(157)
UM	42	14	10	31	3	100	(170)
AW	29	16	10	32	13	100	(100)

Classes: S = salariat (Goldthorpe classes I and II); I = intermediate (IIIa, IVa, IVb); SM = skilled manual (V and VI); UM = unskilled manual (VIIa and IIIb); AW = agricultural workers (IVc, VIIb).

Considered as inflow rather than outflow percentages, that is in terms of class composition rather than class distributions (see Table 7.4), these figures suggest that some 60 per cent of those presently to be found in the salariat are first-generation arrivals in the class. The skilled and unskilled manual classes are also relatively demographically immature. Each comprises only one-third to two-fifths of individuals who are at least second generation in their classes of origin. By comparison, agricultural workers are more likely to have been recruited from the same class of origin, with almost half of those presently on the land hailing from agricultural backgrounds. In general terms the class composition patterns appear to be broadly similar within each sex.

This last observation brings us back to the issue of how one conceptualizes class mobility. More particularly, it raises the question of whether or not patterns of social fluidity (or relative mobility chances) are different for men and women, and in this way reintroduces debate about the unit of class analysis and to whom (or what) one assigns a class location.

One obvious way to address this problem is via a loglinear analysis of the raw mobility data, in order to test the so-called common social fluidity model, which proposes that relative mobility chances are the same for each sex. The results of our analysis are shown in Table 7.5. These appear to confirm that the hypothesis of common social fluidity among the sexes in Russia is sound. As was suggested by the earlier cross-tabulations, there is a significant association between sex and destination, showing that women and men are to some extent distributed to different classes. There is also a strong association between class origins and class destinations, but this does not itself vary by sex. The *ODS* interaction is not significant. In other

Table 7.4 *Goldthorpe class composition in Russia by sex (% by column)*

Origins	Destinations				
	S	IN	SM	UM	AW
Males					
S	37	33	19	13	0
IN	3	0	3	2	0
SM	25	17	36	29	24
UM	26	25	30	42	29
AW	8	25	12	15	47
Total	100	100	100	100	100
(*N*=522)	(190)	(24)	(149)	(142)	(17)
Females					
S	41	31	15	18	15
IN	1	1	2	2	0
SM	25	24	38	22	15
UM	24	26	28	36	19
AW	10	18	17	22	50
Total	100	100	100	100	100
(*N*=627)	(303)	(90)	(60)	(148)	(26)

Class abbreviations: see Table 7.3.

Table 7.5 *Results of testing the model of common social fluidity against data on intergenerational mobility for the sexes in Russia (Goldthorpe class of individuals determined by reference to own employment)*

Model	d.f.	G^2	p	rG^2	delta
1 O+D+S	40	233.67	0.000	–	17.75
2 O+DS	36	135.29	0.000	42.1	13.22
3 DS+OD	20	15.73	0.733	93.3	3.70
4 CSF: OS+DS+OD	16	9.68	0.883	95.9	2.45
5 UNIDIFF	15	9.33	0.860	96.0	2.36

UNIDIFF parameter estimate: −0.1188 (men set at zero).

O = class of origin, five levels (see Table 7.3).
D = class of destination, five levels (see Table 7.3).
S = sex.
rG^2 = % reduction in G^2 for model 1.
delta = % misclassified cases.

words, women are distributed to different class destinations to men because they are women, not because the relationship between origins and destinations varies by sex. Relative class mobility chances are broadly the same for men and women.

Of course, the common social fluidity model offers only a global or generalized test of underlying relative rates, so that small but nevertheless sociologically interesting specific differences in mobility chances can easily be overlooked. A more powerful means of assessing social fluidity in comparative analyses is provided by the so-called uniform difference (or UNIDIFF) model developed by Erikson and Goldthorpe (1992a: 90–2) during the CASMIN Study. This has an added advantage over the standard loglinear approach in that the UNIDIFF test addresses the further issue of whether or not two sets of odds ratios display a monotonic trend in one particular direction. More specifically, it tests for the possibility that the different sets of odds ratios relating to competing pairs of class origins and destinations move uniformly (though not by a constant amount) either towards or away from unity in one mobility table as compared with another, which would suggest (in this particular case) a slight but important difference in underlying relative rates for the sexes.[8]

In fact this more stringent test fails to give a significant improvement in fit over the model of common social fluidity. The deviance in the latter is barely reduced for the sacrifice of one additional degree of freedom. It seems that there is indeed no significant difference in the overall social fluidity regimes for Russian men and women. It is true that the uniform-change parameter points to slightly greater fluidity among females as a whole: if the parameter for men is set at zero, the estimate is negative, indicating a slight decrease in the odds ratios (and therefore marginally greater social fluidity) among women. However, the modest size of this effect, and the failure of the uniform difference model to return a significant improvement in fit, is consistent with the findings reported by Erikson and Goldthorpe themselves (1992a: 246) – who found marginally higher fluidity among women, as compared with men, in only three of the five nations they investigated (and even here they describe the difference in underlying relative rates 'if it exists at all, as very slight indeed').

In this respect, at least, communist Russia – the first and longest-established Western industrial communist state – would appear to be indistinguishable from its capitalist counterparts. As Marshall and his colleagues (1988: 107–8) have shown in the case of Great Britain, the pattern of absolute social mobility rates is different among British men and women, but here too this is attributable to sex segregation in employment rather than differential class mobility rates. The model of common social fluidity across the sexes fits well in both countries. The argument that women are as divided by class processes as are men is no less applicable in Russia than it is in Britain.

Those who advocate a 'conventional' approach to class analysis, maintaining that the household is generally the most appropriate unit of class analysis and that class can be attributed to households according to the standing of their male heads, might at this juncture cite the evidence of similar relative mobility rates among Russian men and women as further support for their arguments. However, since our purpose here is merely to present some basic findings about hitherto largely unexplored patterns of intergenerational social mobility in communist Russia, there seems no need to take a strong stance on the unit of analysis issue in the present context.[9] Our principal interest is in assessing the truth of claims made by some earlier (especially Soviet) sociologists to the effect that patterns of social mobility in the USSR show it to be substantially more open than any of its capitalist counterparts. Thus far, we have demonstrated that communist Russia was not an egalitarian society, if by this it is meant that equality of opportunity prevailed among the different social classes. In fact, chances of social mobility varied appreciably for individuals coming from different social backgrounds, as a calculation of the odds ratios for Table 7.3 will show. However, it has rarely been claimed that the USSR was an equal society, only that it was 'more equal' than its capitalist neighbours. To what extent do our new data support this argument?

One way of addressing this issue of relative openness is to compare intergenerational mobility patterns in the oldest and most mature communist and capitalist societies respectively – in other words Russia and Great Britain. We have therefore examined the results shown above in relation to equivalent data that were collected during the British survey for the International Social Justice Project.[10] Specifically, we are here interested in fitting the model of common social fluidity across the two countries, so testing the hypothesis that patterns of social fluidity or relative mobility chances are the same in Russia and Britain. Table 7.6 shows the results of our analysis for males and females separately. In fact, as can be seen from the table, a model proposing common social fluidity (CSF) provides a sufficient fit in both cases. This tells us that, as one would expect, the distribution of origin and destination classes is different in each society (because of their different occupational structures). However, by including only the further association between origins and destinations we can provide an adequate fit to the data, and one in which the *ODN* interaction term is not required. On the face of it, therefore, the association between social origins and class destinations does not seem to vary much between the two countries. In other words, Russia would not appear to be in aggregate terms a more open society (from the point of view of intergenerational class mobility) than is Britain, since the differences in mobility patterns between the two countries seem largely to be explained by their very different occupational structures. Social fluidity – relative mobility chances or the degree of openness in the class structure – is more or less the same in the most mature of state socialist and democratic capitalist societies.

Again, however, we can take the further step of applying Erikson and Goldthorpe's uniform difference model to these data. In this case, we are interested in the possibility that the odds ratios defining the association between classes of origin and destination tend to move uniformly away from unity in one society (Britain) as compared with the other (Russia), suggesting slightly less social fluidity under the capitalist than the communist regime.

In fact, the UNIDIFF model does not improve significantly upon the fit obtained by the model of common social fluidity in the case of males,

Table 7.6 *Results of testing the model of common social fluidity against data on intergenerational mobility in Russia and Great Britain by sex (Goldthorpe class of individuals determined by reference to own employment)*

Model	d.f.	G^2	p	rG^2	delta
Males					
1 Independence: $ON+DN$	32	139.20	0.000	–	14.48
2 CSF: $ON+DN+OD$	16	13.23	0.656	90.5	3.84
3 UNIDIFF	15	10.73	0.772	92.3	3.13
Females					
1 Independence: $ON+DN$	32	139.98	0.000	–	12.50
2 CSF: $ON+DN+OD$	16	25.36	0.064	81.9	5.35
3 UNIDIFF	15	21.20	0.130	84.9	4.14

UNIDIFF parameter estimates: males 0.3246, females 0.4467 (Russia set at zero).

O = class of origin, five levels (see Table 7.3).
D = class of destination, five levels (see Table 7.3).
N = nation, two levels.
rG^2 = % reduction in G^2 for model 1.
delta = % misclassified cases.

although there is a significant (though rather small) improvement observed among females. Among men, the uniform difference model reduces the deviance by only a further 2.5 for one degree of freedom ($p = >0.10$), although the parameter is positive – which could suggest that, given a much larger sample, mobility chances might be found to be significantly more unequal in Britain than in Russia. In the case of women, the improvement in fit obtained by the UNIDIFF model does just reach statistical significance (the reduction in the log likelihood ratio statistic here is 4.2, for one degree of freedom, $p = <0.05$), and (especially on these relatively small numbers) this does point to somewhat greater inequality of opportunities among British women than among their Russian sisters – since here, too, the uniform difference parameter shows evidence of a systematic increase in the odds ratios, as one moves from considering the Russian data to those for Britain.

Application of this more stringent test does lead us, therefore, to qualify our stark conclusion of common social fluidity in the class mobility regimes of Russia and Britain. In the case of women, there is evidence that communism tended to reduce inequalities of opportunity slightly; as far as men are concerned, Marshall (as a Scot) reserves the right to return a verdict of 'not proven'. However, for both sexes, it has to be recognized that the difference in underlying relative rates in the two countries is (to echo Erikson and Goldthorpe) very slight if in fact it exists at all.[11]

Unfortunately, it is not possible to push our crossnational comparative analysis of intergenerational mobility much further than this, because of the relatively small size of the Russian sample. We simply lack the numbers to test more complex models such as (for example) the 'core model' developed by Erikson and Goldthorpe during the CASMIN Project. What we can conclude is that, contrary to the claims made by many earlier commentators, Soviet Russia was not 'much more open' than its Western capitalist neighbours. It may have been marginally more so among women, but for men the evidence (at least thus far) does not favour arguments for greater equality. Clearly there are differences between the regimes, as can be seen from the deviance remaining after the uniform difference model has been applied, but we can do little more with our particular national samples than confirm that these are not differences in overall social fluidity.

Merit and mobility

Another useful way of pursuing the issue of openness is to consider the role of education in the Soviet system. Historically, the educational system in the USSR has been charged with two policy objectives; namely, the promotion of economic growth on the one hand, and of social homogeneity (via social mobility) on the other. As Yanowitch (1977: 60–1, 79) has noted, there were almost always tensions and compromises between the allocating and egalitarian functions, since access to education was a scarce resource. Economic efficiency called for the distribution of appropriately (and unequally) educated individuals to economic roles in an increasingly differentiated occupational structure. Social homogeneity required the pursuit of equality in educational attainment among children from different social backgrounds, particularly equality in the relative shares of children from working-class and intelligentsia homes in access to advanced levels of schooling, indeed took such equality to be one of the principal indicators of social progress and the steady transition to full communism.[12]

The relative influence of these two orientations has in fact varied throughout Soviet history. Unravelling their effects on educational policies and the history of access to schooling in the USSR is, therefore, a complex matter that need not be pursued here. However, it is worth noting that some commentators have been inclined to stress one or other of these functions at the expense of the other, in order to sustain rather large claims about the nature of Soviet communism. Aitov (1986: 259, 266), for example, paints a picture of the educational system as a harbinger of equality, increasingly accessible to all, and so successful in diminishing class disparities in educational attainment that, together with migration from the countryside to cities, this is one of the 'two basic factors' explaining almost three-quarters of all social mobility. Western observers have, on the whole, been more sceptical. For example, Yanowitch (1977: 66) concludes that the many complexities and tensions within Soviet education make it impossible to characterize in simplistic terms (as elitist or egalitarian), and that the system is best summarized as an 'extended process that simultaneously reproduces social inequalities and offers the prospect of social mobility to considerable numbers of working-class youth'.

Class differentials in educational attainment in the USSR are reasonably well documented – certainly more so than is class mobility itself.[13] Our interest here is in the more general problem of how educational achievement is related to class mobility. The social advancement of children from manual and agricultural working-class backgrounds was one of the declared goals of the Soviet system. Positive discrimination was often practised in favour of these individuals since the demand and support for education tended to be higher among families of intellectuals and managers. This measure of egalitarianism apart, however, the prevailing ethos governing the relationship between the educational and occupational systems was meritocratic (Kende, 1987: 14). In theory, therefore, the association between origins and destinations that was observed in the previous section ought to have been mediated largely by educational attainment. That is, class background should not have substantially influenced a person's opportunity to achieve or maintain an advantaged class position, over and above its effects on his or her educational attainment. Certainly, if claims about the relative openness of the Soviet system are to be upheld, social origins ought to exert less of an influence than in the advanced industrial societies of the capitalist West.

We have pursued this issue by examining the pattern of association between class origins, class destinations and educational attainment. In particular we wish to test the model of meritocracy itself. This assumes perfect mobility conditional upon education. That is, if Soviet citizens were finding their places in the occupational order according to meritocratic principles (and in the absence of ownership and inheritance of private property this was held to be the case), then the impact of class background should not be apparent in class destinations, except as this is mediated by educational credentials. The results shown in Table 7.7 in fact suggest that the meritocracy model (model 3) provides a rather poor fit to our Russian data ($p = 0.008$ and more than 6 per cent of all cases are misclassified). When the OD association is fitted (model 4), the G^2 is reduced significantly, and the model then provides an acceptable fit to the observed data ($p = 0.508$). A reduction of more than 95 per cent of the deviance in the baseline independence model is achieved and the proportion of misclassified cases falls to 3.6 per cent.

The existence of a significant association between class origins and destinations, net of the associations between origins and education and education and destination, tells against the thesis of meritocracy.[14] Inspection of the residuals under the meritocratic model suggests that the process at work is one of class discrimination rather than affirmative class action. For example, the largest residuals occur at middling levels of educational attainment, pointing towards the difficulty of circumventing meritocratic principles where educational credentials are either negligible or very good (university degree level or equivalent). However, where there is evidence of but modest educational attainment (at secondary school or lower tertiary level), the probabilities of social mobility vary according to the class background of

Table 7.7   *Intergenerational mobility and educational attainment in Russia and Great Britain*

Model	d.f.	G^2	p	rG^2	delta
Russia					
1 O+D+E	54	538.59	0.000	–	27.46
2 OE+D	45	417.91	0.000	22.4	25.15
3 OE+ED	36	59.42	0.008	89.0	6.34
4 OE+ED+OD	27	26.19	0.508	95.1	3.60
Great Britain					
1 O+D+E	54	386.98	0.000	–	29.63
2 OE+D	45	304.86	0.000	21.0	26.28
3 OE+ED	36	72.38	0.003	81.2	9.34
4 OE+ED+OD	27	26.76	0.477	93.1	4.55

O   = class of origin, four levels (salariat, intermediate, working, agricultural).
D   = class of destination, four levels (as origins).
E   = education, four levels, corresponding to CASMIN category 1 (low: general elementary and basic vocational qualification); CASMIN category 2 (medium: intermediate vocational and intermediate general qualification); CASMIN categories 3a and 3b (lower tertiary: maturity examination and lower-level tertiary certificate); and CASMIN category 3c (upper tertiary: upper-level tertiary certificate). See König et al. (1988: 58–9).
rG^2 = % reduction in G^2 for model 1.
delta = % misclassified cases.

the individuals concerned. At these levels of attainment, children from salariat backgrounds are over-represented in salariat destinations, and under-represented among manual workers. Thus, under the meritocracy model, children of what we have termed medium (level 2) educational attainment, and from salariat backgrounds, should be distributed to the various class destinations (salariat, intermediate, working, agricultural) in the ratio 42:9:47:2. In our sample the actual distribution was 48:15:37:0. Similarly, at the lower tertiary level (level 3), the predicted proportions 21:16:59:4 can be compared with the observed proportions 34:16:50:0. The obverse pattern tends to prevail among those from manual backgrounds. At these middling educational levels, children of manual workers are more likely to be found in the working class and less likely to be found in the salariat, than would be predicted from the meritocracy model.

Interestingly, as Table 7.7 also shows, this pattern of results is again similar to that found in Britain. In the British case, the meritocracy model (model 3) likewise fails to provide a satisfactory fit to the data, and the *OD* association is also required (model 4). In other words, there is nothing here to suggest that education in the Russian SSR offered a markedly wider avenue of opportunity to children from less privileged class backgrounds than it did in Britain, despite the periodic efforts of Soviet policy makers to weaken, by positive discrimination, the links between class background and educational attainment.[15]

Table 7.8 *Goldthorpe class origins, class destinations (first job) and educational attainment by cohort, Russia*

Model	d.f.	G^2	p	rG^2	delta
1 $O+E+D+C$	63	810.40	0.000	–	30.26
2 $OE+D+C$	57	631.75	0.000	22.0	28.80
3 $OE+ED+C$	51	310.62	0.008	61.7	19.03
4 $OE+ED+OD+C$	47	254.12	0.008	68.6	17.67
5 $OED+C$	35	244.01	0.000	69.9	17.47
6 $OE+ED+OD+CE$	44	51.94	0.192	93.6	6.84
7 $OE+ED+OD+CD$	45	227.65	0.000	71.9	16.67
8 $OE+ED+OD+CE+CD$	42	47.72	0.252	94.1	6.65
9 $OE+ED+CE+ODC$	36	36.91	0.426	95.4	5.52

O = class of origin, three levels (white-collar, working, agricultural).
D = class of destination, three levels (as origins).
E = education, four levels (low, medium, lower tertiary, higher tertiary, as Table 7.7).
C = cohort, two levels (born before 1950, born 1950 and after).
rG^2 = % reduction in G^2 for model 1.
delta = % misclassified cases.

Furthermore, if we then analyse our data on social mobility and educational attainment but broken down by cohort, there is no evidence to suggest that communist Russia was becoming more meritocratic over time (see Table 7.8). Unfortunately, the size of our sample constrains us at this juncture to consider mobility between three classes of origin and destination (white-collar, working and agricultural) in only two cohorts (individuals born before 1950 and those born in 1950 or later), although we maintain the same four levels of educational attainment as in the previous analysis.[16] The best-fitting model (model 6) shows a number of expected results. The *OE* association confirms that the educational attainments of children from different social backgrounds vary. The further association between education and destination (*ED*) confirms that differently qualified individuals go to different class destinations. There is also a significant association between cohort and educational attainment (*CE*): those born in the post-war period from 1950 onwards tend to be more highly qualified than those born in previous years. As before, the association between origins and destinations (*OD*) is significant, and must be included in the model in order to obtain a satisfactory fit to the data; but note that, as the comparison with model 9 shows, the association between class origins and destinations does not itself seem to vary substantially across the two cohorts. The three-way *ODC* interaction term just fails to improve significantly upon the fit of the simpler model.

Conclusion

We would not wish to be guilty of reading too much into our findings. There is no reason to suppose the Russian sample is unrepresentative but (in mobility terms at least) it is relatively small, and for that reason we have been unable either to investigate the fine details of intergenerational mobility or to test more sophisticated models such as those to be found in the CASMIN Project. We must therefore issue the disclaimer that ours is a fairly crude analysis of a rather limited number of cases. Despite its limitations, however, the study has a number of advantages over earlier investigations of social mobility in the USSR. Most obviously, the sample is representative (at least of contemporary Russia) and the data have been coded in a standardized fashion that permits meaningful comparison with other countries.

We have identified a number of distinctive features in Russian patterns of social mobility. The peculiar combination of a state socialist polity and a mature industrial economy has resulted (for example) in a relatively large salariat, a small and shrinking agricultural population, and a large (though diminishing) working class – a unique mobility profile among advanced nations. What apparently is *not* unique to Russia is the mobility regime that underlies these absolute rates of inflow and outflow. Our results suggest that, like many other advanced industrial societies, communist Russia exhibited similar relative mobility rates for men and women. Furthermore, although we can find some evidence that Russian women were more equal in their relative mobility chances than are women in Britain, there are no real grounds for applying that same conclusion to men. Russian males appear to have been almost as class divided as their British counterparts.

Of course, that is a tantalizing 'almost', and it points again to the relatively small size of our sample. There are hints, in the case of our findings for men, that the mobility regime among Russian and British males has not literally been identical. However, we can surely conclude, even on the basis of our rather limited sample, that earlier commentators (notably Soviets themselves) who argued that rates of social mobility in the USSR made it 'much more open' than its capitalist neighbours were in fact mistaken. It is difficult to agree with those such as Aitov (1986: 270) who have argued that Soviet society showed 'tremendous openness', increasing rates of social mobility and only 'residual social inequality', when compared with advanced capitalist states. Rather, we find ourselves inclined to conclude with Markiewicz-Lagneau (1987: 390) that the apparent successes of socialism in promoting social mobility owe little to the distinctive nature of Soviet ideology, and much to the exigencies imposed by forced industrialization under the guidance of a massive and far-reaching state. Readers may recognize in this conclusion a tacit endorsement of Ossowski's (1957) long-suppressed thesis that the effect of socialist revolutions in increasing mobility would come from the stimulus they gave to industrialization rather than any transformation of values. With the demise of communism in Russia itself it is at last possible to investigate seriously the accuracy of this argument. The early evidence is that Ossowski's diagnosis was sound.

Notes

* Gordon Marshall, Svetlana Sydorenko and Stephen Roberts. The analysis was prepared with the assistance of grants from the British Council (Sydorenko) and British Academy/ Leverhulme Trust (Marshall). We would like to thank John Goldthorpe, Anthony Heath and Adam Swift for helpful comments on an earlier version of the chapter.

1 Connor's study is the most inclusive, citing data from the 1960s and early 1970s for Bulgaria, Czechoslovakia, Hungary, Poland, Romania and Yugoslavia. Strmiska's analysis relies on what are, in fact, largely the same surveys. As both authors freely admit, their crossnational findings can only be described as comparable in the loosest sense, since the data are derived from incompatible samples drawn at different times, and embrace a wide range of occupational descriptions and labels coded to broad class categories identified in a variety of ways. In their well-known attempt to transcend these issues of incompatibility, Ganzeboom et al. (1989) compiled 149 intergenerational class mobility tables from 35 countries, but included (admittedly more recent) data for only a few state socialist societies – although, of course, none from the Soviet Union. The more rigorously comparative CASMIN Project, led by Erikson and Goldthorpe (1992a), reports reliable data from the mid 1970s, but only for Hungary, Poland and Czechoslovakia, among the formerly communist states.

2 The most full account will be found in Erikson and Goldthorpe (1992a: ch. 2).

3 For an overview of the literature and issues see Marshall et al., Chapter 5 in this volume.

4 Some might argue that, in a country where women have had high employment rates for a considerable time, the use of fathers' occupations to indicate origin classes should also be seen as problematic. Unfortunately, occupational information on mothers was not collected, so it is not possible to pursue alternatives to the strategy here adopted.

5 The relatively small proportion of agricultural workers in our tables perhaps also reflects, to a lesser extent, a genuine ambiguity in the coding of some rural occupations. Many Russian collective farms are so large that they support a variety of manual and nonmanual jobs in what are, effectively, 'offices and factories in the countryside'. The coding of these occupations into Goldthorpe classes raises the issue of whether the sectoral or hierarchical elements of the situation should be emphasized. The Russian survey agency tended to stress the latter.

6 See, for example, Armstrong (1959), Heitlinger (1979) and Littlejohn (1984: ch. 6).

7 The Goldthorpe class schema is of course not unidimensionally hierarchical. On the distinction between vertical and non-vertical mobility in this context see Erikson and Goldthorpe (1992a: 195). Our results for Russia are based on the hierarchical effects matrix provided by Erikson and Goldthorpe (1992a: 124) and are therefore comparable with those reported for countries included in the CASMIN Project.

8 The same test appears also to have been developed independently by Xie (1992) who refers to it as the 'log-multiplicative layer effect model'.

9 Erikson and Goldthorpe's (1992a: ch. 7) 'dominance' approach to this issue is also less helpful, in the context of investigating crossnational similarities in class mobility regimes, than is the strategy of separating the sexes, since differences in the fit of the various loglinear models across countries are only partly substantive. Because of the way in which dominant 'heads of household' are identified, the findings are arguably also partly artefactual, being affected by (for example) the proportion of class homogeneous households, of female rather than male heads of household, and the extent both of sex segregation in labour markets and of differences in the overall shape of the class structure (as expressed in the destination marginals of the mobility table). For this reason we have confined our analysis to the separate treatment of males and females (but see note 11 below).

10 For technical details of the British study see Chapter 4, note 4 in this volume, and Kluegel et al. (1995).

11 For the sake of completeness, we have repeated our analysis using Erikson and Goldthorpe's dominance criterion to allocate class standing to households in Russia and Great

Britain, but the results do not lead us to any different conclusions. Using this approach, the common social fluidity (CSF) model also provides an acceptable fit to intergenerational mobility data for the two countries (G^2=22.88, d.f.=16, p=0.116, delta=4.26), although the UNIDIFF test again provides a significant but slight improvement on this model (reducing the G^2 by a further 6.31, for one degree of freedom, p = <0.05, delta=2.76). The UNIDIFF parameter estimate is 0.4323 (Russia set at zero). In other words, the fit provided by the CSF model is improved upon by the model of uniform change, and the estimate shows evidence of a monotonic tendency for the odds ratios in Britain to increase as compared with those for Russia. The point is, however, that the increase is small and in no way justifies Soviet claims that social mobility patterns in communist Russia showed it to be 'substantially more open' than capitalist neighbours such as Britain. Our reservations about the use of the dominance approach in this context are stated in note 9 above.

12 Wesolowski and Mach (1986) argue that these two functions need not necessarily be in conflict. In their view, it is possible in a socialist society to reconcile the functions of legitimating the political system and encouraging economic efficiency if one distinguishes two types of social mobility; namely, collective-class type mobility (relevant to political legitimation) and individual-occupational type mobility (an incentive for economic growth).

13 Many of the relevant studies are summarized in Yanowitch (1977: ch. 3) and Lane and O'Dell (1978: ch. 7).

14 Although there is nothing in the meritocracy thesis about differences between the sexes (the argument is about inequalities of class), introducing a control for sex (*S*) does nothing to salvage the meritocratic case. The best-fitting model shows the associations of *OE+SED+OD* (G^2=51.02, d.f.=75, delta=6.47). Nor does the last of these associations itself vary by sex. (Fitting the interaction term *ODS* reduces the deviance in the model by only a further 5.06 for 12 degrees of freedom, p=0.000, delta=5.90.)

15 There is a problem of comparability here, since the British tables (unlike the Russian) include significant numbers of *petite bourgeoisie*, for whom educational credentials are probably a less important mechanism for the attainment of class privilege than is inheritance of property. Yet omitting this social class from the analysis does not substantially alter the results. The actual figures for the meritocracy model are now G^2=70.84, d.f.=36, p=0.001, rG^2=80.8, delta=9.09. Those for the model which includes the association between class origins and destinations are G^2=30.01, d.f.=27, p=0.314, rG^2=91.9, delta=3.67. Similar results, with the same implications for arguments about meritocracy, are reported in Heath et al. (1991a) and by Marshall and Swift, Chapter 9 in this volume.

16 The significance of 1950 is simply that, in general terms, the earlier decades saw rather more vigorous intervention to promote the education of manual and agricultural workers via positive discrimination. The decades since have characteristically placed more emphasis on 'meritocracy'. Because our interest here is in the relative mobility chances of two (admittedly very broad) cohorts, the destination class is indicated by the respondent's first (rather than current) job, in order to control for length of time in employment.

8

Intergenerational Class Processes and the Asymmetry Hypothesis*

The relationship between class and gender is currently a contested issue. Proponents of the so-called conventional approach maintain that the household remains the unit of class composition and that a married woman's class characteristics are determined principally by the occupational position of her husband. It is the conjugal family that shapes class fate, class formation, and class action. In studies of class and mobility, therefore, it is appropriate to consider only the class locations of male 'heads of households'. This view has been subject to growing criticism in recent years. At a time when increasing numbers of women are engaged in employment, many sociologists now favour the view that the individual is the unit of class composition, and allocate class positions to individuals within households on the basis of their own employment.[1]

The controversial 'asymmetry hypothesis' is central to this debate. The hypothesis is clearly formulated in Talcott Parsons's early papers on family and kinship in the United States. Parsons argued that the family is a unit of diffuse solidarity and, therefore, that the members of a given conjugal unit must share a common status in the stratification order. Furthermore, in contemporary industrial societies, it was in fact the occupational position of the husband that determined the standing of the family as a whole. This conviction – which was said to be shared by both marital partners – eliminated intrafamilial status inconsistencies and so obviated the possibility of status conflict. Consequently, as Parsons (1954: 191) puts it, 'there is a typically asymmetrical relation of the marriage pair to the occupational structure', whereby the status-conferring occupational role is confined to that of the husband, so making the household rather than the individual the unit of class composition.

Parsons's proposal was examined intermittently during the 1960s and 1970s. However, with the more recent emergence of feminist perspectives in sociology it has returned to the forefront of debate, especially in the controversial area of class analysis. The issue here has been precisely formulated in terms of how successfully the competing approaches to class analysis can explain observed patterns of socio-political class formation – for example voting behaviour and class identification. Those who favour the conventional strategy would have it that a married woman's class attitudes and behaviour are still best understood in terms of the class position of her husband. Increased female employment carries fewer implications for this argument than its critics have supposed. A woman's attachment to the workforce is typically still the more tenuous. Differences in the relative contributions to household income have also been maintained. It is therefore still reasonable to view the class position of the husband as the stronger determinant of such class characteristics as the voting behaviour of the wife.

By contrast, critics such as Anthony Heath and Nicky Britten (1984) maintain that women's jobs 'do make a difference', in that they shape class attitudes in ways additional to that attributable to the class position of male spouses. Heath and Britten provide evidence which shows that the voting behaviour of females married to working-class males varies according to the class of their own employment. For example, those employed in nonmanual positions but married to manual workers more often vote Conservative than do those in homogeneous working-class households. In reply, conventional class analysts (for example Goldthorpe, 1984b) argue that the central issue is not one of whether there are differences stemming from increased female employment, but the conceptual matter of whether such differences make desirable the abandonment of the conventional view. More specifically, those who favour the conventional approach do not deny that consideration of female employment provides additional insights into women's attitudes and behaviour; however, they insist that this is a sex effect rather than a further consequence of class. The same would be true, for example, of ethnicity or religion. In other words, the issue here is not one of increasing explained variation, but rather one of understanding the *pattern* of association between a woman's class socio-political attributes, her own class position, and that of her spouse.

It is for this reason that we will not be pursuing here that strand in the previous literature which debates the issue of whether or not wives' 'social characteristics' are relevant to the explanation of their class identities or vote. Examples of research along these lines include papers by Abbott and Sapsford (1986), Baxter (1991), and Hayes and Jones (1992a). These and other similar studies seem to us to be entirely misconceived – at least as a means of resolving the dispute about conventional versus individual approaches to class analysis. Orthodox class analysts have never claimed that social class membership *alone* explained class identification – far less that it constituted a key to the full range of socio-cultural preferences. Their argument is simply that, *in so far as* class standing explains these phenomena, then there are less satisfactory and more satisfactory ways of defining the unit of class composition itself. The addition of variables that are (conceptually if not always empirically) independent of class – such as trades union membership, educational qualifications, years of post-compulsory schooling, and such like – will almost certainly explain variance over and above that attributable to class as such.

Against this background Robert Erikson and John Goldthorpe (1992a: 250–3; 1992b) have specified appropriate criteria in terms of which the conventional approach should be seen to stand or fall. They do not deny that a female's class identity may be associated with her own occupational class position. Crucially, however, it should be more strongly associated with the class position of her male partner. Furthermore, when the former association is taken into account, the latter will still be evident. Erikson and Goldthorpe have compiled survey evidence from Britain and a number of other European countries to support these claims.[2]

Their findings for Britain are consistent with those reported by other researchers. For example, Marshall and his colleagues (1988) in the Essex Class Project of the mid 1980s record that the voting behaviour of wives is more strongly influenced by the class position indicated by their husbands' employment than that signalled by their own. The 1979 British General Election Study also revealed the husband's class position to be the better indicator of female voting patterns. For example, females involved in intermediate-class employment and married to service-class males tended to vote Conservative, whereas those with working-class husbands more often favoured the Labour Party. Studies elsewhere have provided similar evidence that would serve to confirm conventional expectations.[3]

One might, therefore, regard the weight of empirical evidence concerning the asymmetry hypothesis as clearly favouring the conventional position. In other words, for the purposes of class analysis, women's class socio-political characteristics are (at least in Britain) attributable largely to the class positions held by their husbands rather than any consequences stemming from their own employment. Recently however, Geoff Payne and Pamela Abbott (1990b) have suggested that this pattern may not simply be a household composition effect, as has been supposed by Goldthorpe and others. More subtle class processes may be at work. They point out, for example, that women who are upwardly mobile through marriage may themselves have been downwardly mobile from their class of origin. That is to say, in order to gain compensation for their downward intergenerational mobility by employment, women may obtain counter-mobility through marriage. Interestingly, for example, Gill Jones (1990) has found that downwardly mobile females from middle-class backgrounds marry younger than do other females from the same class origins. Whether this is due to a clear counter-mobility motive on the part of the former, or is merely an artefact of greater career commitment among the latter, remains unclear. Furthermore, when compared with similarly downwardly mobile men, such females are more likely to achieve counter-mobility by marrying up. Of course, the possibility of marrying up is greater for females, given the degree of sex segregation in the class structure. Nevertheless, given that women are likely to have fewer opportunities to establish employment careers than are men, it may be that marriage offers an 'alternative route' as a means of escaping downward intergenerational mobility.

If intergenerationally downwardly mobile females commonly marry up to achieve counter-mobility, what then of upwardly mobile females? Do these women consolidate their class positions by marrying males engaged in similar employment or do they attach themselves to partners in class positions which reflect their own class backgrounds? If the latter is more often the case, it can then be argued that what is in fact happening in the British class structure is a process of intergenerational 'tidying up', whereby females are reallocated to their original (Payne and Abbott use the term 'proper') class positions through marriage. According to this line of reasoning, those females married to working-class males would themselves more often hail from the working class, while those with professional husbands would correspondingly be more likely to have come from professional or white-collar class backgrounds. In other words a woman's class background would serve to influence her choice of marital partner.

In this way Payne and Abbott raise the possibility that a woman's class background, influencing the choice of her marital partner, underlies her class socio-political preferences. Thus, for example, a woman from service-class origins with a husband employed in this class and who votes for the Conservative Party would do so not simply because of the husband's privileged class position but because her own class background has influenced her choice of marital partner. It is then her class background that may be considered to be the crucial determinant of her vote.

In essence, Payne and Abbott are suggesting that research on the issue of socio-political class formation should now investigate the processes behind extant empirical findings, and in particular explore further the nature of the asymmetry effect. The aim of this chapter is, therefore, to investigate the relationship between intergenerational class processes and household composition effects in explaining the class socio-political characteristics of females in Britain. Given that the class identities and voting behaviour of married women appear to owe more to the class positions of their husbands than to the women's own employment, the central issue is then whether or not a control for the female's class origins detracts from the alleged household composition effect. If this were indeed the case, then one would have to consider the apparent influence of the class of a husband on his spouse's class attitudes as having been, in some part at least, inter-generationally determined.

Data

Our data are taken from the 1991 British Social Justice Survey and the 1987 and 1992 British General Election Surveys. These have similar sample designs and contain all of the relevant information: respondent's class, spouse's class, respondent's class background, and his or her class identification and voting behaviour. The surveys have been pooled in order to gain a sufficiently large sample.[4] This analysis deals only with females currently in employment, who have a male partner (married or cohabiting) also currently employed, and traceable class origins as indicated by the employment of their fathers when they were aged fifteen. Collapsed three-category Goldthorpe classes are used throughout. These embrace the salariat or service class; an intermediate class of routine clerical employees, farmers,

Table 8.1 *Class socio-political characteristics of currently employed females, Goldthorpe class categories, Great Britain (%)*

	Class ID[1]		Voting intention[1]			
	Working class	Middle class	Con.	Lib. Dem.	Lab.	(N)
Female's current class position						
Salariat	38	57	43	25	17	(331)
Intermediate	55	39	47	16	18	(482)
Working	71	25	34	13	35	(489)
Class position of male partner						
Salariat	34	60	51	20	14	(473)
Intermediate	63	32	46	16	19	(396)
Working	76	19	26	15	39	(433)
Female's class origins						
Salariat	37	59	49	21	18	(297)
Intermediate	50	41	52	16	15	(360)
Working	70	27	32	16	32	(645)
Female's first class position						
Salariat	39	53	39	23	18	(161)
Intermediate	57	39	46	16	19	(302)
Working	66	38	31	16	29	(304)

[1] In this and subsequent tables, reported percentages for class identity exclude 'don't know' and those who 'refused class concept'; reported percentages for vote exclude minor parties, non-voters, and those ineligible to vote.

supervisors of manual workers, and the *petite bourgeoisie*; and a working class of skilled and unskilled manual workers and agricultural labourers.

Female class identities and voting

Female class identities and voting are shown in Table 8.1, according to (in turn) the class of the woman's own current employment, that of her male partner, her class origins, and finally the class of her first employment. This last class indicator is included since it is generally acknowledged that a married woman's current class position is often distorted by intermittent engagements in the labour market. For example, women re-entering the labour market after an absence through childbirth are sometimes compelled to do so at a lower occupational level, a phenomenon which has led some observers (for example Dex and Shaw, 1986: 81–7) to suggest that 'class immediately prior to birth of first child' is a better indicator of a woman's true class position. Unfortunately, complete work histories are not available in the surveys used here; however, we can make use of information on a woman's first full-time employment as an (obviously weaker) indicator of her social class prior to marriage and childbearing commitments. The table indicates that the class position of the male partner has particular influence on the female's class sentiments. As expected, those females married to service-class partners are the most likely to view themselves as middle class, and most often vote Conservative. Correspondingly, females attached to working-class males more often favour the Labour Party, and tend to think of themselves as working class. The other class measures relating to the female's own current and first employment, and her class origins, tend to illustrate similar, although less marked, associations of this kind.[5]

Table 8.2a then takes up the particular issue raised by Payne and Abbott. This shows the class attitudes of the females in our samples, according to both the class positions of their male spouses, and also their own class of origin. It is clear that class background strongly influences the choice of marital partner. For example, half of the females from salariat backgrounds have become partnered with a male who is himself employed in the salariat, whereas this is true of only a quarter of those from working-class origins. This is indeed evidence of the intergenerational class process suggested by Payne and Abbott. How then, if at all, does this bear upon the asymmetry effects observed in Table 8.1?

Whilst the strong influence of the male spouse's class is apparent, there is varying evidence that the female's class identity is further distinguished according to her class background. For example, of women attached to salariat males, those who also have salariat origins are clearly the most likely (79 per cent) to view themselves as middle class, while those hailing from working-class origins are the least likely (45 per cent). Similar but less pronounced patterns emerge among females partnered with males employed in other class locations. Amongst females with working-class spouses, it is also true that those from the more privileged class backgrounds are more likely to identify themselves as middle class, although the percentages of those who do so from each of the three class origins are not that dissimilar (25, 24 and 17). This is hardly compelling evidence of a strong inter-generational effect. Class of origin, at least on these results, would seem to have limited impact in distinguishing further between the class identities of females attached to males employed in varying class positions. The picture is similar if one then considers the voting behaviour of these women. Those from working-class backgrounds would appear more often to favour the Labour Party than do those from intermediate or salariat origins. However, there is generally little differentiation between those females from intermediate-class origins, and those hailing from the service class. One would conclude that a female's class background, when considered in conjunction with her male partner's class position, has limited influence on her voting behaviour.

Indeed, when class background is controlled for using logistic regression techniques, the importance of the husband's class position is little diminished (see Table 8.3a). For both class identities and voting behaviour, the relevant odds ratios do change when class origins are taken into account; however, the changes are not substantial enough to suggest that the asymmetry effects reported by conventional class analysis are seriously undermined.[6] For example, as will be evident from model (i), a female partnered with a

Table 8.2   *Class socio-political characteristics of females with currently employed male partners, by Goldthorpe class position of male, and female's class background, Great Britain (%)*

(a) Currently employed females

Class position of male partner	Class background								
	Salariat			Intermediate			Working		
	W	M	(N)	W	M	(N)	W	M	(N)
Salariat	17	79	(159)	35	57	(148)	49	45	(166)
Intermediate	57	41	(86)	49	38	(106)	72	26	(205)
Working	65	25	(52)	70	24	(105)	80	17	(276)
	C	LD	L	C	LD	L	C	LD	C
Salariat	52	25	13	57	18	8	46	16	22
Intermediate	53	15	17	59	16	8	36	16	25
Working	31	17	33	39	13	31	20	15	43

(Total N=1,303)

(b) Previously employed females

Class position of male partner	Class background								
	Salariat			Intermediate			Working		
	W	M	(N)	W	M	(N)	W	M	(N)
Salariat	27	73	(68)	35	63	(49)	36	56	(79)
Intermediate	58	23	(22)	60	26	(59)	76	20	(71)
Working	79	16	(18)	58	37	(41)	78	20	(112)
	C	LD	L	C	LD	L	C	LD	L
Salariat	56	24	8	58	19	9	39	24	28
Intermediate	36	23	10	53	23	11	24	16	33
Working	17	18	58	37	10	31	28	10	41

(Total N=519)

Class identities: W = working class; M = middle class. Voting intentions: C = Conservative; LD = Liberal Democrat; L = Labour.

working-class male is 4.7 times more likely to vote Labour than a female partnered with a service-class male. When female class backgrounds are taken into account this odds ratio is reduced to 4.1 (model (ii)). Similarly, in the case of class identities, when class background is brought into the picture the corresponding odds ratio is reduced from 7.1 to 5.6. It is clear that whether or not an employed and married or partnered woman hails from a working-class background is indeed a further determinant of her class identity and voting behaviour – but this is consistently of much less importance than the class position of her employed male partner.

To what extent does a woman's own employment (rather than her class origins) explain her socio-political preferences? We have already seen that a

Table 8.3 *Results of logistic regression for currently employed and previously employed females, with male partners in current employment, Goldthorpe class categories, Great Britain*

(a) Currently employed females

	Odds ratio (working-class ID), model:			Odds ratio (vote Labour), model:		
	(i)	(ii)	(iii)	(i)	(ii)	(iii)
Male partner's class						
Salariat	ref.	ref.	ref.	ref.	ref.	ref.
Intermediate	3.45*	3.13*	2.78*	1.53*	1.39 ns	1.31 ns
Working	7.14*	5.56*	4.76*	4.70*	4.05*	3.44*
Female's class background						
Salariat		ref.	ref.		ref.	ref.
Intermediate		1.64*	1.52*		0.69 ns	0.66 ns
Working		2.94*	2.50*		1.90*	1.68*
Female's current class						
Salariat			ref.			ref.
Intermediate			1.45*			0.92 ns
Working			1.96*			1.72*

(b) Previously employed females

	Odds ratio (working-class ID), model:			Odds ratio (vote Labour), model:		
	(i)	(ii)	(iii)	(i)	(ii)	(iii)
Male partner's class						
Salariat	ref.	ref.	ref.	ref.	ref.	ref.
Intermediate	5.88*	5.56*	4.76*	2.16*	2.21*	1.94*
Working	5.88*	5.56*	4.35*	5.80*	5.12*	3.98*
Female's class background						
Salariat		ref.	ref.		ref.	ref.
Intermediate		0.94 ns	0.87 ns		0.80 ns	0.75 ns
Working		1.56 ns	1.34 ns		1.95*	1.67 ns
Female's last class						
Salariat			ref.			ref.
Intermediate			1.80*			0.84 ns
Working			2.55*			1.77 ns

Odds ratio (working-class ID) = odds (working-class ID)/odds (middle-class ID)
Odds ratio (vote Labour) = odds (vote Labour)/odds (vote Conservative or Liberal Democrat).
Model (i): class position of male partner is fitted alone.
Model (ii): class background of female is fitted followed by class of male partner.
Model (iii): class background of female and class of male partner are fitted followed by female's own class of employment.
ref.: service class is reference for contrasts with intermediate and working classes.
* = significant at 5% level or better; ns = not significant.

woman's own employment class has a weaker influence than that of her spouse. But it may be the case that a woman's employment has some underlying influence on her vote and class identity. In fact, however, when female employment is included (model (iii)) it is clear that the importance of spouse's class is largely robust to both this and the woman's class of origin.[7] Returning to the above example, a female with a working-class partner is still 3.4 times more likely to vote Labour than a woman with a service-class partner, irrespective of her own employment and class of origin (see Table 8.3a). The corresponding odds ratio for class identity is now reduced from 5.6 (model (ii)) to 4.8 (in model (iii)).

Clearly there is little evidence that females' class backgrounds undermine the influence of the husbands' class positions on these class attitudes. That is to say, a woman's class value system seems to be conditioned largely within the context given by her partner's employment class, rather than her own class origins. Intergenerational class processes would then seem to have limited consequences for the class-related behaviour of females – at least in so far as the asymmetry hypothesis is concerned.

Labour market participation

The above findings relate to women who are actively engaged in the labour market. Of course it has been argued that the observed asymmetry effect should be strongest among females in situations of greatest dependency in households. For example, one might anticipate that the effect of the male partner's occupational standing would be greatest among unwaged domestic labourers, or other women without employment. Similarly, among those in employment, the same might also be true of part-time employees – who typically have inferior incomes, pension prospects, and job security. Thus, for example, Stephen Edgell and Vic Duke (1991) maintain that, among women, 'level of economic activity is related to both political attitudes and behaviour.' Jones (1990) herself makes the rather more general claim that a woman's own occupational class is a better indicator of her life-chances than is that of her husband if she is in full-time employment, but that this does not apply to those employed part-time, or to housewives. Class analysts who have advocated an individual strategy have tended, therefore, as a matter of routine, to distinguish part-time and full-time female employees – and both, in turn, from housewives and other dependants (see Dale et al., 1985; Edgell and Duke, 1991: 29; Jones, 1990: 118–19). How then – if at all – does the degree of labour-market participation among women influence the asymmetry effects reported above?

Five hundred and nineteen women who had previously been in regular employment, who were attached to economically active male partners and who had traceable class origins, were identified in the three surveys. Of these, 82 per cent had classified themselves as housewives, 13 per cent as disabled or retired, and 4 per cent as registered unemployed. Five further women were involved in full-time education or casual employment. The class distribution of these women, based on the female's most recent employment, was 18 per cent salariat, 36 per cent intermediate, and 46 per cent working class. This would indicate that these previously employed women have come disproportionately from less privileged employment.

The class socio-political attributes of these formerly employed females are shown according to both the class position of the male and that of the woman's own class origins in Table 8.2b. The patterns that emerge are similar to those among the currently employed (compare Table 8.2a). This is confirmed by again using regression methods. As was the case with the currently employed, the class position of the male partner emerges as the class indicator which most strongly influences the women's class socio-political characteristics. Furthermore, this influence is only slightly reduced when females' class origins (model (ii)) and then last employment (model (iii)) are included, as can be seen from Table 8.3b. Thus, for example, an economically inactive woman attached to a working-class man is 5.9 times more likely to view herself as working class (rather than middle class) than is such a woman with a salariat partner. Taking into account her class origins reduces these odds to 5.6. The addition of her last employment reduces them further to 4.4. The same general pattern can be observed in the case of voting behaviour. A comparison of the corresponding odds ratios in the two halves of the table indicates that economically inactive women are not systematically more dependent on the class positions of their male partners when nominating their class socio-political preferences. Perhaps surprisingly, we find no marked disparities between our findings for these women, as against those for women currently in paid employment. There is no evidence here to support the argument for a strengthening asymmetry effect, for either class identities or vote, amongst housewives and other economically inactive women.

Finally, then, we should consider the issue of part-time versus full-time employment. In our sample we identified 669 women currently engaged in part-time work, with recorded class origins, and partnered with employed males. Proportionally more of these part-timers were involved in working-class occupations than was the case among their full-time counterparts (53 per cent as compared to 23 per cent). Correspondingly fewer were to be found in service-class jobs (16 per cent as against 35 per cent of those employed full-time). In other relevant respects (class of spouse, social origins, class identities and voting) the two groups of women were broadly similar.

If the logistic regression is then repeated, in order to compare part-time and full-time female employees (see Table 8.4), we do not find that women employed full-time are substantially less likely to define their class interests in terms of the occupational positions of their male partners. Furthermore, when class background is controlled for, the influence of the male partner's class is not seriously undermined in any instance. This pattern is observed for both full-time and part-time female workers and with regard to class identities and voting alike. Again we investigated the possible influence of women's own involvement in the labour market. Table 8.4 indicates that

Table 8.4   *Results of logistic regression for females employed full-time and part-time, with male partners in current employment, Goldthorpe class categories, Great Britain*

(a) Full-time currently employed females

	Odds ratio (working-class ID), model:			Odds ratio (vote Labour), model:		
	(i)	(ii)	(iii)	(i)	(ii)	(iii)
Male partner's class						
Salariat	ref.	ref.	ref.	ref.	ref.	ref.
Intermediate	2.90*	2.50*	2.18*	1.06 ns	0.97 ns	0.85 ns
Working	7.61*	6.09*	4.88*	4.44*	3.94*	3.13*
Female's class background						
Salariat		ref.	ref.		ref.	ref.
Intermediate		1.46 ns	1.38 ns		0.62 ns	0.58 ns
Working		2.51*	2.18*		1.63 ns	1.41 ns
Female's current class						
Salariat			ref.			ref.
Intermediate			1.55*			1.28 ns
Working			2.51*			2.34*

(b) Part-time currently employed females

	Odds ratio (working-class ID), model:			Odds ratio (vote Labour), model:		
	(i)	(ii)	(iii)	(i)	(ii)	(iii)
Male partner's class						
Salariat	ref.	ref.	ref.	ref.	ref.	ref.
Intermediate	3.59*	3.47*	3.29*	1.89*	1.75*	1.75*
Working	6.53*	5.44*	4.94*	5.67*	4.74*	4.31*
Female's class background						
Salariat		ref.	ref.		ref.	ref.
Intermediate		1.71*	1.63 ns		0.88 ns	0.90 ns
Working		3.23*	2.94*		2.43*	2.44*
Female's last class						
Salariat			ref.			ref.
Intermediate			1.27 ns			0.63 ns
Working			1.55 ns			1.05 ns

Notes as for Table 8.3.

part-time employment offers no significant additional explanation, for a woman's socio-political characteristics, once the class of her partner and her class origins have been considered. Among women employed full-time, this additional explanation is clearly significant, but of minor importance. Crucially, however, regardless of a woman's own employment (and class origins) it is the class of her male partner which still dominates her voting and class identity.

Conclusion

In this chapter we have examined the asymmetry hypothesis and have seen the results favour a conventional rather than an individual approach to class analysis. In line with most previous studies for Britain, a married or cohabiting woman's voting behaviour and class identification are seen to be better understood with reference to her male partner's class standing than her own occupational experiences.[8] A woman's first occupational class was found to be no more successful than her present employment in explaining her class socio-political characteristics.

Of course, large numbers of females are employed part-time or engaged in unpaid domestic work, and so we also examined the impact of economic activity levels on the asymmetry effect. Whilst this effect is confirmed in all cases, there would seem (perhaps surprisingly) to be little differentiation in the findings for full-time, part-time and formerly employed females. We can only speculate as to why, in this case at least, women employed full-time do not act in such a way as to present a greater challenge to the asymmetry hypothesis. In Britain, at least, the answer might lie in the segmented nature of labour markets, which results in women generally (whether employed full-time or otherwise) experiencing relatively inferior conditions of employment as compared with men. Is the robustness of the conventional approach to class analysis in this country being sustained, even in the late twentieth century, by the realities of women's employment in Britain?

However, the main issue with which we have been concerned was the suggestion that intergenerational class processes were responsible for observed asymmetry effects. Our findings on this issue are also clear-cut. These processes are clearly evident in the British class structure but then have minimal consequences for the asymmetry effect. A woman's choice of marital partner is influenced by her class background. Those women from the more privileged class origins are more likely to become attached to partners also employed in privileged class positions. However, controlling for women's classes of origin detracts little from the importance of the male partners' class positions, at least with regard to female class identities and voting behaviour. In other words, a female's class socio-political attributes are conditioned largely within the context of her current household, regardless of her class background. This would appear to be the case for all females – irrespective of employment status.

Notes

* Gordon Marshall and Stephen Roberts. We wish to thank Geoff Evans for information about the coding of the election surveys, and David Firth, John Goldthorpe, Anthony Heath, Clive Payne and Adam Swift for helpful comments on an earlier draft of this chapter.

1 For an overview of the now extensive literature about this issue see Marshall et al., Chapter 5 in this volume.

2 It should perhaps be noted here that these authors have also spelled out the asymmetry hypothesis as it applies to men; namely, that a man's socio-political characteristics are strongly associated with his own class position, and that when this association is controlled for, any association between his class socio-political attributes and his wife's class position 'is weak, if, in fact, it exists at all'. This side of the argument is largely undisputed – both proponents and critics of the conventional approach would expect a man's class characteristics to be dominated by his own rather than his partner's class – and for this reason we direct our attention in this analysis towards the more controversial case of partnered women.

3 See Marshall et al. (1988: 67, 71–2) and, more generally, Jackman and Jackman (1983: 140–52), Felson and Knoke (1974), Rossi et al. (1974) and Hodge and Treiman (1968).

4 When several social surveys are combined in this way, this raises the issue of compatibility of responses across the various studies. We have therefore investigated the validity of pooling these surveys and find no significant interaction effects across the studies. Further details concerning questionnaire design and administration, sampling, and other technical aspects of the British Social Justice Survey will be found in Kluegel et al. (1995). For technical details of the British General Election Surveys see Heath et al. (1991b).

5 Class of first employment was not available in the 1992 British General Election Survey. The result shown in the table therefore refers only to females included in the other two surveys.

6 In the case of voting, the table shows the results of modelling the chances of voting Labour rather than Liberal Democrat or Conservative considered together, since logistic regression methods are appropriate for dichotomous response variables. We have however repeated the analysis, taking Liberal Democrat versus Conservative voting as the dependent variable, and find a pattern of class effects which, as one would expect from the results shown in Table 8.1, is less pronounced. Note also that the election surveys record voting behaviour at their respective general elections. The British Social Justice Survey inquired as to voting intention 'if there were a general election tomorrow'.

7 This finding holds true whether one considers a woman's current or first employment, although for ease of presentation, only the results for the former are included in Table 8.3a.

8 It should be noted that this finding is not necessarily generalizable to other nation states. For a ten-country comparative analysis of asymmetry effects (but one which does not pursue the issue of intergenerational class processes) see Marshall et al., Chapter 5 in this volume.

Part IV
SOCIAL JUSTICE

9

Social Class and Social Justice*

What is the relation between social class and social justice? Few would deny that the distribution of rewards in Britain displays a marked inequality of outcome. But, while some maintain that unequal outcomes reflect unequal opportunities, others insist that existing inequalities are the hallmark of a meritocracy. From the former point of view, class advantage testifies to social injustice; from the latter, social class and social justice are wholly compatible.

In this chapter we examine alternative conceptions of distributive justice in the light of social mobility outcomes and patterns of educational attainment in modern Britain. The data are taken from a national random sample of individuals interviewed during the mid 1980s as part of the Essex Class Project. Our analysis suggests that, even when educational attainment is held constant, class of origin effects are apparent in class destinations. Most noticeably, among individuals having modest or no educational credentials, those from relatively privileged class backgrounds are less likely to arrive at working-class destinations than are similarly qualified men and women from disadvantaged class backgrounds. In other words class privilege offers at least some protection against educational failure. Moreover, a gender effect is also obvious, since women tend to fare worse than their male class and educational peers.

We argue that this evidence undermines the claim that the class structure of Britain can be justified as meritocratic or as consistent with equality of opportunity for all. Class background influences a person's opportunity to achieve or maintain an advantaged position over and above its effects on his or her educational attainments. This is not surprising, since those from relatively advantaged backgrounds are more likely to have access to resources other than educational achievement, which can serve to protect them from the consequences of educational failure. It suggests that the attempt to justify inequality of outcome as consistent with meritocracy is sociologically naive since it ignores the ways in which the former militates against the achievement of the latter. Only by political intervention to ensure that the allocation of individuals to occupations is strictly meritocratic can the two be rendered compatible. Our conclusion is that the class structure of this country remains an obstacle along the path towards distributive justice – even if this is understood in terms of limited conceptions such as equality of opportunity with reward proportional to desert or merit.

What is class and how might class be just?

What is meant by social class? For the purposes of the present investigation we attempt to foreclose discussion of this contested concept by referring throughout to the class categories devised by John Goldthorpe and his colleagues for the Oxford Social Mobility Project during the mid 1970s.[1] This particular approach to class analysis has of course been subject to a number of criticisms. However, despite the controversy surrounding Goldthorpe's work, the most important feature of his class schema – its distinction between more and less privileged market and work situations – has in fact been widely endorsed. No one has seriously disputed his claim that the incomes, economic security, chances of advancement, authority and autonomy attached to service-class occupations are typically greater than those pertaining to intermediate occupations, which in turn are characteristically superior to those found among the working class (Goldthorpe, 1980: 39). Indeed, empirical investigation of the actual market and work situation of respondents to the Essex study confirmed that this was the case, and that the indicators used by Goldthorpe himself offered generally reliable measurement of the theoretical dimensions underlying his scheme.[2] From the point of view of the present analysis this is all that matters: the Goldthorpe categories reflect real differences in the distribution of desirable goods and attributes accruing to occupational roles. We shall call these categories social classes.

How then may we define social justice? Here things are rather more complicated. Philosophers and political theorists have articulated numerous conceptions of justice and endorsed a wide range of distributive principles. We do not seek to defend any particular formulation. It is sufficient for our purposes simply to note that, among the variety of principles advanced in this way, those of desert, merit, entitlement, equality of outcome, equality of opportunity, and functional inequality would seem to be most relevant to the topic of social class.[3]

These principles have been combined in complex ways, both in particular political ideologies and in the writings of academic political theorists. Socialists are generally thought to place particular emphasis on need and equality of outcome, but it is well known that Marx considered the desert-oriented distributive principle 'to each according to his labour' as appropriate to the first or lower stage of socialism, to be superseded by the maxim 'to each according to his need' only in a second or higher stage. Liberals tend to endorse the value of equality of opportunity, with inequalities of outcome deemed legitimate if they reflect differences in merit, but cannot agree about the conditions that are necessary to ensure equality of opportunity or about what constitutes merit. Some liberals hold a more extreme libertarian position (often confused in popular terminology with conservatism), and argue both that people are entitled to do as they choose with whatever resources they have acquired legitimately, and that this is more important than equality of opportunity. Old-style conservatives tend simply to regard hierarchy as a good thing, either because inequality is a necessary prerequisite of culture and civilized values, or because they respect tradition and inequality is traditional. From this point of view all talk of the principles of social justice, and perhaps even the notion of social justice itself, is inappropriately rationalist in tenor.[4]

Given such complexity, it is wise to eschew labels, since these merely simplify in such a way as to invite confusion. Rather, we will identify directly the particular issues which emerge in relating social justice to inequality, as manifest in the form of social class. How might a class structure understood in the way outlined above be defended as just? Since the existence of such a structure implies the unequal distribution of power and advantage, it would seem that any understanding of justice as equality of outcome must rule out the possibility of a just class society, and clearly much opposition to class has derived from such an understanding. But other principles of justice, which may be regarded as serving precisely to provide criteria by which one may justify inequalities of outcome, offer more promising alternatives. Four such principles can be identified. The unequal distribution of power and advantage embodied in a class structure might be deemed just if it reflected differential desert or merit; or represented the distribution of holdings to which people were legitimately entitled; or was an outcome derived from a situation of initial equality of opportunity; or was functional, either for all members of society, or specifically for the worst off. Let us consider each of these in turn.

The idea that unequal distribution might be legitimate because people deserve or merit unequal rewards has a great deal of intuitive appeal. If justice consists in giving people their due, and those dues are different, then justice seems clearly to require unequal outcomes. However, this approach does raise the question of what it is that constitutes bases of desert or merit, and which qualities of individuals it would be just to reward. A central issue here would seem to be the distinction between those attributes for which the individual can claim responsibility and those which are his or hers merely by chance. If it is the case that I possess particular talents or skills merely as a result of the natural lottery then it is by no means clear that justice is served by rewarding such possession. On the other hand, if I work hard and choose to attend evening classes to obtain qualifications, then it seems that I am indeed more deserving than someone who does neither. Matters are further complicated if one believes, as for example does John Rawls (1972: 310–15), that the ability to work hard is itself a chance attribute and thus an improper basis for reward. In any case, the point is that the defence of class inequality in terms of the principles of merit or desert would have to show that the class structure reflected morally relevant differences between individuals, not just any differences whatsoever.

The idea that inequality might be just because people are entitled to unequal resources can be distinguished from the previous approach because it is possible to hold that people are entitled to certain goods without in any sense deserving them. Robert Nozick (1980: 160–4, 224–7) most clearly and systematically articulates this view. He maintains that, even if one accepts each individual's natural assets as arbitrary in that they cannot be said to deserve them, people are still entitled to the fruits of these assets and to whatever else other people freely choose to give them. Gary Lineker may not deserve the millions he makes from his soccer skills because he did not deserve the skills, but if people choose to pay to watch him, and what they pay to do so was justly acquired by them in the first place, then Lineker is entitled to those millions, and the state acts unjustly in demanding a share of his wealth for redistributive purposes. Here we see a libertarian emphasis on property rights and freedom of choice which is quite different from the idea that people should get what they deserve. If a millionaire chooses to bequeath his money to an untalented layabout then justice as entitlement demands that he be permitted to do so, and forbids taxation of the inheritance, despite the fact that any normal conception of justice as desert or merit is here clearly violated. Desert-based conceptions of justice are, in Nozick's terms, 'patterned' and necessarily conflict with those free exchanges and just transfers which justify an individual's entitlement to resources.

Contemporary thinkers of the new right tend to conflate the principles of entitlement and desert. This is obvious, for example, in their defence of the market as a distributive mechanism. On the one hand, the market is praised because people get out what they put in, with hard work and entrepreneurial skill being particularly rewarded. On the other hand the market is also thought to give people freedom of choice. Quite apart from questions about what exactly it is that the market does reward, and precisely what choices it does leave people free to make, the point is that these are quite different defences which are here being confused. Academic political theorists – though not politicians – have acknowledged the ways in which these different principles can conflict. This is true of Nozick himself, not only with regard to the difference between entitlement and desert, but also in respect of the potential contradiction between entitlement and equality of opportunity.

The principle of equality of opportunity is in any case open to a variety of interpretations. Does it demand that, however unequal their abilities, people should be equally empowered to achieve their desired goals? This would imply that the unmusical individual who wants to be a concert pianist should receive a great deal more training than the child prodigy. Should people have equal resources to devote to their life-plans – irrespective of their abilities? Or, less drastically, does this principle merely require that people with the same abilities should have equal opportunities to achieve their desired goals – an interpretation which is consistent with the idea that the talented should have more opportunities than the untalented? Nozick's point (1980: 255) is that, however we understand the principle of equality of opportunity, it is clearly at odds with the idea of justice as entitlement. This is most obvious where rights of bequest and inheritance are concerned. Is the class system to be justified as consistent with equality of opportunity or with justice as entitlement?

Friedrich Hayek is another theorist who recognizes the inadequacy of certain contemporary defences of those inequalities produced by the market. His critique points to our fourth and final justification of inequality. For Hayek, it is clear that one cannot justify market outcomes as reflecting merit or desert, for luck plays too large a role in determining who gets what. Fortunately, however, the fact that such outcomes are unintended and unforeseen aggregate consequences means that they are not the kind of thing which it is appropriate to regard as just or unjust. Indeed, the whole idea of social justice is a 'mirage', which requires us to make the mistake of seeing society as an agent. Interestingly, Hayek (1976: 64, 74) thinks that the defence of market outcomes at the level of the general public rests upon the erroneous belief that such outcomes reward merit, and he suggests that such a belief is necessary if people are to tolerate the inequalities that the market produces. However, his own justification of the market mechanism is quite different, and points instead to its alleged efficiency. For Hayek, inequality is justified because it is functional, and works to the advantage even of those who have least:

> Productivity is high because incomes are unequally divided and thereby the use of scarce resources is directed and limited to where they bring the highest return. Thanks to this unequal distribution the poor get in a competitive market economy more than they would get in a centrally directed system. (1978: 67)

Sociologists will of course be reminded here of functionalist explanations of stratification.

The connections between efficiency and justice (two axioms which may seem antithetical rather than complementary) are best illustrated in the writings of John Rawls. His famous 'difference principle' asserts that inequalities are justified only if they serve to increase the advantage of the least favoured group in society. What makes this a principle of justice is the idea that justice consists in considering society from an impartial standpoint, in Rawls's case from an 'original position' in which agreement is reached by hypothetical people deprived of information about their talents and attributes, behind a 'veil of ignorance'. According to Rawls, people constrained in this way to choose impartially would be concerned to maximize the well-being of the least advantaged members of society, lest they themselves fall into that group. In other words, they will agree to permit inequalities, but only if they contribute to the welfare of the poor. The functional theory of stratification thus becomes a principle of justice via the additional claim that justice requires us to give priority to the most disadvantaged members of society.

This attempt to reconcile inequality with justice is distinct from those considered above since there is no suggestion here that people deserve their advantages. Nor are they entitled to whatever resources people choose freely to give them: the restriction on inequalities precisely rules out many of those that Nozick would permit. The relationship to equality of opportunity is more complex, since it is possible to argue for equality of opportunity on the grounds that it is necessary to an efficient allocation of resources, rather than because it rewards merit or gives people what they deserve. For example, replying to the charge that it is absurd to describe as fair a competition between individuals unequally endowed with those attributes necessary for success, Simon Green has argued that

> There is nothing unfair about a competition between any number of individuals in which one wins and others lose solely due to the impact of genetically endowed talent if (and only if) the competition is conceived as a source of information about the respective abilities of each competitor. If that information is subsequently used to the benefit of all competitors then the competition is not only useful, but also justified. (1988: 7)

It would be a mistake to regard those who win the competition as morally superior to those who lose, but we are none the less justified in giving them a greater share of resources, because otherwise we fall foul of the problem of concealment. What incentive will people have to reveal their talents if there is no reward for exercising them? Or, as Green (1988: 9) puts it, 'to induce an individual to reveal his talents it will be necessary to offer incentives which will – in effect – represent rewards for gratuitous endowments.' Equality of opportunity is important because without it we are deprived of the social benefits that would result from the exercise of those talents that have not had equal opportunity to compete.

Green therefore defends the idea that people should have equal opportunities to compete for unequal rewards as being consistent with the view that we do not deserve our talents or what we get from them. While it would be possible to reward people for their morally worthy efforts, rather than their arbitrary abilities, the result would be absurdly inefficient and in some cases dangerous. Inequalities are justified, not because they are deserved but because they are essential to overcoming the problem of concealment, while equality of opportunity is necessary to ensure that society benefits from the talents of all its members. The goal is meritocracy, but meritocracy is valued because we all benefit if people are doing what they do best, not because meritocracy gives each person his or her due.

This defence of inequality of outcome with equality of opportunity as together consistent with social justice raises, in rather sharper form, some of the same issues as the functionalist account of stratification. What theory of motivation is presupposed by this kind of approach? On the one hand, this is a theory for those who are motivated by a sense of justice, here understood as a concern for the well-being of the least privileged members of society. It is this concern that justifies otherwise undeserved inequalities on the grounds of efficiency. But, if people are concerned to promote the well-being of the poor, why do they need incentives to reveal and employ their talents optimally? The logic is somewhat contradictory since this is an argument for altruists which assumes that people are self-interested. Perhaps, however, we might distinguish between two kinds of inequality that could be justified in this way; namely, those that are intrinsically necessary, and those that are necessary on motivational grounds. Among the former might be inequalities of authority, power and expertise, considered functional for efficient organization and management. The latter would comprise those rewards deemed necessary to induce people to take up such positions. The justification of the latter, but not of the former, is dependent upon a particular view of human motivation as necessarily self-interested. It is interesting in this regard to note that Goldthorpe's class scheme seeks to group together occupations on the basis of a combination of both market situation and work situation. If we can equate the former with the point about motivation, and the latter with the more fundamental technical exigencies of production, then we can see that these two aspects of the class system might be differentially related to particular conceptions of justice.

But it is not our purpose here to assess the relative merits of these different attempts to reconcile social inequality with social justice. We wish only to point out that they are indeed different. For what we find in most non-philosophical attempts to justify inequality is a combination of arguments from desert, merit, entitlement, equality of opportunity and functionalism, with no clear recognition that these may involve different, and in some cases mutually incompatible, assumptions. On the one hand, there is nothing wrong with people climbing the social ladder providing they do so through their own efforts, while on the other they are entitled to pass their advantage on to their children. Unequal outcomes are justified simultaneously on the grounds that they are needed to give people incentives, and so contribute to social justice by helping the poor, and because they give individuals what they deserve. Conceptions of justice that legitimize some forms of inequality may undermine others. We should not allow those who quite rightly point out that justice does not necessarily require equality of outcome themselves to blur important distinctions.

Social mobility and social justice

This last point can readily be illustrated by reference to the debate about the publications of the Essex Class Project. In their monograph (Marshall et al., 1988: ch.6), the Essex team report that 70 per cent of those interviewed perceived the distribution of income and wealth in Britain to be unfair, with most people expressing a preference for a redistribution in favour of the relatively deprived. One interesting aspect of the findings is that similar proportions within each social class support a more equal distribution of rewards. Even among those in privileged class positions, a majority felt the distribution of wealth to be unjust, and endorsed a more egalitarian outcome. Marshall and his colleagues also maintained that class was the most common source of social identity among their respondents, with 90 per cent able to place themselves in class terms, almost three-quarters describing class as an inevitable feature of modern society, and a similar proportion stating that they thought it hard for a person to move from one social class to another.

These common-sense perceptions are consistent with the mobility data themselves. This is not to deny that the Essex researchers found substantial net upward social mobility among their interviewees. For example, of those men in top Goldthorpe service-class (class I) locations, fully one-third were from working-class backgrounds. More than 20 per cent of men from working-class origins had achieved service-class destinations. However, these figures make no allowance for changes in the occupational structure itself, notably the expansion of skilled white-collar jobs associated with the move from a manufacturing to a service economy. Marshall and his colleagues therefore argued that the 'room at the top' created by the transformation in the occupational division of labour had not, in fact, been accompanied by greater equality in the chances of advancement. Calculating the odds ratios for different mobility trajectories, and then inspecting these across age cohorts, they observe that the chances of a man from a service-class background securing service-class rather than working-class employment are more than seven times greater than those of a man from working-class origins – and that these relative chances have remained the same over successive mobility cohorts. A similar pattern is evident among women.

The contrast between absolute and relative mobility rates is essentially the difference between total numbers and proportions. Although many men and women from working-class origins have been upwardly socially mobile, the more privileged social classes remain proportionately more successful in using their advantages to prevent downward mobility among their off-spring, so that the overall association between an individual's class of origin and his or her class destination is remarkably stable throughout most of the present century. In other words the degree of 'openness' or 'fluidity' in the structure has been more or less constant. In consequence, the Essex researchers conclude that 'the post-war project of creating in Britain a more open society, through economic expansion, educational reform and egalitarian social policies, has signally failed to secure its objective' (Marshall et al., 1988: 138). Social class – and therefore social injustice – is seen to be a pervasive feature of life in this country.

Critics espousing alternative conceptions of justice were quick to challenge this interpretation of the evidence. Peter Saunders (1989a; 1989b; 1990a) has mounted the most systematic attack. He registers three objections to the Essex study. The first is that the particular question posed in the survey – 'Do you think the distribution of income and wealth in

Britain is fair?' – implicitly endorses an egalitarian and thus, as he would see it, socialist view of justice. Why is it, Saunders asks, that Marshall and his colleagues did not field questions premised on different conceptions of justice? Saunders himself does not frame these, but since he rehearses the arguments of Hayek and Nozick at length, clearly has in mind items concerning (for example) the entitlement of individuals to retain goods legitimately acquired, the justice of those who work hardest deserving the greatest rewards, and the market as an efficient distributive mechanism. Saunders also objects to the notion of relative mobility, describing it as an attempt to 'move the goalposts' in the face of absolute mobility figures which suggest that the class system is less rigid than was hitherto supposed. The resolute commitment of the Essex team to odds ratios and relativities overlooks the fact that, although capitalism is premised on inequality, it is also a dynamic system from which everyone benefits through economic expansion. The military metaphor of the 'forward moving column' is appropriate, though avoided by Marshall and his associates, since their focus is exclusively on equality of outcome. Finally, Saunders offers a rather technical criticism of the argument that social class is a 'basic social identity' in modern Britain, maintaining instead that this finding is an artefact of survey methodology. Respondents to the Essex study were allegedly 'bombarded with questions about class right from the start of the interview', so it is hardly surprising that they subsequently described both themselves and their society in class terms.

Marshall and Rose (1989; 1990) have replied to these detailed criticisms elsewhere. But neither they, nor the team responsible for the Oxford Social Mobility Project (which has attracted similar comment), have pursued Saunders's underlying objection to their approach to class analysis in general; namely, that 'to show that a society is unequal is by no means the same as showing that it is unfair'. The whole mobility paradigm rests, according to Saunders (1990a: 51, 81–3), on the mistaken assumption that everybody has the same abilities and aptitudes. Class analysts tend therefore to compare actual patterns of mobility with a norm according to which social origins have no effect on destinations. This criterion of perfect openness 'assumes that genetic or natural advantages (including factors like differential parental support and encouragement) either do not exist or are randomly distributed between different social strata'. It is an ideal which does not admit of the possibility that talents are unequally distributed, with the most gifted people tending to rise to the highest social positions, and then passing on some of their genetic advantages to their children.

We are not qualified to pursue the biological aspects of this argument. But it is not clear to us why the question – 'Do you think that the distribution of income and wealth is fair?' – should be thought to be biased in favour of a Rawlsian rather than a Nozickian conception of justice. Presumably respondents committed to an entitlement-based, or even a desert-based conception can answer this question as well as anybody else. It may be that Saunders is objecting to the emphasis on the term 'fairness' as opposed to, say, 'entitlement' or 'desert', but in that case it is odd that he formulates his own claim in terms which argue that inequality can be *fair* rather than rejecting the concept altogether. Alternatively, he may see the question as containing an implicit bias in favour of patterned or 'end state' conceptions of justice, but this again would seem to be unwarranted since it is perfectly open to a respondent to object to a particular distribution on the grounds that it was not arrived at in a procedurally just way. Finally, and more generally, Saunders seems to conflate precisely the different kinds of justifications of inequality that it seems to us important to distinguish. On the one hand, inequality is defended on the Hayekian, and of course Rawlsian, grounds that it promotes productivity and serves to advantage everybody over time; on the other, it is defended because it gives people what they are entitled to, or (something else again) reflects the fact that people deserve differently. These justifications may coincide, as for instance where people freely give resources (to which they are entitled) to others who have particular talents (which they deserve) and in so doing promote the long-run well-being of the least advantaged, but they need not necessarily do so.

However, these points notwithstanding, Saunders is of course quite correct to say that inequality *per se* is not necessarily unjust. Indeed it has been our concern to indicate the variety of ways in which this might be the case. In the remainder of this chapter, therefore, we focus on that strand of justification which seems to be dominant in his argument; namely, the suggestion that different rates of mobility across classes reflect an unequal distribution of justice-relevant talents and abilities, and that it is inappropriate or biased to premise one's analysis on the assumption that such advantages are randomly distributed throughout the population.

It is true also that class analysts have been reluctant to grasp this nettle firmly. The history of the Oxford Social Mobility Project itself illustrates the problem. Following the division of labour within this project, the task of analysing the association between class origins and class destinations fell principally to John Goldthorpe, who duly published his findings as *Social Mobility and Class Structure in Modern Britain* (1980). The results show the same seeming paradox of increasing rates of absolute mobility, combined with constant relative mobility chances, as were later to be reported by the Essex team on the basis of their own survey. Goldthorpe makes no mention of the impact of education on mobility regimes. The data on education were scrutinized instead by A.H. Halsey, Anthony Heath and John Ridge. Their analysis, as reported in *Origins and Destinations* (1980), concentrates on the relationship between the social origins and educational destinations of the adult men in the Oxford sample. This volume offers convincing evidence that the pattern of educational achievement is much influenced by the structure of the educational system itself. The workings of the 'tri-partite' system, persistence of the private sector, and practice of 'streaming' within comprehensive schools all function to perpetuate class differences in attainment, even among children of equal ability. Typical, for example, is the finding that

> among pupils with identical social backgrounds and family climates, those with superior measured intelligence have chances of getting to a selective school which are not greatly better than those of lesser-ability pupils. Conversely, among pupils of identical measured ability, social origin is a good discriminator of pupils' chances of getting to selective schools. (Halsey et al., 1980: 163; see also Heath and Clifford, 1990)

The likelihood of getting some kind of selective secondary schooling is roughly three times greater among service-class children than among those from working-class backgrounds – an inequality of opportunity which has remained stable throughout the post-war period. Again, however, there is no attempt to relate educational to occupational outcomes.

These conclusions are controversial for a number of reasons, not least of which is that the analysis of the impact of social origins on educational achievement rests on estimates of the distribution of IQ scores among children from different class backgrounds, estimates which (as the authors themselves admit) are of questionable validity. However, more interesting from the present point of view is the fact that, in the division of academic labour between Goldthorpe and Halsey, responsibility for investigating the relationship between educational attainment, social origins, and class destinations seems to have been overlooked, at least in so far as one can judge from the subsequent publications. Thus, for example, Goldthorpe concludes from his study of social mobility that

> an enormous discrepancy emerges if one compares the chances of men whose fathers held higher-level service-class positions being themselves found in such positions rather than in working-class ones with the same relative chances of men who are of working-class origins. Where inequalities in class chances of this magnitude can be displayed, the presumption must be, we believe, that to a substantial extent they do reflect inequalities of opportunity that are rooted in the class structure, and are not simply the outcome of the differential 'take-up' of opportunities by individuals with differing genetic, moral, or other endowments that do not derive from their class position. (1980: 252)

But, as critics such as Saunders have been quick to point out, this is merely a presumption. It could equally well be the case that the abilities and motivations of those who are upwardly mobile are simply different from those left behind. For example, children from middle-class backgrounds may receive greater parental encouragement to do well, and so perform better than their working-class peers in terms of both educational and occupational achievement.

Halsey, Heath and Ridge have in fact made separate attempts to link the findings from the educational side of the Oxford project to Goldthorpe's conclusions about social mobility, but with limited success from the point of view of resolving the argument about social class and social justice. For example, Halsey (1977) examined the relationship between father's education, father's occupation, son's education, son's first occupation and son's present occupation, and concluded that education both exerts an important independent influence on first job and acts as a crucial transmitter of the prior influence of social background throughout an occupational career. The direct effect of class origin on class destination is small, relative to that of education, although origins affect destinations indirectly via educational attainment. Is Britain therefore a meritocracy? Halsey argues that no such principle of justice links the occupational and education spheres:

> what has happened is the weighting of the dice of social opportunity according to class, and 'the game' is increasingly played through strategies of child rearing refereed by schools through their certifying arrangements . . . education is increasingly the mediator of the transmission of status between generations . . . education is the principal agent of achievement. But at the same time the institutional process over which it exercises increasing sway is just as importantly one in which ascriptive forces find ways of expressing themselves as 'achievement'. (1977: 184)

At this juncture, Halsey can point to the persistence of class differentials in access to certain types of schooling, and thus the seeming inequality in opportunities to gain credentials. However, for critics such as Saunders, these differentials merely testify to the unequal distribution of talent and effort. Clearly, middle-class children work harder, either because of their upbringing or because they are more able. This sort of political arithmetic is quite consistent with meritocratic theories of justice.

Similar objections can be raised against the analysis offered by Heath and Ridge (1983; see also Heath, 1981: chs 4 and 5), since it seems to demonstrate that privileged origins cannot protect men from the occupational consequences of educational failure, and conversely that working-class boys who gain educational credentials are likely to be upwardly mobile. Meritocratic theory aside, however, it is hard to see how these attempts to marry the Oxford findings about educational opportunity to Goldthorpe's data about the fluidity of mobility regimes can possibly succeed, since the partners to the union profess contradictory views about what the marriage should entail. Halsey, Heath and Ridge employ the so-called Hope-Goldthorpe categories as the basis for measuring occupational advancement, a process which they then attempt to model via a conventional path analysis of the relationships between the relevant class and educational variables. However, these analytical techniques are disowned by Goldthorpe himself: indeed, his whole research programme is designed specifically to discredit them.

The Hope-Goldthorpe classification is a social grading of occupations. The complex procedures by which this scheme was constructed need not detain us here. These involved a series of rating exercises in which members of the general public and professional experts were asked to rank occupations in terms of their 'social standing'. The results were scaled and a composite value was produced for each job. The crucial point to note is that the resulting classification purports to measure 'the "general desirability" of occupations, understood as a synthetic, emergent judgement from a specific population' (Goldthorpe and Hope, 1974: 132). It was designed in order to replicate in Britain the inquiry by Peter Blau and Dudley Duncan (1967) into the American occupational structure. These authors studied 'status attainment'; that is, the extent to which the occupational status of individuals is affected by their family of origin, education, race, and other attributes. Blau and Duncan conceptualized mobility as the movement of individuals up or down an occupational hierarchy arranged according to differences in the 'prestige' or 'social standing' of the various jobs.

Goldthorpe's own class analysis, on the other hand, rests on the premise that individuals are born into distinct 'social classes', membership of which tends to have important consequences for life-chances, values, and patterns of association. Classes, as we have seen, are defined by the criteria of 'market situation' and 'work situation'. Goldthorpe has stated (Goldthorpe and Bevan, 1977; Goldthorpe, 1985) that he rejected the earlier Hope-Goldthorpe scale in favour of the later Goldthorpe classes for two reasons. The first is that mobility data themselves militate against viewing occupational trajectories as embedded within a social continuum. There is a systematic patterning of intergenerational and career trajectories which casts doubt on the assumption that individuals are free to move up and down an ordered hierarchy according to their labour-market capacities. The evidence suggests, instead, a context of class structure. Secondly, the status attainment paradigm epitomized in the work of Duncan and his associates rests on undemonstrated assumptions about the social relationships of deference, acceptance, or derogation implied in socio-economic status scales; ignores the methodological difficulties caused by the composite or synthetic nature of these scales themselves; and is incapable of distinguishing adequately the various structural influences on mobility from those which originate in personal attributes. The mathematical techniques of loglinear modelling can isolate these influences, and so offer class analysts a method for analysing contingency tables which is as powerful as the path-analytic technique available to the status attainment school, without the requirement of ordinal data (and therefore prior assumptions) about a 'social hierarchy'.

Against this background, it is not difficult to see why the issue of social justice has tended to fall between the two stools of educational attainment on the one hand, and class analysis on the other. Discussion of the former typically occurs within the context of the status attainment paradigm. Class analysis in general – and European study of social mobility in particular – rejects both the conceptual framework and the research techniques of precisely that paradigm. On this issue we are inclined to side with Goldthorpe.[5] To take only the most obvious example, it is generally accepted that one of the socially and politically most significant mobility trajectories in recent Western history has taken large numbers of individuals from self-employed agricultural backgrounds to urban manual-employee destinations. It is hard to conceptualize this as a movement either 'up' or 'down' the class structure – far less scale it in terms of interval units in a continuous hierarchy of socially desirable occupations.

Is the British class structure meritocratic?

Our own approach, by comparison, is to address Saunders's meritocratic defence of inequality in terms that relate directly to social class, by examining the relationship between class trajectories and educational attainment. If people find their place in the occupational order according to meritocratic principles, then the impact of class background should not be apparent in class destinations, except as this is mediated by educational achievement.

The Essex survey suggests that this is not in fact the case. The data are shown in Table 9.1a. Social class is here recorded in terms of the collapsed Goldthorpe categories – service, intermediate, and working. The table reports intergenerational mobility experiences. Social background is indicated by the class of the respondent's chief childhood supporter when he or she was at the same age as the interviewee. Destination is the class of the respondent at the time of the interview. Educational attainment has been scaled as high, medium, or low. (The rating procedure is explained in the table.) Males and females are also distinguished and the results are given in both cross-tabular and loglinear form.

The contingency tables paint the picture in terms of outflow or class distribution, showing the amount and pattern of mobility experienced by men and women from the various social origins, controlling for educational attainment. Class of origin effects are evident in destinations. Among males, high educational achievement guarantees equal chances of entry into service-class occupations, irrespective of social background. However, at lower educational levels, service-class origins offer at least some protection against downward class mobility. Thus, for example, among men with middling credentials, 43 per cent of those with service-class backgrounds themselves achieve service-class destinations, with only 26 per cent downwardly mobile into the working class. The corresponding figures among men from working-class backgrounds are 15 and 48 per cent respectively. Similarly, 33 per cent of poorly qualified men from service-class homes arrive at service-class destinations, while 40 per cent are found in the working class. Among poorly qualified males from proletarian backgrounds the percentages are 11 and 64.

Class effects are also obvious among women. Indeed, even among highly educated females, those from service-class backgrounds are noticeably more likely to secure service-class occupations than are equally well-qualified women having origins in the working class. But gender effects are also apparent. Among highly educated men the service-class to service-class transition is accomplished by 92 per cent of respondents. Only 78 per cent of similarly qualified women succeed in this way. Similarly, the working-class to service-class trajectory is experienced by 91 per cent of highly credentialled men, but only 57 per cent of comparable women. Among respondents having middling and minimal credentials, women are less likely than men to be found in the service class and more likely to arrive at

Table 9.1 *Intergenerational mobility and educational attainment, Great Britain*

(a) Mobility trajectories (%)

Educational attainment	Origins	Male S	I	W	(N)	Female S	I	W	(N)	All S	I	W	
High	S	92	3	5	100 (38)	78	22	0	100 (27)	86	11	3	100
	I	90	5	5	100 (40)	63	35	2	100 (49)	75	21	3	100
	W	91	9	0	100 (32)	57	39	4	100 (23)	76	22	2	100
Medium	S	43	32	26	100 (47)	30	61	9	100 (23)	39	41	20	100
	I	31	41	29	100 (101)	22	63	16	100 (64)	27	49	24	100
	W	15	37	48	100 (110)	21	60	19	100 (78)	17	47	36	100
Low	S	33	27	40	100 (15)	0	57	43	100 (7)	23	36	41	100
	I	13	33	54	100 (92)	13	37	50	100 (46)	13	34	53	100
	W	11	25	64	100 (157)	2	43	56	100 (108)	7	33	60	100

(b) Loglinear analysis

Model		d.f.	G^2	p	rG^2	Δ
Origin, education, destination						
1	$O+E+D$	20	533.24	0.0000	–	26.39
2	$O+ED$	16	141.88	0.0000	73.4	13.74
3	$OE+ED$	12	30.16	0.0027	94.3	5.72
4	$OE+ED+OD$	8	4.26	0.8343	99.2	1.89
Origin, education, destination, sex						
1	$S+O+E+D$	46	650.39	0.0000	–	30.79
2	$S+O+ED$	42	253.68	0.0000	61.0	19.39
3	$S+OE+ED$	38	155.25	0.0000	76.1	13.51
4	$SOE+ED$	30	139.91	0.0000	78.5	14.09
5	$OE+SED$	30	70.54	0.0000	89.2	9.21
6	$SOE+SED$	24	59.44	0.0001	90.9	7.79
7	$SOE+SED+OD$	20	27.58	0.1194	95.8	4.81
8	$OE+SED+ODS$	20	30.44	0.0628	95.3	5.77
9	$SOE+ED+ODS$	20	38.84	0.0071	94.0	5.66
10	$SOE+SED+ODS$	16	23.57	0.0990	96.4	4.05

O = class of origin (S = service; I = intermediate; W = working).
D = class of destination (S = service; I = intermediate; W = working).
S = male, female.
E = educational attainment (low, medium, high). Low: holds no formal qualifications: CSE grades 2–5; or job training (e.g. HGV driving licence) only. Medium: holds CSE grade 1; GCE O or A level or Scottish equivalents; Overseas School Leaving Certificate; ONC, OND, City and Guilds; HNC, HND, City and Guilds; RSA clerical or commercial; or full apprenticeship qualification. High: holds teacher training qualification; full nursing qualification; other technical or business qualification; professional qualification; degree or higher degree; or other vocational qualification equivalent to a degree.
rG^2 = % reduction of G^2 achieved by new parameter.
Δ = % misclassified cases.

intermediate destinations, irrespective of social origins. Of course, there is nothing surprising in these figures, since we know from studies elsewhere that women are heavily concentrated in the routine clerical occupations that comprise Goldthorpe class III.

However, in a contingency table such as this it is difficult to identify all of the significant associations, and it is now standard practice to analyse these sorts of data using the established techniques of loglinear modelling. Table 9.1b shows the results of this exercise where the sex of respondents is both excluded and included as a variable in the analysis. Consider, first of all, the simpler case in which the data are collapsed over sex (upper panel). We can see clearly from the table that the meritocracy model (model 3), which posits that the association between class origins and destinations is mediated entirely through educational attainment, provides a rather poor fit to the data: $p = <0.01$ and almost 6 per cent of all cases are misclassified. When the OD parameter is fitted (model 4), the G^2 is reduced significantly, and the model provides a good fit to the observed data ($p = 0.83$). A reduction of more than 99 per cent of the G^2 for the baseline independence model is achieved and barely 2 per cent of cases are misclassified.

The existence of a significant direct association between class origins and destinations (the OD term) tells against the thesis of meritocracy, since the latter assumes perfect mobility conditional upon education, and therefore no direct origin–destination term in the model. Furthermore, inspection of the residuals under the meritocracy model shows that the misclassified cases deviate systematically in a way that tends to support our own view that class inequalities in Britain cannot easily be justified in meritocratic terms. For example, by far the largest residuals are found among men and women having medium-level educational qualifications, mainly (in terms of our scale) O levels and/or A levels but no significant higher education. At this middling level of educational attainment, individuals of service-class origins are over-represented in service-class destinations (observed $N = 27$, expected $N = 17$) and under-represented in working-class destinations (observed $N = 14$, expected $N = 20$). Conversely, similarly qualified men and women from working-class origins are under-represented in service-class destinations (observed $N = 32$, expected $N = 46$) and over-represented in working-class destinations (observed $N = 68$, expected $N = 54$). This suggests that it is harder to circumvent meritocratic principles, at least in so far as these are represented by occupational rewards for educational attainment, where educational credentials are either negligible or (at the other extreme) rather good. The greatest scope for deviating from meritocratic principles, thus interpreted, would seem to be where there is evidence of some (modest) educational attainment – evidence which is, presumably, open to varying interpretations, and seems to be of differing worth to different individuals, according to their class background.

There is nothing in the meritocracy literature about the influence of gender on the apportioning of rewards: the thesis of meritocracy is specifically addressed to the issue of class. In any event, however, partitioning the data according to sex does nothing to salvage the meritocratic case. As can be seen from the lower panel in Table 9.1b, the best-fitting model (model 7) fits the parameters $SOE+SED+OD$, and again it is not possible to achieve a satisfactory fit to the data without including a direct OD association. (Models 8 and 9 provide a clearly less good fit than model 7. Nor does the additional three-way interaction term ODS, in model 10, give a significant improvement – losing four degrees of freedom for a reduction in the G^2 of only 4.01.) The implication of model 7 accords well with theoretical expectations: compared with men, women tend to attain lower credentials, across all classes of origin (SOE). They also arrive at different destinations in the class structure, even where educational attainment is held constant, because of sex segregation and discrimination in the labour market (SED). Net of both of these effects, however, there is still an unmediated association between origins and destinations (which, as a comparison of models 7 and 10 shows, does not vary significantly by sex). In short, it is simply not possible to fit a meritocracy model to these data (whether or not they are collapsed over sex), since class origins can significantly affect class destinations, irrespective of educational attainments, and especially where these are middling.

Of course the analysis is not conclusive. It uses the collapsed Goldthorpe categories, rather than the more sensitive sevenfold classification, but the numbers in some of the cells are still rather small. Of more substantive theoretical import, the grouping of manifold educational qualifications into three levels is rather crude, and it may be that more of the variation in destination would be explained by education, and less attributable to origin alone, in a model which had a more nuanced approach to the measurement of education. If people from service-class origins are disproportionately achieving qualifications at the top end of our 'medium' category, for example, then it could be this properly meritocratic criterion which goes some way towards explaining their relative advantage in terms of destinations.

It is also of course the case that our model regards educational achievement as a proper indicator of merit. While this may seem uncontroversial, and certainly a great deal of the discussion of meritocracy (whether of a desert-based or functional kind) has assumed that it is education which ought to determine the allocation of individuals to occupational positions, it is nevertheless possible to argue that a person's educational achievement is only one aspect of merit among many. For example, it may be that the ability to work hard is something which is properly rewarded in occupational terms, but it is in principle distinct from the educational qualifications a person actually achieves. If one held that the ability to work hard was itself something quite separate from educational achievement, was sufficient to justify differential reward in meritocratic terms, and was differentially distributed across classes, then one might regard the effect of origin on destination net of education not as reflecting lack of meritocracy but as indicating the reward of an aspect of merit not captured by our model. Perhaps middle-class parents pass on to their children, whether genetically or environmentally, not only talents relevant to education (such as intelligence and motivation to achieve in school) but also talents directly relevant to occupation (such as the will to work hard more generally). In that case, a person of middle-class origins who fails in educational terms may still be more likely to 'merit' an advantaged destination than someone of working-class origins, and our unexplained direct effect may not tell against meritocracy broadly understood. It does seem to us, however, that the onus is on the meritocrats to show that the unmediated effect of origin on destination is consistent with meritocratic principles, and represents, say, intelligence or effort not reflected in educational credentials, rather than (as we would interpret it) the transmission of class advantages by particularistic means which cannot be justified in meritocratic terms.[6]

These caveats aside we do address squarely a particular conception of social justice which legitimates class inequalities on the grounds that they are reflections of differential merit. Investigating the extent to which intergenerational class trajectories are shaped by meritocratic principles, specifically the criterion of treating equal educational credentials equally, we find that, with respect to our indicators at least, equals are here treated unequally. It seems to be the case that, in modern Britain, class of origin and sex can, at least in some measure, undermine the meritocratic principle of equality of opportunity upon which some theories of justice seek to justify inequalities of outcome. People from different class origins have unequal chances, not only of educational but also of occupational success, despite taking actual credentials into consideration. In short, even if we accept the suggestion that unequal educational achievements reflect genuine differences in ability and talent across classes, and that justice requires that such differences be rewarded in class terms, we still cannot defend existing class inequalities as just.

Conclusion

The use of odds ratios as a technique for measuring the degree of openness in societies has generated considerable controversy. The virtue of describing social mobility in relative rather than absolute terms has, therefore, been widely disputed. Similarly, the constitution of social identities in advanced industrial societies remains a matter of debate, in particular the issue of how best to explore empirically the salience of class as compared with other collective loyalties. In both cases the disagreements are as much about matters of methodology as matters of fact.[7]

In our discussion of the relations between social class and social justice we have tried to avoid these larger disputes by pursuing a single substantive proposition advanced by critics of class analysis. Identifying a variety of ways in which one might seek to argue that class inequality was just –

because people deserve differentially, or because a process of free exchange may lead to unequal outcomes, or because it is consistent with people having equal opportunities, or because such inequality serves the long-term advantage of the least privileged – we focus on the particular claim that the association between origin and destination may reflect differences in ability and talent that are connected to class origins. Only on the assumption that the distribution of meritorious attributes was random with respect to class origin would one be licensed to infer that such association indicates a lack of equality of opportunity or meritocracy. Once we recognize that social justice may require that people be rewarded for their possession of such attributes, and that their possession may be associated with class origin, then we must acknowledge that justice – treating like cases alike – is entirely compatible with class-structured mobility regimes.

Our data suggest, however, that in the distribution of occupational rewards for educational attainment, equals may well be treated unequally. Class origins can compensate for educational failure and men tend to be favoured over women. Nor, the caveats outlined above aside, is there any reason to suppose that our results are merely artefactual. For example, those men who had started from service-class origins and arrived at service-class destinations despite their lack of educational attainment are not to be explained away as proprietors, a status which would nevertheless grant access to a privileged class standing. They are, instead, civil servants, office managers and general managers; all of whom left school at age 15 and without having obtained formal qualifications; none of whom have since passed any examinations or gained other recognized credentials. Our findings tend therefore to undermine the suggestion that Britain is an unequal but meritocratic and therefore essentially just society.[8]

We have already suggested that those concerned to legitimize class inequality need more carefully to distinguish between the various justifications that they tend to conflate. To say that people deserve their advantaged class position, or that they are entitled to it because it results from a process of free exchange, or that it reflects differences in talent and ability which need to be rewarded differentially if the economic system is to serve the advantage of all, is to say three quite different things. In another context we would argue further that it is only the last of these that provides a plausible ideal conception of justice: with Rawls, we find it hard to see that people deserve reward for attributes that are theirs as a result of genetic or environmental fortune, and against Nozick we would argue that what matters about individual freedom is not so intimately related to property rights and to freedom of exchange as to tell conclusively for an altogether historical and unpatterned conception of justice. So, in our view, if the class structure is to be defended as just it must be on the grounds that the inequalities which constitute it help, in the long run, the least advantaged members of society. The argument here, for unequal outcomes together with meritocracy or equality of opportunity, would be that both are needed to induce and allow people to utilize their talents in the socially optimal way. It would take empirical research of a quite different kind to address fully the issue of whether the class structure of modern Britain is consistent with this conception of justice. It is sufficient, in this context, simply to note that, for reasons which are well grounded in the substantive research conducted by sociologists and educationalists over the course of several decades, we are sceptical of the claim that differences in educational achievement altogether reflect differences in merit. To the contrary, there are good reasons for supposing that the education system acts as a mediator of advantage in an unjustifiable way, so that those most qualified are not necessarily those most able. Even if occupational outcomes did reflect educational achievements, as our data suggest they do not entirely, we would still be suspicious of the view that this indicated a meritocratic class structure.

Can the attempt to defend class inequality as consistent with social justice concede the empirical case and retreat to the claim that, while we do not yet have meritocracy, a combination of substantially unequal class positions and meritocratic procedures remains a coherent and viable goal? While in the ideal case it seems possible to imagine a society where a structure of unequal positions does not interfere with a strictly meritocratic allocation of individuals to places in that structure, we can surely read our results as supporting the suggestion that such an ideal is sociologically naive. As Frank Parkin puts it:

> Although the processes of rewarding and recruitment are analytically separable they are closely intertwined in the actual operation of the stratification system. This is to a large extent to do with the prominent part played by the family in 'placing' individuals at various points in the class hierarchy. There is a marked tendency for those who occupy relatively privileged positions to ensure that their own progeny are recruited into similar positions. (1972: 13–14)

The processes referred to by Parkin are not merely contingent, as if we could reasonably expect them to be otherwise, but rather reflect tendencies inherent in the social institutions of class and the family. Families enjoying an advantaged position in the class structure are concerned to transmit the advantage across generations, and the very fact of their advantage means that they will tend to have access to resources which facilitate such transmission. If children from advantaged backgrounds suffer educational failure, their class position makes it likely that they will be able to call upon other resources, perhaps most importantly in the form of class-related social networks, which can protect them from the consequences. The only way to counteract such social processes would be political intervention to ensure that the procedures whereby individuals are allocated to occupations are strictly meritocratic. Defenders of the claim that unequal outcomes can be just because compatible with equality of opportunity must recognize that, in the absence of such intervention, class inequality will tend rather to impede than to instantiate social justice.

Notes

* Gordon Marshall and Adam Swift. The authors wish to thank John H. Goldthorpe for his generous help in preparing this chapter.

1 For detailed discussion of Goldthorpe's approach to class analysis see Clark et al. (1990). See also Marshall et al., Chapter 4 in this volume.

2 See Marshall et al. (1988: ch. 4) and, for more recent independent analysis, Evans (1992; 1996a).

3 Campbell (1988) offers an overview of the extensive political and philosophical literature on social justice.

4 For a good account of the particular conceptions of justice developed within political ideologies see Goodwin (1987: ch. 13).

5 For a discussion of the status attainment paradigm in general, including the place of education as an explanatory variable in this research, see Matras (1980). On the competing European tradition of class mobility studies see Kurz and Müller (1987).

6 Although we are not here primarily concerned with the question of equality of opportunity as between the sexes, the following points arise by analogy with our discussion of class and meritocracy, and are worth noting. First, even if we suppose (for the sake of argument) that the differential distribution of educational attainment between men and women of similar class origins reflects differences in intelligence and motivation, still we cannot, by appeal to this supposition alone, defend the differential allocation of men and women to class destinations as meritocratic. The significance of the *SED* interaction term shows that there is an association between sex and destination even when we control for educational achievement. Second, it is of course possible to argue that the differential allocation of similarly qualified men and women to places in the class structure reflects aspects of 'merit' not picked up by educational qualifications. If men are more likely to work hard in their jobs, or less likely to leave their jobs (even temporarily, to raise a family) than are women with similar levels of education, then it might be claimed that their superior rewards in the labour market are indeed merited. We do not have space to pursue these thoughts here – and neither, of course, relates directly to our central finding that there is, for both men and women, an association between origins and destinations that is unmediated by education.

7 On odds ratios, and the respective merits of absolute and relative approaches to the study of social mobility, see Payne (1987a; 1987b). The debate about class identities, and in particular the arguments of the Essex Class Project, is pursued in the exchange between Pahl (1991), Crompton (1991) and Marshall (1991).

8 This conclusion is further substantiated by the more robust findings reported in Heath et al. (1991a). A manuscript copy of this article was kindly made available to us by its authors as the first published version of the present text was in press. Heath and his colleagues examine data from the General Household Survey, analysing the relationship between educational attainment (four categories), sex, Goldthorpe class origins and destinations. In general terms their findings simply reinforce our own. They conclude for example, that 'even among people with similar educational levels, those from service-class origins are more likely to be found in the service class themselves than are those from working-class origins. Britain is by no means a pure meritocracy.' Gender differences also persist, although a comparison of the 1973 and 1985 data-sets suggests that these are declining in importance. By comparison, changes in the direct effects of social origin on occupational attainment and in class relativities in general are both small, and in neither case reach statistical significance.

10

Was Communism Good for Social Justice? A Comparative Analysis of the Two Germanies*

One distinctive feature of David Lockwood's sociology is his emphasis on the comparative method. *Solidarity and Schism* (1992) is a clear endorsement of Durkheim's dictum that 'comparative sociology is not a particular branch of sociology; it is sociology itself, in so far as it ceases to be purely descriptive and aspires to account for facts' (1964: 139). In this chapter I endeavour to follow David's example by presenting a crossnational comparative analysis of class inequality in the former Federal and Democratic Republics of Germany. More specifically, I attempt to determine whether or not 50 years of communism increased equality of opportunity in East Germany, to a degree greater than that found in its capitalist sister-state to the west.

The German experience offers an unusual research opportunity to students of social stratification. Here was an advanced industrial nation, reduced almost literally to ruins by modern warfare, which was then rebuilt in separate parts according to distinctive socio-political blueprints. One, in the West, continued to follow the capitalist route to economic prosperity. The other, in the East, pursued a communist path in its search for social justice. Now, some 50 years later, the results can be examined in detail. In a strict sense this has not been a sociological experiment – but, at this macro level of system integration, it is probably as close to it as we in the discipline are ever likely to come. Certainly, we have been presented with an opportunity for comparative analysis of an especially rigorous kind, in which (to use Melvin Kohn's terminology) the nation state provides a context for investigating how social institutions operate under varying circumstances; and, in this particular case, the *ceteris paribus* clause describes an unusual situation in which – political regimes apart – most other things were at the outset indeed equal.[1]

My purpose is therefore rather modest. It is simply to determine whether or not one particular communist state delivered on its promise of creating a more open society. I will argue that the study of social mobility rates suggests little progress was made towards achieving this goal.

Equality of outcome and equality of opportunity

All communist regimes have experimented with a variety of systems of remuneration and distribution in the attempt to reduce inequalities of outcome or condition among citizens. One thinks here, for example, of early Russian drives towards the levelling of wages and benefits; of the short-lived hopes of substituting moral for material incentives in post-revolutionary Cuba; and of periodic (sometimes catastrophic) attempts in China to restructure the allocation of rewards without inducing either economic stagnation or administrative chaos. The long-term consequences of these and other initiatives have been debated at length. There is some evidence – though keenly disputed – that communist redistribution may have diminished inequalities of outcome, as these have historically been evident in the disposition of wealth, health care, housing and the like. However, the jury of international scholarship is still out on this issue, and I do not intend here to anticipate any decisions at which it may yet arrive.[2]

But the communists themselves never mistook egalitarianism for socialism. No less an authority than Stalin insisted that

> Equalitarianism owes its origin to the individual peasant type of mentality, the psychology of share and share alike, the psychology of primitive 'communism'. Equalitarianism has nothing in common with Marxist socialism. Only people who are unacquainted with Marxism can have the primitive notion that the Russian Bolsheviks want to pool all wealth and then share it out equally.[3]

In this respect, Stalin and others who wrote in similar vein were simply rehearsing the tenets formulated by Marx himself, who considered the desert-oriented principle of rewarding each 'according to his labour contribution' to be appropriate to the first or lower (and present) stage of socialism. This second-best criterion was to be superseded by the maxim 'to each according to his needs' only in a subsequent (and, in the event, never realized) higher stage.[4]

Perhaps ironically, therefore, appeals to social justice in later communist writings typically took the form of the liberal principle of increasing equality of opportunity to earn rewards proportionate to merit. Having conceded that inequalities of outcome, although perhaps diminished, would continue to be a necessary feature of socialist societies for the foreseeable future (at least if economic growth were to be secured), elites then offered the alternative argument that socialism nevertheless promoted distributive justice by giving people more equal access to unequally rewarded positions, in a society still (temporarily and regrettably) characterized by a hierarchy of offices carrying different levels of material advantage.[5]

As Walter Connor (1979: 25) has observed, most socialist societies were therefore characterized by an unresolved conflict between different conceptions of justice, evident in the policy disputes that separated those whom he describes as 'ideological egalitarians' from their 'pragmatic reformist' opponents. Examples abound, but one obvious illustration is provided by Soviet policy towards entry into higher education, which alternated between egalitarian and meritocratic initiatives. What we now call positive (or reverse) discrimination was often practised in the attempt to guarantee equal outcomes in the distribution of university places. Children of workers and peasants were compensated for cultural and other disadvantages by being awarded studentships irrespective of their educational achievements. At other times, performance in competitive examinations was the principal criterion of admission, and the concerns of individual merit were given priority over those of class preference. In this instance, as in other attempts to resolve the tensions between equality of outcome and equality of opportunity, most socialist governments pursued a middle course – 'retaining the promise of greater equality in the future, and claiming that much of it has been achieved, while citing the socialist performance principle as a contemporary guide to reward'.[6]

This tension is sometimes presented as a contrast between two types of mobility that are said to characterize actually existing socialism; namely, collective (or class) mobility and individual (or social) mobility. The former refers to what Wlodzimierz Wesolowski and Bogdan W. Mach (1986: 25, 27) describe as 'the collective mobility of the unprivileged classes'; that is, greater 'equality of condition', the principle supposedly governing state intervention in the process of distributing goods. Individual mobility, on the other hand, relates to 'mobility through qualifications and occupations [and] posits the creation of similar opportunities for achieving unequally rewarded positions. It derives from the pragmatic and reformist version of socialism or its meritocratic version.' As Wesolowski and Mach concede, Marxist sociologists have been loath to discuss equality of opportunity, on the grounds that Marx himself regarded this as a bourgeois ideal that was irrelevant to the classless communist societies of the future. However, as they also acknowledge, parity in the chances for individual social mobility was 'an important problematic' in the real socialist societies of Eastern Europe, especially since 'propaganda suggests that there has been a close approximation to the ideal of equal opportunities.'[7]

The meritocratic defence of social inequality under socialism is also a prominent theme in the sociological literature on stratification. For example, in their review of the history and functions of social mobility under real socialism, Wesolowski and Mach observe that

> During the first stage of a socialist regime, a stress on equality of positions as the main characteristic of the new order is of strategic importance for those in authority. Later a new problem confronts this type of regime. It consists in associating egalitarian promise with mobility through qualifications, in order to foster societal support for an inegalitarian, but meritocratic, system generating achievement motivation and capable of growing and innovating. (1986: 30)[8]

Like Connor, Wesolowski and Mach can see 'some unclarity' in the relationship between these two principles, since equality of opportunity points to individual occupational mobility (mainly through qualifications) while equality of conditions seems to call for collective mobility (secured by state intervention to redistribute resources).

Soviet and other socialist scholars of the post-Stalinist period therefore employed the language of class (or strata) and of class inequality (or differentiation) readily enough. But they steadfastly maintained that there were important differences in the degree of openness in class structures East and West. In particular the former offered far greater equality of opportunity than did the latter.[9] This assessment was based mainly on the evidence provided by some methodologically suspect studies in particular industrial enterprises, towns, or regions within the former Soviet Union. I have reviewed this rather disparate material elsewhere.[10] By comparison, a summary of the literature on intergenerational social mobility in the GDR is easily compiled, since there is none – or, at least, nothing that has been published or circulated in the West.[11] Most commentators have therefore remained open-minded about the relative inequalities of opportunity in the two Germanies.[12]

Of course, arguments have been proffered about the extent to which equality of opportunity was enhanced under communism or state socialism generally, and it is not unreasonable to suppose that these were intended also to apply to the GDR. On the one hand, for example, Frank Parkin (1972: 165) has referred to the 'relative openness' and 'high degree of social fluidity' of 'Soviet or socialist type societies', and concluded that 'mobility opportunities in Eastern Europe are more favourable than those in the West.' On the other hand, conclusions such as this tend to fly in the face of the most recent evidence, which suggests that the pattern of relative mobility chances (or degree of social fluidity) is basically the same across all industrial societies. For example, having examined the intergenerational social mobility data for a selection of both capitalist and state socialist societies, David B. Grusky and Robert M. Hauser (1984: 26) insist that their results 'make it quite clear that the cross-nationally common element heavily predominates over the cross-nationally variable one'. Similarly, and more recently still, Erikson and Goldthorpe (1992a: 389) have concluded that 'the total amount of the association between class origins and destinations that is cross-nationally variable is . . . only very small relative to the amount that is cross-nationally common.'

Against this background, the lack of reliable evidence for the GDR is particularly unfortunate, since that country provides a potentially critical test case. East Germany was the only state socialist society (with the possible other exception of the Czech lands within former Czechoslovakia) that was industrialized before communism was established. This is important, because many disputes about the relative openness of capitalist and state socialist societies hinge upon a disagreement about the extent to which rates of intergenerational social mobility under real socialism were a consequence of communist social policy, rather than of the industrialization process itself.[13] The GDR not only is exempt from this limitation but, as was suggested above, offers the additional bonus of a controlled comparison with the capitalist Federal Republic to the west.

The empirical issue to be confronted here is therefore straightforward enough. Were the former communist societies of Europe in fact more open than their Western capitalist counterparts? This is a question to which comparison of the two Germanies provides a particularly appropriate response.

Social mobility in the two Germanies

I attempt to answer this question using data collected as part of the International Social Justice Project (ISJP). The Federal and Democratic Republics of Germany were included in this study as separate countries about which information was collected by means of nationally representative random sample surveys of adults aged 18 or above. Interviews were conducted on a face-to-face basis by a professional survey organization during 1991. A response rate of 71 per cent was obtained in each study. This yielded 1,837 and 1,019 cases in the West and East respectively. The occupational data from these surveys were coded to the German employment status (*Berufstellungen*) and 1968 ISCO (International Standard Classification of Occupations) categories, to which specially designed algorithms were then applied, in order to generate Goldthorpe (CASMIN) class variables which were crossnationally comparable.

What does the analysis of our data in terms of these classes reveal? We begin with the distribution of origin and destination classes among respondents to the surveys (Table 10.1). In this table, the class distributions of males and females are given separately in terms of their own employment, and in relation to that of their fathers when respondents were aged 15.

It will be seen that, as might be expected, the marginal distributions are similar across the former nations. In the case of males, the proportion with class origins in the salariat is slightly higher in the West than the East (24 per cent as against 19), whereas the obverse is the case for those from skilled manual backgrounds (31 per cent and 34 per cent respectively). The latter pattern is also found among females. Among both sexes, and hardly surprisingly, somewhat higher proportions of West Germans have *petit bourgeois* origins. Turning to class destinations, we see that the differences between the two countries are greater, although here too they can hardly be described as pronounced. The percentage of respondents found in salariat destinations is higher among men in the West but among women in the East – although this latter finding is probably due more to the fact that we cannot separate the upper and lower elements of this class (classes I and II) than to any real differences in the class distributions of women East and West. (Women in both countries would tend be found in the lower rather than the upper salariat.) Women are also much more likely than are men to be found in routine clerical work and in unskilled (rather than skilled) manual occupations. Comparing the origin and destination distributions within countries, we find the expected sectoral shifts in favour of non-manual employment among West German men, although there has been no obvious corresponding tendency for the proportion involved in manual

Table 10.1   *Distribution of respondents by Goldthorpe class of origin and destination and by sex, and delta (dissimilarity index) values for origin and destination distributions, FRG and GDR*

(a) Class of origin (% by column)[1]

	Males		Females	
Goldthorpe class[2]	FRG	GDR	FRG	GDR
I+II	24	19	24	25
IIIa	8	7	11	9
IVa+IVb	11	9	14	8
IVc	10	12	9	10
V+VI	31	34	25	32
VIIa+IIIb	15	16	15	12
VIIb	2	2	2	5

(b) Class of destination (% by column)[1]

	Males		Females	
Goldthorpe class[2]	FRG	GDR	FRG	GDR
I+II	37	31	30	34
IIIa	12	7	30	22
IVa+IVb	8	6	5	4
IVc	2	4	1	4
V+VI	28	37	7	9
VIIa+IIIb	13	14	27	24
VIIb	1	2	1	4

(c) Deltas for origin and destination distributions, and pairwise comparison of nations

FRG: origins and destinations	males = 21	females = 37
GDR: origins and destinations	males = 14	females = 34
FRG: compared with GDR: origins	males = 7	females = 12
destinations	males = 13	females = 12
Males compared with females	FRG = 32	GDR = 30

[1] Percentages may not sum exactly because of rounding.
[2] Classes are salariat (I+II); routine clerical employees (IIIa); *petite bourgeoisie* (IVa+IVb); farmers and smallholders (IVc); skilled manual workers (V+VI); unskilled manual workers (VIIa+IIIb); agricultural workers (VIIb).

work to diminish among their counterparts in the East. The percentage of farmers and smallholders (class IVc) has declined in East and West alike.

The overall correspondence between the marginal distributions is evident in the low crossnational dissimilarity indices (deltas) shown in the table. For example, if the deltas for the sexes are calculated pairwise across the countries, the resulting values of 7 and 13 (for male origin and destination distributions respectively) are among the lowest found in any earlier

Table 10.2 *Decomposition of total mobility rates (TMR) into total vertical (TV) and total non-vertical (TNV) mobility, and of total vertical mobility into total upward (TU) and total downward (TD) mobility, by sex, FRG and GDR*

	TMR	TV	TNV	TV/TNV	TU	TD	TU/TD
Males							
FRG	63	50	13	3.8	34	16	2.1
GDR	70	56	14	4.0	37	19	1.9
Females							
FRG	75	56	19	2.9	29	27	1.1
GDR	72	55	17	3.2	30	25	1.2

analogous pairwise comparison of industrial nations (see Erikson and Goldthorpe, 1992a: 193). Interestingly enough, the male/female deltas within each country are also close, at 32 for the FRG and 30 in the case of the GDR. In other words, the degree of class differentiation by sex is both remarkably similar, given the different socio-political regimes of the two countries; and, in the case of East Germany, perhaps surprisingly high (since previous surveys tend to show that the current class distributions of men and women are more similar in state socialist societies than in those of the capitalist West). In this respect, at least, the GDR would seem to be rather more like the Federal Republic than like the other state-socialist countries of Eastern Europe – and the degree of employment segregation by sex in the former West Germany was high even by the standards of capitalist societies (see Erikson and Goldthorpe, 1992a: 243).

Similarly, if we then calculate the observed mobility rates for each country (Table 10.2), these too are markedly alike. In this table, we report total mobility rates (TMR), in turn divided into total vertical (TV) and total non-vertical (TNV) mobility. Vertical mobility is then partitioned further into total upward (TU) and total downward (TD) mobility. Among males, the vertical to non-vertical ratio is a little higher in the GDR, although the ratio of upward to downward mobility is marginally greater in the Federal Republic. In the case of women both ratios are somewhat higher for the East. But, in all cases, one is again talking here about slight differences in an overall pattern of results which is similar across the two former nation states.

Turning now to the models, one obvious issue can be clarified at the outset, if we compare the relative mobility chances among men and women under the different socio-political regimes. We can see, by returning to Table 10.1, that there are some differences between the sexes, in both countries, where individuals are treated in terms of their own employment experiences. In particular, women are more likely than are men to be found in routine clerical employment, and less likely to obtain skilled manual jobs. In other words, women's class destinations differ from those of men, because of widely recognized processes yielding sex segregation in labour markets.

Table 10.3 *Results of testing the model of common social fluidity against
data on intergenerational mobility for the sexes (individual's Goldthorpe
class determined by reference to own employment), FRG and GDR*

Model	G^2	d.f.	p	rG^2	delta	beta
FRG						
Independence: *OS+DS*	329.36	72	0.000	–	17.88	
CSF: *OS+DS+OD*	26.33	36	0.881	92.0	4.68	
UNIDIFF	26.16	35	0.860	92.1	4.65	ns
GDR						
Independence: *OS+DS*	152.49	72	0.000	–	13.56	
CSF: *OS+DS+OD*	33.49	36	0.589	78.0	5.98	
UNIDIFF	33.49	35	0.541	78.0	5.97	ns

O = class of origin, seven levels (see Table 10.1).
D = class of destination, seven levels (see Table 10.1).
S = sex.
G^2 = log likelihood ratio.
rG^2 = % reduction in G^2 achieved (treating the conditional independence model as a baseline).
delta = % misclassified cases.
beta = UNIDIFF parameter estimate; males set at zero; ns = not significant.

How do these processes affect relative class mobility chances? The
evidence shown in Table 10.3 suggests that they do not. Here I fit three
models to the data for class social mobility and sex. In both countries the
independence model (*OS+DS*) provides a poor fit to the data. Men and
women may be distributed to different class destinations but this does not
exhaust the relationships in our mobility tables. In fact a model of common
social fluidity (CSF) provides an adequate fit to the data for both parts of
Germany. This model allows for the associations in the independence
model but posits a further association between a person's class of origin
and his or her class destination (*OD*). That association is itself invariant
across the sexes. The interaction between a person's class origins, destinations, and sex (the *ODS* term in the model) is not significant and
therefore not required to obtain a satisfactory fit to the data.

Moreover, as the final set of results shows, Erikson and Goldthorpe's
(1992a: 90–2) UNIDIFF model does not improve significantly upon the fit
obtained by the generalized or global model of common social fluidity –
scarcely reducing the deviance (in the case of the GDR not at all) for the
sacrifice of the additional degree of freedom. Application of this more
stringent test does not therefore lead us to qualify our conclusion that
relative class mobility chances are the same for each sex within the two
countries. In substantive terms, this means that the pattern of relative
mobility rates (or social fluidity) underlying women's intergenerational
mobility is similar to that which characterizes men's mobility, so that the
same set of class-linked inequalities is evident among males and females
alike. This proposition holds true in both parts of formerly divided
Germany. In other words, while the raw mobility data confirm that the

position of women within the class structure is different from that of men, these differences in absolute rates are almost entirely attributable to differences in the marginal (destination) distributions in the tables. In other words, while sex segregation in the occupational structures of each country means that men and women tend to arrive at different destinations, class inequalities scarcely vary by sex.

These results neatly confirm Christel Lane's argument (1983: 490, 501) that, in the GDR, great progress was made towards providing women with 'the preconditions to make them equal to men in the labour market' – although perhaps not in the way she intended this claim to be taken. Lane may be correct when she suggests that *sexual* equality had advanced further in East Germany than in the more progressive capitalist societies, in the sense that females were not as widely discriminated against in terms of educational opportunities, were more likely to receive equal pay for equal work, and in general terms benefited from a centralized political system which 'made possible the relatively fast and rational redistribution of resources in favour of women'. But it is also true that, under communism, women in the GDR appear to have been treated equally alongside men in the sense that, and to the extent that, the degree of *class* inequality in mobility chances was as pronounced among females as it was among males. If East German women were liberated then they were free only to share in the same class-related inequalities of opportunity as were to be found among their male partners.[14]

The next question follows logically from the last. If relative mobility chances are the same for males and females within the two countries, how then do they compare in crossnational perspective? An appropriate way of exploring this issue is to fit a model of common social fluidity to each pair of mobility tables for the sexes. The results are shown in Table 10.4. Here one is testing the hypotheses that relative mobility rates are the same among men in the GDR and FRG and, likewise, the same among women.

In these tests, the independence model posits only an association between the distribution of class origins and each of the two nations (ON), and between the distribution of class destinations and nations (DN). In other words the marginal distributions are allowed to vary across the countries. This model, as expected, fits badly for both sexes. However, and again for both sexes, a model of common social fluidity provides an acceptable fit to the data. In the case of males, for example, this model returns a G^2 of 48 on 36 degrees of freedom, and misclassifies almost 7 per cent of cases ($p = 0.084$). Among females fewer than 6 per cent of individuals are wrongly classified by the model ($p = 0.593$). These figures represent improvements of some 82 per cent (for men) and 85 per cent (for women) on the simpler independence model. In other words, relative mobility chances were broadly similar in both parts of Germany, such that by far the largest part of the association between social background and class destinations in the two societies was common to both.

Table 10.4 *Results of testing the model of common social fluidity in the*
FRG and GDR by sex (individual's Goldthorpe class determined by
reference to own employment)

Model	G^2	d.f.	p	rG^2	delta	beta
Males						
Independence: *ON+DN*	261.02	72	0.000	–	16.39	
CSF: *ON+DN+OD*	48.18	36	0.084	81.5	6.80	
UNIDIFF	34.54	35	0.490	86.8	5.30	−0.7040
Females						
Independence: *ON+DN*	220.83	72	0.000	–	16.02	
CSF: *ON+DN+OD*	33.40	36	0.593	84.9	5.85	
UNIDIFF	26.55	35	0.847	88.0	5.33	−0.5408

O	= class of origin, seven levels (see Table 10.1).
D	= class of destination, seven levels (see Table 10.1).
N	= nation, two levels.
G^2	= log likelihood ratio.
rG^2	= % reduction in G^2 achieved (treating the conditional independence model as a baseline).
delta	= % misclassified cases.
beta	= UNIDIFF parameter estimate; FRG set at zero.

However, mobility chances were not literally identical in the East and
West, since (as will be seen from the table) the uniform difference
parameter offers a significant improvement on the more general model of
common social fluidity. Here, at last, we find some indication that communism enhanced equality of opportunities for mobility. The UNIDIFF
parameter estimate is not only significant but negative, indicating a
decrease in the odds ratios for the GDR compared with those for the
FRG, and therefore a somewhat increased level of overall social fluidity in
the East. It is important not to exaggerate this effect. More than four-
fifths of the association between origins and destinations in each society
was common to both. Nevertheless, by applying the fairly searching test
of the uniform difference model, it is just about possible to sustain the
argument that the political regime of the Democratic Republic did after
all secure systematically but *marginally* greater equality of opportunity
among men and women than did the democratic regime immediately to
the west.

Cohorts and the core model

This is probably as far as the analysis can be pushed using these data. A
more sophisticated treatment would require larger samples.

I have, for example, attempted to fit the CASMIN 'core model' to the
male mobility data for the GDR. This is a topological model that seeks
to capture a series of specific effects that are exerted on the pattern of
relative rates. Rather than postulate common social fluidity, Erikson and

Goldthorpe (1992a: chs 4 and 5) proposed a model embracing four effects that are predicted from sociological theory; namely, those of hierarchy, inheritance, sector and affinity. Unfortunately the GDR sample from the ISJP is simply too small to permit reliable analysis in these terms. The model returns a $G^2(S)$ – a log likelihood ratio statistic standardized on the size of the smallest sample in the CASMIN study – of 45.7 (the critical value of this measure is 40), delta=7.8, p=0.29. Only two of the eight parameter estimates for the effects in the model reach statistical significance; namely, those which relate to the generally increased propensity for individuals to be found in their class of origin rather than any other (*in1*), and a sectoral effect (*se*) that captures the enhanced probability of movements of an intrasectoral as against an intersectoral kind (especially in relation to the distinction between agricultural and non-agricultural class positions). However, all but two of the parameters estimated for the GDR are of the same sign as the crossnationally common parameters in the model, the exceptions being those for the *hi2* and *in2* terms. These anticipate respectively that long-range vertical mobility will be especially low, and that there will be a distinctively high degree of immobility within classes IVa+IVb (the *petite bourgeoisie*), IVc (farmers and smallholders), and I+II (the salariat).

If the data for the GDR and FRG are pooled, in effect creating a data-set for a unified Germany, the national variant of the CASMIN core model proposed by Erikson and Goldthorpe for the FRG provides an improved but still inadequate fit (G^2S is now 44, delta=4.1, p=0.11); all of the parameter estimates have the signs expected under the model; and three further effects reach or come close to the level of statistical significance. These are the *in2* and *hi2* terms themselves (which are now signed positively and negatively respectively, as in the CASMIN core model), and the *af1* term (which describes a disaffinity between the salariat and the class of agricultural workers). Only the *hi1*, *in3*, and *af2* terms fail to reach levels of statistical significance; that is, those effects proposing respectively a reduced probability of social mobility (*ceteris paribus*) where intergenerational crossing of lines of hierarchical division is involved; an especially high propensity towards father–son succession in farming; and a series of affinities that derive from specific continuities between classes (specifically the salariat and routine clerical classes, the two agricultural classes, and those where there is the greatest possibility of transferring capital between generations). The actual estimates are as follows (ns = not significant): *hi1* = ns; *hi2* = –0.42; *in1* = 0.32; *in2* = 1.25; *in3* = ns; *se* = –1.1; *af1* = –0.39; *af2* = ns (compare Erikson and Goldthorpe, 1992a: 147).

This can be taken only as weak evidence which does no more than hint that not only was the overall degree of social fluidity the same in both societies, but the pattern of relative mobility chances might also have been similar. Set in this context the CSF models must appear crude. Nevertheless, despite the relatively small numbers, there is no reason to believe that the principal findings here reported are unreliable.

Table 10.5 *Results of testing the model of common social fluidity in the
FRG and GDR by sex (individual's Goldthorpe class determined by
reference to own employment), with social class collapsed to three levels*

Model	G^2	d.f.	p	rG^2	delta	beta
Males						
Independence	90.95	8	0.000	–	12.16	
CSF	9.49	4	0.050	89.6	3.55	
UNIDIFF	1.16	3	0.767	98.7	1.33	–0.6787
Females						
Independence	78.80	8	0.000	–	11.32	
CSF	5.58	4	0.231	92.9	2.89	
UNIDIFF	3.37	3	0.338	95.7	2.45	ns

Class origin and class destination each have three levels: salariat (I+II), intermediate
(III+IV+V), and working (VI+VII). Details otherwise are as in Table 10.4.

For example, anyone worried about sparseness in the tables may be
reassured to learn that we can collapse the class categories from seven to
three, but this makes no substantive difference to the outcome. The same
basic pattern reappears in the results (see Table 10.5). That is to say, a
common social fluidity model fits adequately for both sexes, and the
uniform difference model then offers an improved fit – but one which is
now statistically significant for males only (since the simpler CSF model fits
so well among females). In other words, the mobility regimes in both parts
of Germany for both sexes were largely common, although – according
to the more sensitive criterion of the UNIDIFF model – there is some
evidence of systematic but only slightly greater equality of opportunity
(especially among men) in the East.

Similarly, if attention is concentrated on those individuals who were born
after the end of the Second World War, we again find essentially common
social fluidity across the two socio-political regimes (Table 10.6). These are
the respondents whose whole experience was exclusively of one system or
the other, and yet it is hard to find evidence that the Honecker generation
benefited from greater equality of opportunity than did those who lived
through the West German 'economic miracle', despite the declared communist policy of dismantling class barriers and extending opportunities for
talented individuals from less privileged backgrounds. Indeed, the
marginally increased fluidity earlier detected in East Germany (by the
UNIDIFF model) is largely invisible among those born in the GDR during
the communist period, although this is probably because the common
social fluidity models for males and females fit so well – itself, perhaps,
something of an artefact of the reduced numbers in the analysis (569 males
and 596 females distributed across 18 cells in each model).

It is possible, by looking at the residuals, to see where the data deviate
most from the CSF model. In the case of West German males, the model
of common social fluidity fitted in Table 10.4 underestimates the numbers

Table 10.6 *Results of testing the model of common social fluidity in the FRG and GDR by sex (individual's Goldthorpe class determined by reference to own employment), with social class collapsed to three levels, among respondents born in 1946 or later*

Model	G^2	d.f.	p	rG^2	delta	beta
Males						
Independence	30.63	8	0.000	–	9.84	
CSF	1.35	4	0.855	95.6	1.96	
UNIDIFF	0.42	3	0.933	98.6	0.89	ns
Females						
Independence	32.07	8	0.000	–	9.30	
CSF	1.76	4	0.783	94.5	2.23	
UNIDIFF	1.75	3	0.629	94.5	2.24	ns

Details as in Tables 10.4 and 10.5.

intergenerationally stable in the salariat (observed 108, expected 98), but overestimates those who will be downwardly mobile from the salariat to the skilled working class (observed 27, expected 33). Other residuals are smaller and show no obvious pattern. In the case of East Germany, intergenerational stability in the salariat is overestimated, whereas the obverse is the case in relation to downward mobility from the salariat to the skilled working class (observed 29 and 28, expected 39 and 21, respectively). Other discrepancies are smaller and again lack a general pattern.

In short, our analysis of the data from the ISJP suggests that the overall pattern of association between class origins and class destinations was similar in both parts of formerly divided Germany; and, furthermore, to the limited extent that this was not the case, then the discrepancy lay mainly in the fact that the propensity for long-range mobility was marginally greater under state socialism than under democratic capitalism. This is hardly surprising, given the intervention in higher education practised by socialist states, specifically the policy of sponsoring and promoting children from working-class and agricultural backgrounds, despite their relative failure in the competition for university places. But what is surely striking in all of this is that, despite its declared policy of facilitating long-range mobility into the salariat by opening up higher education to the sons and daughters of workers, the communist regime in East Germany made so little impact on the basic structure of unequal relative mobility chances between the various classes. Inequalities of opportunity were, despite half a century of determined communism, in effect diminished only at the margins.

The ideology of meritocratic socialism

This chapter started from the premise, concisely stated by Wesolowski and Mach, that 'individual and collective mobility, both as social benefaction and as a correlate of economic necessity, is part of the ideology of state socialism.' 'To read the newspapers,' they observe,

> is enough to realize that the problem of mobility is really important in Eastern European countries. Their communist parties consider social promotion, both for individuals and for groups, as one of the bigger blessings brought about by the new regime. The possibility of moving from the peasantry to the working class and from either of these to the highly qualified professions of the intelligentsia is ideologically construed as a way of evening out historical wrongs. (1986: 20–1)

The evidence bearing upon collective mobility – equality of outcome – is a matter of unresolved debate about which I have not ventured an opinion. However, if the above analysis of social fluidity is sound, then the most that can be claimed on behalf of state socialism in East Germany is that it promoted a marginal increase in equality of opportunity. Relative mobility chances for individuals in the former GDR were in fact basically the same as those to be found in capitalist West Germany.[15]

At this point I am reminded of Ferge's remarks about the gap between rhetoric and reality under actually existing socialism. 'It can happen,' she observes,

> that while the political declarations or the social policy decisions of a country are expressly committed to social change and to the reduction of inequalities, the *ex post facto* statistical and sociological analysis of facts shows a different tendency, with no change or even an increase in inequalities. Thus one must draw one's conclusions about the real balance of power and the interests served by it from these facts. (1979: 30)

My own conclusions about the facts of social mobility chances in the two Germanies are, I hope, evident enough. By way of closing remarks, however, it is interesting to consider the views of German respondents themselves, specifically with respect to these same issues of equality, opportunity and rewards. They provide an interesting coda to Ferge's declaration in favour of sociology as against ideology.

Consider, for example, the proportions in each country who agreed or disagreed with the various statements shown in Table 10.7. Again the data are taken from the ISJP surveys. The columns in the table report the percentage of those interviewed in the FRG and GDR who agreed with each item, minus the percentage who disagreed, together with the resulting difference between the two nations.[16] It is clear from the first item that neither set of interviewees was much inclined to support equality of outcome in the distribution of income and wealth. The pattern of responses to the next four items suggests that, by contrast, a substantial majority in both countries were in favour of equality of opportunity, and of a competition with unequal outcomes, so long as rewards were proportional to merit. Thus, as the last of these items demonstrates, differences in skill and intelligence were not commonly attributed to luck but seen instead as talents deserving of differential reward. In sum, the degree of support for broadly meritocratic principles of reward applied to a competition in which

Table 10.7 *Support for distribution principles and perceptions of inequality, FRG and GDR (%)*

	FRG	GDR	Difference
The fairest way of distributing wealth and income would be to give everyone equal shares	−37	−42	5
It's only fair if people have more money or wealth, but only if there are equal opportunities	72	70	2
People are entitled to keep what they have earned – even if this means some people will be wealthier than others	83	91	8
People who work hard deserve to earn more than those who do not	89	96	7
It is just luck if some people are more intelligent or skilful than others, so they don't deserve to earn more money	−27	−35	8
In [country] people have equal opportunities to get ahead	21	−35	56
In [country] people get rewarded for their efforts	56	1	55
In [country] people get rewarded for their intelligence and skills	66	27	39
Do you think you are paid much less than you deserve, somewhat less than you deserve, about what you deserve, somewhat more than you deserve, or much more than you deserve?	45	80	35[1]

[1] Percentages are of those who felt they were paid less than they deserved minus those who felt they were paid more.

all have equal chances to win is similar among East Germans and West Germans alike, as the final column in the table makes clear.

However, when we turn from the realm of moral principles to that of beliefs about the extent to which the existing distribution of rewards is in accordance with those principles, the differences between the two countries become pronounced. Respondents in the East, on being invited to comment upon life in the former GDR, were markedly more likely to describe a society in which people did not have equal opportunities to get ahead, were not rewarded for their efforts or talents, and therefore earned much less than they deserved, than were respondents in the West when asked to make the same assessments in relation to the former Federal Republic. East Germans perceived their society as one in which chances for advancement were unequal and the ensuing rewards for success unjustly distributed because undeserved. In other words, it is people's perceptions of what is the case that are here crossnationally divergent, rather than their conceptions of what constitutes social justice. The East German ideology of merito-cratic socialism seems to have reinforced popular support for broadly meritocratic principles, as applied to a competition in which all have equal opportunities, and so created expectations which were at odds with the reality of everyday life in the GDR itself.

It is not difficult to imagine why the popularly perceived gap between principle and practice became so pronounced. Meritocratic aspirations will have been raised to an unrealistic level by the rhetoric of enhanced social fluidity under communism. Meritocratic principles were openly flouted in the policies announcing positive discrimination on behalf of workers and peasants. There was also widespread public awareness of the covert and overt discrimination that was practised in favour of men, productive workers, and members of the Party. Be that as it may, it seems certain that in the context of state socialism, the perceived failure of the East German authorities to deliver on their promise of creating an open society will have exacerbated the already considerable problems of regime legitimation, since it was the state itself that took responsibility for distributive outcomes and for effecting social change.

This conclusion is implicit in Wesolowski and Mach's commentary on the functions of social mobility under state socialism. 'In socialist systems,' they observe, 'state intervention takes the form of reorganizing social life.' Furthermore,

> since the state authorities in 'reorganizing society' intervene strongly in all macro-structures, the problem of legitimation becomes global as a result. The authorities which feel qualified to recreate reality are perceived by the population as responsible for everything . . . In revolutionary systems, which initially derived their legitimacy, at least in part, from promising extensive social change, the issue of maintaining and of widening the legitimacy resting on such foundations is crucial. (1986: 25)

The meritocratic aspirations of West Germans, and their perception of the Federal Republic as a society in which people in broad terms did obtain their due deserts, are characteristic of those found in most advanced capitalist societies.[17] In these societies, the popular belief that inequality results from equal opportunities and reflects meritocratic reward serves to legitimate market outcomes, since success and failure are routinely attributed to individual talents and effort (or their absence).[18]

However, in the GDR, the potential for legitimation inherent in meritocratic beliefs was undermined by the supreme power claimed by (and attributed to) the state. East Germans seem to have endorsed meritocratic principles as strongly as West Germans (the ideology of meritocratic socialism serving to reinforce these aspirations); but, at the same time, also held expectations about the role of government (and its responsibility for delivering on policy promises) which were consistent with living in a centrally planned society. When these expectations were not fulfilled (at least with regard to equality of opportunity) then the state became the obvious culprit.[19]

It seems to me that the German experience underlines the importance of David Lockwood's observations about the necessity of taking into account the *content* of people's beliefs in prospective explanations of social integration. In *Solidarity and Schism* (1992: 22, 41, 134–5, 156, 298–9, 310), David points out that Durkheimians and Marxists alike have tended to ignore the variability of belief systems, and to assume instead their formal equivalence from the point of view of accounting for social solidarity. In other words, for many theorists of social order, one set of overarching values and norms has been as good as any other. All have been given the same role in explanations of social cohesion. However, some belief systems are simply more conducive to social order than are others, and the point about meritocratic beliefs in general, and the notion of equality of opportunity in particular, is that (as David also notes) these individualize the causes of success and failure. By claiming all responsibility for distributive outcomes in the name of socialism, the East German authorities effectively denied that possibility, and ensured instead that these causes were identified within the state itself.

If I may finish on a speculative note, one might argue therefore that these findings about attitudes to social justice help explain why the GDR collapsed quite so quickly, after it became clear that the Soviets would not intervene militarily to support the communists. The East German ruling elite, having attempted to legitimate their regime in broadly meritocratic terms (as being consistent with equality of opportunity), failed to satisfy the popular expectations for social mobility that were generated by their own political rhetoric. The GDR was perceived by its citizens to be a grossly unmeritocratic social order. For this reason, popular discontent could easily be focused upon the central authorities, rather than internalized by attributing failure to individual responsibility – especially since the state claimed for itself such an extensive role in the ordering of distributive outcomes. Of course, the legitimation deficit suffered by the former GDR had many and more obvious sources than the failure of the central authorities to change the public perception of relative mobility chances, most notably perhaps in the West German television channels that were available each evening to some 85 per cent of East German residents. I would not wish to exaggerate the significance of social mobility (or immobility) in any account of the collapse of real socialism.[20] Still, if my argument is sound, then it does tend to confirm the wisdom of David Lockwood's advice to take seriously both the content of belief systems and the methodology of comparative analysis.

Postscript

While the first published version of this chapter was in press the researchers involved in the East German Life History Study (Max Planck Institute for Human Development and Education, Berlin) also published some reports on social mobility in the GDR (see Huinink and Solga, 1994; Mayer and Solga, 1994; Solga, 1995). Comparison of our findings involves the usual problems deriving from the use of somewhat different statistical techniques and class schemes. Nevertheless, their results are consistent with my own, and confirm that the picture, painted by the SED, of East Germany as an 'open society' was (to paraphrase their conclusion) 'more myth than reality' – since overall social fluidity in the GDR was no greater than in the FRG and probably declined over time. (The key findings are reported in Solga, 1995: Table 8; Mayer and Solga, 1994: Tables 2 and 3.)

Notes

* I would like to thank John H. Goldthorpe, A.H. Halsey, Marion Headicar, and Laurence A. Whitehead for helpful advice and comments on an earlier draft of this chapter. The surveys were funded by the Deutsche Forschungsgemeinschaft and supervised by Bernd Wegener (Humboldt University of Berlin). The data were merged by Duane Alwin at the Institute for Social Research (University of Michigan at Ann Arbor) with financial support from the National Science Foundation.

1 Kohn's (1989: 20–4) fourfold classification of types of comparative research is described in his edited collection of essays on crossnational research in sociology. On the post-war similarities between the economic and social structures of (what were to become) the FRG and GDR see Mellor (1978).

2 It seems unlikely that this complex question will have a simple answer. After reviewing the evidence, I am inclined to agree with the authors of one study who concluded that 'in sum it appears a valid generalization that, if private ownership of the means of production is replaced by collective ownership, some types of inequality are eliminated, some others remain, and some new sorts of inequalities emerge in social life' (Kolosi and Wnuk-Lipiński, 1983: 3). The evidence relating to the Soviet Union is reviewed in Lane (1982: ch. 3). That for socialist Eastern and Central Europe more generally is reported in Kende and Strmiska (1987). On Cuba see the essays collected in Mesa-Lago (1971). The Chinese experience is summarized by Parish (1981). On the GDR see Hauser et al. (1994).

3 Stalin (1955: 120–1). On this issue critical Marxists tend to share in the view of the orthodoxy. See, for example, Ferge (1979: 40–1).

4 This interpretation of Marx's theory of justice is stated concisely in Elster (1985: 229–30). Later Marxist thinking on the issue of social justice is summarized in Lukes (1985: ch. 4). For overviews of the wider literature see Cohen (1986) and Scherer (1992). According to many observers, the distributive inequalities of condition found under real socialism were the result not only of rewarding 'each according to his work', but also of giving unequal rewards for equal work. For example, Wlodzimierz Wesolowski (1988: 3–7) has argued that because of the widespread tendency to discriminate against women, and to favour members of the Party in general and workers in so-called productive sectors of the economy in particular, under state socialism the 'gender, sector and *nomenklatura* principles undermine the model assumption of equal pay for equal work.'

5 Rogovin (1986: 137) summarizes the official view in these terms: 'The concepts of social justice and social equality are not identical . . . equality in, say, material status of members of society may be unjust, especially when it is due to wage equalization although the respective work done may be unequal in quality and quantity. The principal form of a just distribution in the position of individuals and social groups under socialism is a differentiation based on the consistent observation of the principle of distribution according to work performed.'

6 See also Meier (1989: 169–70) who notes: 'The educational system in all socialist societies has to fulfil at least two universal functions: to provide as much social equality . . . as seems necessary for the stability and legitimation of the socialist order, and to produce an educated labour force . . . both a pool of highly trained and selected talents and a specialized, educated "normal" labour force . . . Educational systems in both the Soviet Union and the GDR have

experienced situations in which the egalitarian principle of guaranteeing equal educational rights and chances to students from all classes and strata in practice came into conflict with the meritocratic principle by which recruitment for the different trades and professions is managed. The twofold universal use of education periodically creates tensions that hardly can be ignored. Educational planning from above tries to orchestrate the conflicting purposes in such situations by giving priority to one or the other goal and reversing the rank order of functions from time to time.'

7 Wesolowski (1988: 17) later argued explicitly that *both* 'the reduction of social differences' and 'processes of intergenerational mobility' should be taken as 'indicators and elements of socialist changes' in any study of stratification under real socialism. Ferge (1979: 42–4, 305–6) makes the same point in almost the same words.

8 David Lane (1976: 178) has rightly noted that the Soviet ideology of meritocracy also embodied strong functionalist overtones. Wesolowski's (1988: 11–12) own restatement of the normative theory of stratification under socialism is a good example of how the meritocratic and functionalist defences of inequality became intertwined. In his account, socialism 'is based on the assumption that the division of labour is an inseparable feature of every modern society and that this is linked with two of its correlates: the unequal distribution of power and the unequal distribution of material goods. The division of labour manifests itself, among other things, in a multiplicity of specific jobs, some of which require greater qualifications, or expert knowledge, and others – lesser qualifications . . . One may say that jobs which differ as regards qualifications and knowledge give unequal inputs to the well-being of society. Likewise, the differentiation between managerial and non-managerial positions gives unequal inputs to the progress and welfare of society as a whole. The principle of socialist justice calls for higher remuneration of both jobs with higher qualifications and positions of power. In this model not only the actual results of different jobs and actions are taken into consideration. But also the effort made to become better qualified likewise counts . . . Jobs and functions that require greater preparations should be more highly evaluated . . . In this way the model postulates: (1) that there are "more valuable" jobs and functions; (2) that these deserve higher rewards.'

9 See, for example, the claims of Rutkevitch and Filipov (1973: 235) and Aitov (1986: 256, 270), discussed by Marshall et al. in Chapter 7 in this volume. See also Hegedüs (1977: 59, 71) and Charvát et al. (1978: 162), who offer the same argument, in almost the same terms. Reviewing this field a decade or so later, Wesolowski and Mach (1986: 27) observed that, in real socialist societies, 'those in power appear to have adopted a convenient stance. According to them, so much has been done to equalize opportunities and the process of levelling the social position of classes is proceeding so rapidly that there is no need to query how the equality of opportunities should be implemented in practice. To a certain extent thought has leapt into a world better than the one which has been created in reality. However, questions about the degree to which opportunities have been made equal cannot be avoided.'

10. See Marshall et al., Chapter 7 in this volume. Greater social fluidity was of course not the only alleged difference between classes in the West and stratification under real socialism. An earlier (now unfashionable) argument was that status crystallization (the correlation between education, occupation, income, housing conditions and such like) was lower under state socialism than democratic capitalism (see Alestalo et al., 1980). The Soviet literature also offers extensive discussion about such issues as cross-class co-operation, intraclass differentiation or fractions, and the relationship with the Party. These are not germane to the issue of social justice and need not be considered here. A good summary of the official theories of class under state socialism will be found in Matthews (1972). The more recent views of critical socialists are outlined in Böröcz (1989).

11 A few studies of *intra*generational mobility in the GDR were published (for example Braunreuther, 1966) – although, for ideological reasons, career mobility (or 'fluctuation') was examined mostly in terms of movement between types of economic enterprise.

12 Invariably, studies which purport to analyse equality of opportunity in East Germany focus only upon the narrower question of equality in *educational* opportunities, in the restricted sense of class differentials in access to (usually higher) education – data on educational

participation rates being, by comparison with those on intergenerational class mobility, more readily available. See, for example, Williamson (1979) and Glaessner (1984).

13 Compare, for example, the different assessments of intergenerational mobility in soviet-type societies offered by Strmiska (1987) and Teckenberg (1990). These authors differ mainly in their interpretation of the evidence concerning social fluidity. Some earlier researchers fail to make the fundamental distinction between absolute mobility rates and relative mobility chances. See, for example, the analysis of Czechoslovakian mobility offered in Charvát et al. (1978) and the study of Estonia by Kenkman et al. (1986).

14 I am inclined not to share Lane's optimism about the degree to which equality between the sexes was established in East Germany for reasons that are made clear by Helga Michalsky (1984: 262), who concludes her review of the evidence with the observation that most policies of sexual equality in the GDR 'remained almost entirely at the stage of declamatory principles', leaving 'traditional behaviour patterns in both sexes [which] mean that even in education the old clichés on the different roles of the sexes are handed on'. See also Sørensen and Trappe (1995).

15 Although I have maintained the distinction between equality of outcome and equality of opportunity for the heuristic purposes of this chapter, I would also argue (following Parkin, 1972: 13–14) that in practice, unequal outcomes have implications for equality of opportunity. The same point is made in different ways by Wesolowski and Mach (1986: 30), Kolosi and Wnuk-Lipiński (1983: 144), and Ferge (1979: 154).

16 Responses to the questions were precoded, typically on a five-point Likert scale, ranging from strongly agree and agree through a neutral category to disagree and strongly disagree.

17 The best overview of what is now a substantial field of empirical research into public perceptions of distributive justice will be found in Miller (1992).

18 See, for example, Hayek (1976: 64, 74), who notes that although one cannot justify market outcomes as reflecting desert (since luck plays too large a role in determining who gets what), nevertheless the solidarity of market societies depends to an important degree on the erroneous popular belief that market outcomes do in fact reward merit. Hayek judges such a belief to be necessary if people are to tolerate the inequality that the market produces.

19 This interpretation of East German popular culture is consistent with the findings reported by Roller, who concludes from survey evidence gathered in late 1990 that 'East Germans supported the achievement principle of the market economy to the same degree as the West Germans. At the same time, they harboured higher expectations regarding the role of government, expectations that are more congruent with a planned economy' (1994: 115).

20 Interestingly enough, however, Koralewicz-Zebik (1984: 225) has made exactly the same argument in relation to Poland. She maintains the evidence suggests that 'changes in the perception of inequalities in Poland . . . show that . . . greatest frustration was due to a decomposition of the system of meritocratic justice, accepted by the majority of Poles, combined with the expansion of other, unaccepted, criteria for rewards. Thus the growth of increasing inequalities was accompanied by a total withdrawal of the legitimization of inequalities.' For an overview of East German legitimation problems see Stent (1986).

References

Abbott, P. and Sapsford, R. (1986) 'Class identification of married working women', *British Journal of Sociology*, 37: 535–49.

Abbott, P. and Sapsford, R. (1987) *Women and Social Class*, London: Tavistock.

Abercrombie, N. and Warde, A. (1988) (with Soothill, K., Urry, J. and Walby, S.) *Contemporary British Society*, Cambridge: Polity Press.

Abercrombie, N., Hill, S. and Turner, B.S. (1980) *The Dominant Ideology Thesis*, London: George Allen and Unwin.

Acker, J. (1973) 'Women and social stratification: a case of intellectual sexism', *American Journal of Sociology*, 78: 936–45.

Ahrne, G. and Wright, E.O. (1983) 'Classes in the United States and Sweden: a comparison', *Acta Sociologica*, 26: 211–35.

Aitov, N.A. (1986) 'The dynamics of social mobility in the Soviet Union', in M. Yanowitch (ed.), *The Social Structure of the USSR: Recent Soviet Studies*, Armonk, NY: M.E. Sharpe, pp. 254–70.

Alestalo, M., Slomczyński, K.M. and Wesolowski, W. (1980) 'Patterns of stratification', in E. Allardt and W. Wesolowski (eds), *Social Structure and Social Change: Finland and Poland Comparative Perspective*, Warsaw: Polish Scientific Publishers, pp. 117–46.

Alexander, S. (1976) 'Women's work in nineteenth-century London: a study of the years 1820–50', in J. Mitchell and A. Oakley (eds), *The Rights and Wrongs of Women*, Harmondsworth: Penguin, pp. 59–111.

Allen, S. (1982) 'Gender, inequality and class formation', in A. Giddens and G. Mackenzie (eds), *Social Class and the Division of Labour*, Cambridge: Cambridge University Press, pp. 137–47.

Aponte, R. (1990) 'Definitions of the underclass: a critical analysis', in H.J. Gans (ed.), *Sociology in America*, Newbury Park, CA: Sage, pp. 117–37.

Arber, S. (1996) 'Integrating non-employment into research on health inequalities', *International Journal of Health Studies*, 26: 445–81.

Armstrong, J.A. (1959) *The Soviet Bureaucratic Elite*, New York: Praeger.

Arutiunian, Iu.V. (1973) 'Social mobility in the countryside', in M. Yanowitch and W.A. Fisher (eds), *Social Stratification and Mobility in the USSR*, White Plains, NY: International Arts and Sciences Press, pp. 320–53.

Auletta, K. (1982) *The Underclass*, New York: Random House.

Bagguley, P. and Mann, K. (1992) 'Idle thieving bastards? Scholarly representations of the "underclass"', *Work, Employment and Society*, 6: 113–26.

Bartley, M., Carpenter, L., Dunnell, K. and Fitzpatrick, R. (1996) 'Measuring inequalities in health: an analysis of mortality patterns using two social classifications', *Sociology of Health and Illness*, 18: 455–74.

Bauman, Z. (1982) *Memories of Class*, London: Routledge and Kegan Paul.

Bauman, Z. (1988) 'Sociology and postmodernity', *Sociological Review*, 36: 790–813.

Bauman, Z. (1992) *Intimations of Postmodernity*, London: Routledge.

Baxter, J. (1991) 'The class location of women: direct or derived?', in J. Baxter, M. Emmison and J. Western (eds), *Class Analysis and Contemporary Australia*, Melbourne: Macmillan, pp. 202–22.

Baxter, J., Emmison, M. and Western, J. (eds) (1991) *Class Analysis and Contemporary Australia*, Melbourne: Macmillan.

Beck, U. (1992) *Risk Society*, London: Sage.

Bell, D. (1976) *The Coming of Post-Industrial Society*, Harmondsworth: Penguin.

Bell, D. (1979) *The Cultural Contradictions of Capitalism*, London: Heinemann.

Berger, S. (ed.) (1981) *Organizing Interests in Western Europe*, Cambridge: Cambridge University Press.

Blau, P.M. and Duncan, O.D. (1967) *The American Occupational Structure*, New York: Wiley.

Blossfeld, H.-P. and Shavit, Y. (eds) (1992) *Persistent Inequality: Changing Educational Stratification in Thirteen Countries*, Boulder, CO: Westview Press.

Bonney, N. (1988) 'Gender, household and social class', *British Journal of Sociology*, 29: 28–46.

Böröcz, J. (1989) 'Mapping the class structures of state socialism in East-Central Europe', *Research in Social Stratification and Mobility*, 8: 279–309.

Bradley, H. (1996) *Fractured Identities*, Cambridge: Polity Press.

Braunreuther, K. (1966) *Soziologische Probleme der Fluktuation von Arbeitskräften*, Berlin: Akademie Verlag.

Braverman, H. (1974) *Labour and Monopoly Capital*, London: Monthly Review Press.

Breen, R. and Rottman, D.B. (1995a) *Class Stratification: a Comparative Perspective*, London: Harvester Wheatsheaf.

Breen, R. and Rottman, D.B. (1995b) 'Class analysis and class theory', *Sociology*, 29: 453–73.

Breiger, R. (1981) 'The social class structure of occupational mobility', *American Journal of Sociology*, 87: 578–91.

Brittan, S. (1978) *The Economic Consequences of Democracy*, London: Temple Smith.

Britten, N. and Heath, A. (1983) 'Women, men and social class', in E. Gamarnikow, D.H.J. Morgan, J. Purvis and D.E. Taylorson (eds), *Gender, Class and Work*, London: Heinemann, pp. 46–60.

Brown, P. and Scase, R. (1994) *Higher Education and Corporate Realities*, London: UCL Press.

Bulmer, M. (1975) *Working-Class Images of Society*, London: Routledge and Kegan Paul.

Burgoyne, C., Swift, A. and Marshall, G. (1993) 'Inconsistency in beliefs about distributive justice: a cautionary note', *Journal for the Theory of Social Behaviour*, 23: 327–42.

Butler, D. and Kavanagh, D. (1985) *The British General Election of 1983*, London: Macmillan.

Butler, D. and Rose, R. (1960) *The British General Election of 1959*, London: Macmillan.

Callinicos, A. (1990) 'Reactionary postmodernism?', in R. Boyne and A. Rattansi (eds), *Postmodernism and Society*, Basingstoke: Macmillan.

Campbell, T. (1988) *Justice*, London: Macmillan.

Charvát, F., Linhart, J. and Večernik, J. (1978) 'Some remarks on the application of mobility approach in a socialist society', in W. Wesolowski, K. M. Slomczyński and B.W. Mach (eds), *Social Mobility in Comparative Perspective*, Warsaw: Polish Academy of Sciences Press, pp. 159–71.

Clark, J., Modgil, C. and Modgil, S. (eds) (1990) *John H. Goldthorpe – Consensus and Controversy*, Bristol, PA: Falmer.

Clark, T.N. and Lipset, S.M. (1991) 'Are social classes dying?', *International Sociology*, 6: 397–410.

Clegg, S., Boreham, P. and Dow, G. (1986) *Class, Politics, and the Economy*, London: Routledge and Kegan Paul.

Cohen, R.L. (ed.) (1986) *Justice: Views from the Social Sciences*, New York: Plenum.

Connor, W.D. (1979) *Socialism, Politics and Equality: Hierarchy and Change in Eastern Europe and the USSR*, New York: Columbia University Press.

Cortina, J. M. (1993) 'What is coefficient alpha? An examination of theory and applications', *Journal of Applied Psychology*, 78: 98–104.

Coulter, F., Cowell, F. and Jenkins, S. (1992) 'Differences in needs and asssessment of income distribution', *Bulletin of Economic Research*, 44: 77–124.

Crewe, I. (1984) 'The electorate: partisan dealignment ten years on', in H. Berrington (ed.), *Change in British Politics*, London: Frank Cass, pp. 183–215.

Crewe, I. (1987) 'On the death and resurrection of class voting: some comments on *How Britain Votes*', *Political Studies*, 34: 620–38.

Crompton, R. (1979) 'Trade unionism and the insurance clerk', *Sociology*, 13: 403–26.

Crompton, R. (1980) 'Class mobility in modern Britain', *Sociology*, 14: 117–19.

Crompton, R. (1991) 'Three varieties of class analysis: comment on R.E. Pahl', *International Journal of Urban and Regional Research*, 15: 108–13.

Crompton, R. (1993) *Class and Stratification*, Cambridge: Polity Press.

Crompton, R. (1995) 'Women's employment and the "middle class"', in T. Butler and M. Savage (eds), *Social Change and the Middle Classes*, London: UCL Press, pp. 58–75.

Crompton, R. and Jones, G. (1984) *White-Collar Proletariat*, London: Macmillan.

Crompton, R. and Mann, M. (eds) (1986) *Gender and Stratification*, Cambridge: Polity Press.

Crompton, R. and Sanderson, K. (1990) *Gendered Jobs and Social Change*, London: Unwin Hyman.

Crook, S., Pakulski, J. and Waters, M. (1992) *Postmodernization*, London: Sage.

Crossick, G. (1978) *An Artisan Elite in Victorian Society*, London: Croom Helm.

Dale, A., Gilbert, G.N. and Arber, S. (1985) 'Integrating women into class theory', *Sociology*, 20: 384–409.

Daniel, W.W. and Millward, N. (1983) *Workplace Industrial Relations in Britain*, London: Heinemann.

Daunton, M.J. (1983) *House and Home in the Victorian City*, London: Edward Arnold.

Davidoff, L. (1979) 'The separation of home and work? Landlords and lodgers in nineteenth- and twentieth-century England', in S. Burman (ed.), *Fit Work for Women*, London: Croom Helm, pp. 64–97.

De Graaf, N.D. and Heath, A. (1992) 'Husbands' and wives' voting behaviour in Britain: class-dependent mutual influence of spouses', *Acta Sociologica*, 35: 311–22.

Delphy, C. and Leonard, D. (1986) 'Class analysis, gender analysis and the family', in R. Crompton and M. Mann (eds), *Gender and Stratification*, Cambridge: Polity Press, pp. 57–73.

Dex, S. (1985) *The Sexual Division of Work*, Brighton: Wheatsheaf.

Dex, S. and Shaw, L.B. (1986) *British and American Women at Work*, London: Macmillan.

Duke, V. and Edgell, S. (1984) 'Public expenditure cuts in Britain and consumption sectoral cleavages', *International Journal of Urban and Regional Research*, 8: 177–201.

Duke, V. and Edgell, S. (1987) 'The operationalization of class in British sociology: theoretical and empirical considerations', *British Journal of Sociology*, 38: 445–63.

Dunleavy, P. (1979) 'The urban bases of political alignment: social class, domestic property ownership, and state intervention in consumption processes', *British Journal of Political Science*, 9: 403–43.

Dunleavy, P. (1980a) *Urban Political Analysis*, London: Macmillan.

Dunleavy, P. (1980b) 'The political implications of sectoral cleavages and the growth of state employment', *Political Studies*, 28: 364–83, 527–49.

Dunleavy, P. (1987) 'Class dealignment in Britain revisited: why odds ratios give odd results', *West European Politics*, 10: 400–19.

Dunleavy, P. and Husbands, C.T. (1985) *British Democracy at the Crossroads*, London: George Allen and Unwin.

Durkheim, E. (1952 [1897]) *Suicide*, New York: Free Press.

Durkheim, E. (1964 [1895]) *The Rules of Sociological Method*, New York: Free Press.

Eder, K. (1993) *The New Politics of Class*, London: Sage.

Edgell, S. (1993) *Class*, New York: Routledge.

Edgell, S. and Duke, V. (1991) *A Measure of Thatcherism*, London: Harper Collins.

Edwards, R. (1979) *Contested Terrain*, London: Heinemann.

Elster, J. (1985) *Making Sense of Marx*, Cambridge: Cambridge University Press.

Emmison, M. and Western, M. (1990) 'Social class and social identity: a comment on Marshall et al.', *Sociology*, 24: 241–53.

Erikson, R. (1984) 'Social class of men, women and families', *Sociology*, 18: 500–14.

Erikson, R. (1990) 'Politics and class mobility: does politics influence rates of social mobility?', in I. Persson (ed.), *Generating Equality in the Welfare State: The Swedish Experience*, Oslo: Norwegian University Press, pp. 247–67.

Erikson, R. and Goldthorpe, J.H. (1988) 'Women at class crossroads: a critical note', *Sociology*, 22: 545–53.

Erikson, R. and Goldthorpe, J.H. (1992a) *The Constant Flux*, Oxford: Clarendon Press.

Erikson, R. and Goldthorpe, J.H. (1992b) 'Individual or family? Results from two approaches to class assignment', *Acta Sociologica*, 35: 95–105.

Erikson, R. and Jonsson, J.O. (1996) 'Explaining class inequality in education: the Swedish test case', in R. Erikson and J.O. Jonsson (eds), *Can Education Be Equalized? The Swedish Case in Comparative Perspective*, Oxford: Westview Press, pp. 1–63.

Esping-Andersen, G. (1985) *Politics Against Markets*, Princeton: Princeton University Press.

Esping-Andersen, G. (1990) *The Three Worlds of Welfare Capitalism*, Cambridge: Polity Press.

Esping-Andersen, G. and Korpi, W. (1984) 'Social policy as class politics in post-war capitalism: Scandinavia, Austria and Germany', in J.H. Goldthorpe (ed.), *Order and Conflict in Contemporary Capitalism*, Oxford: Clarendon Press, pp. 179–208.

Evans, G. (1992) 'Testing the validity of the Goldthorpe class schema', *European Sociological Review*, 8: 211–32.

Evans, G. (1993) 'Class, prospects and the life-cycle: explaining the association between class position and political preferences', *Acta Sociologica*, 36: 263–76.

Evans, G. (1996a) 'Putting men and women into classes: an assessment of the cross-sex validity of the Goldthorpe schema', *Sociology*, 30: 209–34.

Evans, G. (1996b) 'Social class and interest formation in post-communist societies', in D.J. Lee and B.S. Turner (eds), *Conflicts about Class*, London: Longman, pp. 225–44.

Evans, G., Heath, A. and Payne, C. (1991) 'Modelling trends in the class/party relationship, 1964–87', *Electoral Studies*, 10: 99–117.

Featherman, D.L. and Selbee, L.K. (1988) 'Class formation and class mobility: a new approach with counts from life history data', in M. Riley and B. Huber (eds), *Social Structure and Human Lives*, Newbury Park, CA: Sage, pp. 247–63.

Featherman, D.L., Jones, F.L. and Hauser, R.M. (1975) 'Assumptions of social mobility research in the US: the case of occupational status', *Social Science Research*, 4: 329–60.

Featherman, D.L., Selbee, L.K. and Mayer, K.U. (1989) 'Social class and the structuring of the life course in Norway and West Germany', in D.I. Kertzer and K.W. Schaie (eds), *Age Structuring in Comparative Perspective*, Hillsdale, NJ: Erlbaum, pp. 55–93.

Featherman, D.L., Spenner, K.I. and Tsunematsu, N. (1990) 'Class and the socialization of children: constancy, change or irrelevance?', in E.M. Hetherington, R.M. Lerner and M. Perlmutter (eds), *Child Development in Life-Span Perspective*, Hillsdale, NJ: Erlbaum, pp. 67–90.

Featherstone, M. (1991) *Consumer Culture and Postmodernism*, London: Sage.

Felson, M. and Knoke, D. (1974) 'Social status and the married woman', *Journal of Marriage and the Family*, 36: 516–21.

Ferge, Z. (1979) *A Society in the Making*, White Plains, NY: M.E. Sharpe.

Foster, J. (1974) *Class Struggle and the Industrial Revolution*, London: Methuen.

Franklin, M.N. (1985) *The Decline of Class Voting in Britain*, Oxford: Clarendon Press.

Gallie, D. (1988) 'Employment, unemployment and social stratification', in D. Gallie (ed.), *Employment in Britain*, Oxford: Blackwell, pp. 465–74.

Gallie, D. (1994a) 'Patterns of skill change: upskilling, deskilling, or polarization?', in R. Penn, M. Rose and J. Rubery (eds), *Skill and Occupational Change*, Oxford: Oxford University Press, pp. 41–76.

Gallie, D. (1994b) 'Are the unemployed an underclass? Some evidence from the social change and economic life initiative', *Sociology*, 28: 737–57.

Gambetta, D. (1987) *Were They Pushed or Did They Jump? Individual Decision Mechanisms in Education*, Cambridge: Cambridge University Press.

Gans, H.J. (1993) 'From "underclass" to "undercaste": some observations about the future of the postindustrial economy and its major victims', *International Journal of Urban and Regional Research*, 17: 327–35.

Ganzeboom, H., Luijkx, R. and Treiman, D.J. (1989) 'Intergenerational class mobility in comparative perspective', *Research in Social Stratification and Mobility*, 8: 3–84.

Garnsey, E. (1978) 'Women's work and theories of class stratification', *Sociology*, 12: 223–43.

Giddens, A. (1991) *Modernity and Self-Identity*, Cambridge: Polity Press.

Glaessner, G.-J. (1984) 'The education system and society', in K. von Beyme and H. Zimmerman (eds), *Policymaking in the German Democratic Republic*, Aldershot: Gower, pp. 190–211.

Glasgow, D.G. (1980) *The Black Underclass: Poverty, Unemployment, and the Entrapment of Ghetto Youth*, San Francisco: Jossey-Bass.

Goldthorpe, J.H. (1971) 'Theories of industrial society: reflections on the recrudescence of historicism and the future of futurology', *Archives Européennes de Sociologie*, 12: 263–88.

Goldthorpe, J.H. (1978) 'The current inflation: towards a sociological account', in J.H. Goldthorpe and F. Hirsch (eds), *The Political Economy of Inflation*, London: Martin Robertson, pp. 186–214.

Goldthorpe, J.H. (with Llewellyn, C. and Payne, C.) (1980) *Social Mobility and Class Structure in Modern Britain*, Oxford: Clarendon Press.

Goldthorpe, J.H. (with Llewellyn, C. and Payne, C. (1987) *Social Mobility and Class Structure in Modern Britain* (2nd edn), Oxford: Clarendon Press.

Goldthorpe, J.H. (1982) 'On the service class: its formation and future', in A. Giddens and G. Mackenzie (eds), *Social Class and the Division of Labour*, Cambridge: Cambridge University Press, pp. 162–85.

Goldthorpe, J.H. (1983) 'Women and class analysis: in defence of the conventional view', *Sociology*, 17: 465–88.

Goldthorpe, J.H. (1984a) 'The end of convergence: corporatist and dualist tendencies in modern western societies', in J.H. Goldthorpe (ed.), *Order and Conflict in Contemporary Capitalism*, Oxford: Clarendon Press, pp. 315–43.

Goldthorpe, J.H. (1984b) 'Women and class analysis: reply to the replies', *Sociology*, 18: 491–99.

Goldthorpe, J.H. (ed.) (1984c) *Order and Conflict in Contemporary Capitalism*, Oxford: Clarendon Press.

Goldthorpe, J.H. (1985) 'Soziale Mobilität und Klassenbildung: Zur Erneuerung einer Tradition soziologischer Forschung', in H. Strasser and J.H. Goldthorpe (eds), *Die Analyse sozialer Ungleichheit*, Opladen: Westdeutscher Verlag, pp. 174–204.

Goldthorpe, J.H. (1988 [1979]) 'Intellectuals and the working class in modern Britain', in D. Rose (ed.), *Social Stratification and Economic Change*, London: Hutchinson, pp. 39–56.

Goldthorpe, J.H. (1992) 'Employment, class and mobility: a critique of liberal and Marxist theories of long term change', in H. Haferkamp and N. Smelser (eds), *Modernity and Social Change*, Berkeley, CA: University of California Press, pp. 122–46.

Goldthorpe, J.H. (1995) 'Le "noyau dur": fluidité sociale en Angleterre et en France dans les années 70 et 80', *Revue française de sociologie*, 36: 61–79.

Goldthorpe, J.H. (1996a) 'Class and politics in advanced industrial societies', in D.J. Lee and B.S. Turner (eds), *Conflicts about Class*, London: Longman, pp. 196–208.

Goldthorpe, J.H. (1996b) 'Class analysis and the reorientation of class theory: the case of persisting differentials in educational attainment', *British Journal of Sociology*, 47: 481–505.

Goldthorpe, J.H. and Bevan, P. (1977) 'The study of social stratification in Great Britain, 1946–1976', *Social Science Information*, 16: 209–302.

Goldthorpe, J.H. and Hope, K. (1974) *The Social Grading of Occupations*, Oxford: Clarendon Press.

Goldthorpe, J.H. and Payne, C. (1986) 'Trends in intergenerational mobility in England and Wales, 1972–1983', *Sociology*, 20: 1–24.

Goldthorpe, J.H., Lockwood, D., Bechhofer, F. and Platt, J. (1969) *The Affluent Worker in the Class Structure*, Cambridge: Cambridge University Press.

Goodwin, B. (1987) *Using Political Ideas*, Chichester: Wiley.

Gorz, A. (1982) *Farewell to the Working Class*, London: Pluto Press.

Graetz, B. (1991) 'The class location of families: a refined classification and analysis', *Sociology*, 25: 101–18.

Gray, R.Q. (1974) 'The labour aristocracy in the Victorian class structure', in F. Parkin (ed.), *The Social Analysis of Class Structure*, London: Tavistock, pp. 19–38.

Gray, R.Q. (1976) *The Labour Aristocracy in Victorian Edinburgh*, Oxford: Clarendon Press.

Gray, R.Q. (1981) *The Aristocracy of Labour in Nineteenth Century Britain*, London: Macmillan.

Green, S.J.D. (1988) 'Is equality of opportunity a false ideal for society?', *British Journal of Sociology*, 39: 1–27.

Grusky, D.B. and Hauser, R.M. (1984) 'Comparative social mobility revisited: models of convergence and divergence in 16 countries', *American Sociological Review*, 49: 19–38.

Habermas, J. (1975) *Legitimation Crisis*, Boston: Beacon Press.

Habermas, J. (1979) *Communication and the Evolution of Society*, London: Heinemann.

Hagan, J. and Albonetti, C. (1982) 'Race, class and the perception of criminal injustice in America', *American Journal of Sociology*, 88: 329–55.

Haller, M. (1981) 'Marriage, women and social stratification: a theoretical critique', *American Journal of Sociology*, 86: 766–95.

Haller, M. (1990) 'European class structure: does it exist?', in M. Haller (ed.), *Class Structure in Europe: New Findings from East–West Comparisons of Social Structure and Mobility*, London: M.E. Sharpe, pp. xi–xxii.

Halsey, A.H. (1977) 'Towards meritocracy? The case of Britain', in A.H. Halsey and J. Karabel (eds), *Power and Ideology in Education*, New York: Oxford University Press, pp. 173–96.

Halsey, A.H., Heath, A.F. and Ridge, J.M. (1980) *Origins and Destinations*, Oxford: Clarendon Press.

Harris, C.C. and Morris, L.D. (1986) 'Households, labour markets and the position of women', in R. Crompton and M. Mann (eds), *Gender and Stratification*, Cambridge: Polity Press, pp. 86–96.

Harrison, R. (1965) *Before the Socialists*, London: Routledge and Kegan Paul.

Harvey, D. (1990) *The Condition of Postmodernity*, Oxford: Blackwell.

Hauser, R.M. (1978) 'A structural model of the mobility table', *Social Forces*, 56: 919–53.

Hauser, R.M., Dickinson, P.J., Travis, H.P. and Koffel, J. M. (1975) 'Temporal change in occupational mobility: evidence for men in the United States', *American Sociological Review*, 40: 279–97.

Hauser, R., Frick, J., Mueller, K. and Wagner, G.G. (1994) 'Inequality in income: a comparison of East and West Germans before reunification and during transition', *Journal of European Social Policy*, 4: 277–95.

Hayek, F. (1976) *The Mirage of Social Justice*, London: Routledge and Kegan Paul.

Hayek, F. (1978) 'The atavism of social justice', in F. Hayek, *New Studies in Philosophy, Politics, Economics and the History of Ideas*, London: Routledge and Kegan Paul, pp. 57–68.

Haynes, C. and Jones, F.L. (1992a) 'Class identification among Australian couples: are wives' characteristics irrelevant?', *British Journal of Sociology*, 43: 463–83.

Haynes, C. and Jones, F.L. (1992b) 'Marriage and political partisanship in Australia: do wives' characteristics make a difference?', *Sociology*, 26: 81–101.

Heath, A. (1981) *Social Mobility*, London: Fontana.

Heath, A. (1990) 'Class and political partisanship', in J. Clark, C. Modgil and S. Modgil (eds), *John H. Goldthorpe: Consensus and Controversy*, Bristol, PA: Falmer, pp. 161–9.

Heath, A. (1992) 'The attitudes of the underclass', in D.J. Smith (ed.), *Understanding the Underclass*, London: Policy Studies Institute, pp. 32–47.

Heath, A. and Britten, N. (1984) 'Women's jobs do make a difference', *Sociology*, 18: 475–90.

Heath, A. and Clifford, P. (1990) 'Class inequalities in education in the twentieth century', *Journal of the Royal Statistical Society, Series A*, 153: 1–16.

Heath, A. and Clifford, P. (1996) 'Class inequalities and educational reform in twentieth-century Britain', in D.J. Lee and B.S. Turner (eds), *Conflicts about Class*, London: Longman, pp. 209–24.

Heath, A. and Ridge, J. (1983) 'Schools, examinations and occupational attainment', in J. Purvis and M. Hales (eds), *Achievement and Inequality in Education*, London: Routledge and Kegan Paul, pp. 239–57.

Heath, A., Jowell, R. and Curtice, J. (1985) *How Britain Votes*, Oxford: Pergamon.

Heath, A., Jowell, R. and Curtice, J. (1986) 'Understanding electoral change in Britain', *Parliamentary Affairs*, 39: 150–64.

Heath, A., Jowell, R. and Curtice, J. (1987a) 'Trendless fluctuation: a reply to Crewe', *Political Studies*, 35: 256–77.

Heath, A., Jowell, R. and Curtice, J. (1987b) 'Class dealignment and the explanation of political change: a reply to Dunleavy', *West European Politics*, 11: 146–8.

Heath, A., Mills, C. and Roberts, J. (1991a) 'Towards meritocracy? Recent evidence on an old problem', in C. Crouch and A. Heath (eds), *Social Research and Social Reform*, Oxford: Clarendon Press, pp. 217–43.

Heath, A., Jowell, R., Curtice, J., Evans, G., Field, J. and Witherspoon, S. (1991b) *Understanding Political Change: The British Voter, 1964–1987*, Oxford: Pergamon.

Hegedüs, A. (1977) *The Structure of Socialist Society*, London: Constable.

Heitlinger, A. (1979) *Women and State Socialism*, London: Macmillan.

Herrnstein, R.J. and Murray, C. (1994) *The Bell Curve: Intelligence and Class Structure in American Life*, New York: Free Press.

Hibbs, D. (1982) 'Economic outcomes and political support for British governments among the occupational classes', *American Political Science Review*, 76: 259–79.

Hiller, D.V. and Philliber, W.W. (1978) 'The derivation of status benefits from occupational attainments of working wives', *Journal of Marriage and the Family*, 40: 63–9.

Himmelweit, H.T., Humphreys, P. and Jaeger, M. (1985) *How Voters Decide*, Milton Keynes: Open University Press.

Hindess, B. (1987) *Politics and Class Analysis*, Oxford: Basil Blackwell.

Hirsch, F. (1977) *Social Limits to Growth*, London: Routledge and Kegan Paul.

Hobsbawm, E.J. (1964) *Labouring Men*, London: Weidenfeld and Nicolson.

Hobsbawm, E.J. (1981) 'The forward march of Labour halted?' and 'Observations on the debate', in M. Jacques and F. Mulhearn (eds), *The Forward March of Labour Halted?*, London: New Left Books, pp. 1–19, 167–82.

Hodge, R.W. and Treiman, D.J. (1968) 'Class identification in the United States', *American Journal of Sociology*, 73: 535–47.

Holton, R.J. and Turner, B.S. (1989) 'Has class analysis a future? Max Weber and the challenge of Liberalism to *Gemeinschaftlich* accounts of class', in R.J. Holton and B.S. Turner, *Max Weber on Economics and Society*, London: Routledge and Kegan Paul, pp. 160–96.

Hope, K. (1981) 'Trends in the openness of British society in the present century', *Research in Social Stratification and Mobility*, 1: 127–69.

Huinink, J. and Solga, H. (1994) 'Occupational opportunities in the GDR: a privilege of the older generations?', *Zeitschrift für Soziologie*, 23: 237–53.

Ishida, H. (1993) *Social Mobility in Contemporary Japan*, Stanford, CA: Stanford University Press.

Jackman, M.R. and Jackman, R.W. (1983) *Class Awareness in the United States*, Berkeley, CA: University of California Press.

Jones, F.L. (1991) 'Common social fluidity: a comment on some recent criticism', Australian National University: Research School of Social Sciences.

Jones, F.L., Kojima, H. and Marks, G. (1994) 'Comparative social fluidity: trends over time in father-to-son mobility in Japan and Australia, 1965–1985', *Social Forces*, 72: 775–98.

Jones, G. (1990) 'Marriage partners and their class trajectories', in G. Payne and P. Abbott (eds), *The Social Mobility of Women*, Bristol, PA: Falmer, pp. 101–19.

Jones, G.S. (1983) *Languages of Class: Studies in English Working-Class History 1832–1982*, Cambridge: Cambridge University Press.

Jonsson, J.O. (1991a) 'Towards the merit-selective society?', University of Stockholm: Swedish Institute for Social Research.

Jonsson, J.O. (1991b) 'Class formation: the holding power and socio-demographic composition of social classes in Sweden', University of Stockholm: Swedish Institute for Social Research.

Jonsson, J.O. and Mills, C. (1993) 'Social class and educational attainment in historical perspective: a Swedish–English comparison, parts I and II', *British Journal of Sociology*, 44: 213–47, 403–28.

Joyce, P. (1980) *Work, Society and Politics*, London: Macmillan.

Kende, P. (1987) 'Introduction', in P. Kende and Z. Strmiska (eds), *Equality and Inequality in Eastern Europe*, Leamington Spa: Berg, pp. 1–17.

Kende, P. and Strmiska, Z. (eds) (1987) *Equality and Inequality in Eastern Europe*, Leamington Spa: Berg.

Kenkman, P.O., Saar, A. and Titma, M.Kh. (1986) 'Generations and social self-determination', in M. Yanowitch (ed.), *The Social Structure of the USSR: Recent Soviet Studies*, Armonk, NY: M.E. Sharpe, pp. 180–214.

Kerr, C. (1983) *The Future of Industrial Society*, Cambridge, MA: Harvard University Press.

Kerr, C., Dunlop, J.T., Harbison, F.H. and Myers, C.A. (1960) *Industrialism and Industrial Man*, Cambridge, MA: Harvard University Press.

Kirk, N. (1985) *The Growth of Working-Class Reformism in Mid-Victorian England*, London: Croom Helm.

Kluegel, J., Mason, D.S. and Wegener, B. (eds) (1995) *Social Justice and Political Change*, New York: Aldine, de Gruyter.

Kohn, M. (1989) 'Introduction', in M. Kohn (ed.), *Cross-National Research in Sociology*, Newbury Park, CA: Sage, pp. 17–31.

Kolosi, T. and Wnuk-Lipiński, E. (1983) *Equality and Inequality under Socialism*, London: Sage.

König, W., Lüttinger, P. and Müller, W. (1988) 'A comparative analysis of the development and structure of educational systems', CASMIN Working Paper 12, University of Mannheim.

Koralewicz-Zebik, J. (1984) 'The perception of inequality in Poland 1956–1980', *Sociology*, 18: 225–37.

Korpi, W. (1978) *The Working Class in Welfare Capitalism: Work, Unions and Politics in Sweden*, London: Routledge.

Korpi, W. (1983) *The Democratic Class Struggle*, London: Routledge and Kegan Paul.

Kuhn, A. and Wolpe, A. (eds) (1978) *Feminism and Materialism*, London: Routledge and Kegan Paul.

Kurz, K. and Müller, W. (1987) 'Class mobility in the industrial world', *Annual Review of Sociology*, 13: 417–42.

Lakatos, I. (1970) 'Falsification and the methodology of scientific research programmes', in I. Lakatos and A. Musgrave (eds), *Criticism and the Growth of Knowledge*, Cambridge: Cambridge University Press, pp. 91–196.

Lane, C. (1983) 'Women in socialist society with special reference to the German Democratic Republic', *Sociology*, 17: 489–505.

Lane, D. (1976) *The Socialist Industrial State*, London: George Allen and Unwin.

Lane, D. (1982) *The End of Social Inequality?*, London: George Allen and Unwin.

Lane, D. and O'Dell, F. (1978) *The Soviet Industrial Worker*, Oxford: Martin Robertson.

Lash, S. (1990) *Sociology of Postmodernism*, London: Routledge.

Leiulfsrud, H. and Woodward, A. (1987) 'Women at class crossroads: repudiating conventional theories of family class', *Sociology*, 21: 393–412.

Lewis, O. (1964) *The Children of Sanchez*, Harmondsworth: Penguin.

Lipset, S.M. (1960) *Political Man*, London: Heinemann.

Lipset, S.M. (1981) 'Whatever happened to the proletariat?', *Encounter*, 56: 18–34.

Littlejohn, G. (1984) *A Sociology of the Soviet Union*, London: Macmillan.

Littler, C.R. and Salaman, G. (1982) 'Bravermania and beyond: recent theories of the labour process', *Sociology*, 16: 251–69.

Llewellyn, C. (1981) 'Occupational mobility and the use of the comparative method', in H. Roberts (ed.), *Doing Feminist Research*, London: Routledge and Kegan Paul, pp. 129–58.

Lockwood, D. (1958) *The Blackcoated Worker*, London: Unwin.

Lockwood, D. (1974) 'For T.H. Marshall', *Sociology*, 8: 363–7.

Lockwood, D. (1975) 'Sources of variation in working-class images of society', in M. Bulmer (ed.), *Working-Class Images of Society*, London: Routledge and Kegan Paul, pp. 16–31.

Lockwood, D. (1992) *Solidarity and Schism*, Oxford: Clarendon Press.

Lukes, S. (1984) 'The future of British socialism?', in B. Pimlott (ed.), *Fabian Essays in Socialist Thought*, London: Heinemann, pp. 269–83.

Lukes, S. (1985) *Marxism and Morality*, Oxford: Clarendon Press.

Lyotard, J.-F. (1986) *The Postmodern Condition: A Report on Knowledge*, Manchester: Manchester University Press.

Macdonald, K. and Ridge, J. (1987) 'Social mobility', in A.H. Halsey (ed.), *Trends in British Society since 1900* (2nd edn), London: Macmillan, pp. 129–47.

Mann, M. (1970) 'The social cohesion of liberal democracy', *American Sociological Review*, 35: 423–31.

Markiewicz-Lagneau, J. (1987) 'The education ethos and the meritocratic ethos', in P. Kende and Z. Strmiska (eds), *Equality and Inequality in Eastern Europe*, Leamington Spa: Berg, pp. 379–406.

Marmot, M.G. (1994) 'Social differentials in health within and between populations', *Daedalus*, 123: 197–216.

Marsh, C. (1986a) 'Occupationally-based measures of social class', London: Social Research Association.

Marsh, C. (1986b) 'Social class and occupation', in R.G. Burgess (ed.), *Key Variables in Social Investigation*, London: Routledge and Kegan Paul, pp. 123–52.

Marsh, C. and Blackburn, R.M. (1992) 'Class differences in access to higher education in Britain', in R. Burrows and C. Marsh (eds), *Consumption and Class*, London: Macmillan, pp. 184–211.

Marshall, G. (1983) 'Some remarks on the study of working-class consciousness', *Politics and Society*, 12: 263–301.

Marshall, G. (1990) *In Praise of Sociology*, London: Unwin Hyman.

Marshall, G. (1991) 'In defence of class analysis: a comment on R.E. Pahl', *International Journal of Urban and Regional Research*, 15: 114–18.

Marshall, G. and Rose, D. (1989) 'Reply to Saunders', *Network*, 44 (May): 4–5.

Marshall, G. and Rose, D. (1990) 'Out-classed by our critics?', *Sociology*, 24: 255–67.

Marshall, G. and Swift, A. (1996) 'Merit and mobility: a reply to Peter Saunders', *Sociology*, 30: 375–86.

Marshall, G., Swift, A. and Roberts, S. (1997) *Against the Odds? Social Class and Social Justice in Industrial Societies*, Oxford: Clarendon Press.

Marshall, G., Rose, D., Newby, H. and Vogler, C. (1988) *Social Class in Modern Britain*, London: Hutchinson.

Marshall, G., Rose, D., Vogler, C. and Newby, H. (1985) 'Class, citizenship and distributional conflict in modern Britain', *British Journal of Sociology*, 36: 259–84.

Marshall, T.H. (1973 [1949]) 'Citizenship and social class', in T.H. Marshall, *Class, Citizenship, and Social Development*, Westport, CT: Greenwood Press, pp. 65–122.

Martin, R. and Wallace, J. (1984) *Working Women in Recession*, Oxford: Oxford University Press.

Mascie-Taylor, C.G.N. (1990) 'The biology of social class', in C.G.N. Mascie-Taylor (ed.), *Biosocial Aspects of Social Class*, Oxford: Oxford University Press, pp. 117–42.

Massey, D. (1984) *Spatial Divisions of Labour*, London: Macmillan.

Matras, J. (1980) 'Comparative social mobility', *Annual Review of Sociology*, 6: 401–31.

Matthews, M. (1972) *Class and Society in Soviet Russia*, London: Allen Lane.

Mayer, K.U. and Solga, H. (1994) 'Mobilität und Legimität. Zum Vergleich der Chancenstrukturen in der alten DDR und der alten BRD oder: Haben Mobilitätschancen zu Stabilität und Zusammenbruch der DDR beigetragen?', *Kölner Zeitschrift für Soziologie und Sozialpsychologie*, 46: 193–208.

Mayer, K.U., Featherman, D.L., Selbee, L.K. and Colbjornsen, T. (1989) 'Class mobility during working life: a cross-national comparison of Germany and Norway', in M. Kohn (ed.), *Cross-National Research in Sociology*, Newbury Park, CA: Sage, pp. 218–39.

McLennan, G. (1981) '"The labour aristocracy" and "incorporation": notes on some terms in the social history of the working class', *Social History*, 6: 71–81.

McRae, S. (1986) *Cross-Class Families*, Oxford: Clarendon Press.

Meier, A. (1989) 'Universals and particularities of socialist educational systems: the transition from school to work in the German Democratic Republic and the Soviet Union', in M. Kohn (ed.), *Cross-National Research in Sociology*, Newbury Park, CA: Sage, pp. 167–84.

Mellor, R.E.H. (1978) *The Two Germanies*, London: Harper and Row.

Mesa-Lago, C. (ed.) (1971) *Revolutionary Change in Cuba*, Pittsburgh: University of Pittsburgh Press.

Michalsky, H. (1984) 'Social policy and the transformation of society', in K. von Beyme and H. Zimmerman (eds), *Policymaking in the German Democratic Republic*, Aldershot: Gower, pp. 242–71.

Michels, R. (1962 [1911]) *Political Parties*, New York: Free Press.

Miles, R. (1982) *Racism and Migrant Labour*, London: Routledge and Kegan Paul.

Miller, D. (1992) 'Distributive justice: what the people think', *Ethics*, 102: 555–93.

Mills, C.W. (1959) *The Sociological Imagination*, Oxford: Oxford University Press.

Moorhouse, H.F. (1978) 'The Marxist theory of the labour aristocracy', *Social History*, 3: 61–82.

Moorhouse, H.F. (1979) 'History, sociology, and the quiescence of the British working class', *Social History*, 4: 481–90.

Moorhouse, H.F. (1981) 'The significance of the labour aristocracy', *Social History*, 6: 229–33.

Morris, L.D. (1993) 'Is there a British underclass?', *International Journal of Urban and Regional Research*, 17: 404–12.

Murgatroyd, L. (1982) 'Gender and occupational stratification', *Sociological Review*, 30: 573–602.

Murgatroyd, L. (1984) 'Women, men and the social grading of occupation', *British Journal of Sociology*, 35: 473–97.

Murphy, J.W. (1988) 'Making sense of postmodern sociology', *British Journal of Sociology*, 39: 600–14.

Murray, C. (1984) *Losing Ground: American Social Policy, 1950–1980*, New York: Basic Books.

Murray, C. (1990) *The Emerging British Underclass*, London: Institute of Economic Affairs.

Myles, J. and Turegun, A. (1994) 'Comparative studies in class structure', *Annual Review of Sociology*, 20: 103–24.

Newby, H., Rose, D., Vogler, C. and Marshall, G. (1985) 'From class structure to class action: British working-class politics in the 1980s', in B. Roberts, R. Finnegan and D. Gallie (eds), *New Approaches to Economic Life*, Manchester: Manchester University Press, pp. 86–102.

Nicholson, L. (1992) 'On the postmodern barricades: feminism, politics, and theory', in S. Seidman and D.G. Wagner (eds), *Postmodernism and Social Theory*, Cambridge, MA: Blackwell, pp. 82–99.

Nozick, R. (1980) *Anarchy, State and Utopia*, Oxford: Basil Blackwell.

Offe, C. (1976) *Industry and Inequality*, London: Edward Arnold.

Offe, C. (1984) *Contradictions of the Welfare State*, London: Hutchinson.

Offe, C. (1985) 'Work: the key sociological category?', in C. Offe, *Disorganized Capitalism*, Cambridge: Polity Press, pp. 129–50.

Olson, M. (1965) *The Logic of Collective Action*, Cambridge, MA: Harvard University Press.

OPCS (1980) *Classification of Occupations, 1980*, Office of Population Censuses and Surveys, London: HMSO.

Osborn, A.F. and Morris, T.C. (1979) 'The rationale for a composite index of social class and its evaluation', *British Journal of Sociology*, 30: 39–60.

Ossowski, S. (1957) 'Social mobility brought about by social revolutions', ISA, Fourth Working Conference on Social Stratification and Mobility, Geneva.

Östberg, V. (1996) *Social Structure and Children's Life Chances*, Stockholm: Swedish Institute for Social Research.

Pahl, R.E. (1984) *Divisions of Labour*, Oxford: Blackwell.

Pahl, R.E. (1989) 'Is the emperor naked? Some comments on the adequacy of sociological theory in urban and regional research', *International Journal of Urban and Regional Research*, 13: 709–20.

Pahl, R.E. (1991) 'R.E. Pahl replies', *International Journal of Urban and Regional Research*, 15: 127–9.

Pakulski, J. (1993) 'The dying of class or of Marxist class theory?', *International Sociology*, 8: 279–92.

Pakulski, J. and Waters, M. (1996) *The Death of Class*, London: Sage.

Parish, W.L. (1981) 'Egalitarianism in Chinese society', *Problems of Communism*, 30 (January–February): 37–53.

Parkin, F. (1972) *Class Inequality and Political Order*, London: Paladin.

Parsons, T. (1954 [1943]) 'The kinship system of the contemporary United States', in T. Parsons, *Essays in Sociological Theory*, New York: Free Press, pp. 177–96.

Pawson, R. (1990) 'Half-truths about bias', *Sociology*, 24: 229–40.

Payne, G. (1987a) *Employment and Opportunity*, London: Macmillan.

Payne, G. (1987b) *Mobility and Change in Modern Society*, London: Macmillan.

Payne, G. and Abbott, P. (eds) (1990a) *The Social Mobility of Women*, Bristol, PA: Falmer.

Payne, G. and Abbott, P. (1990b) 'Beyond male mobility models', in G. Payne and P. Abbott (eds), *The Social Mobility of Women*, Bristol, PA: Falmer, pp. 159–74.

Pelling, H. (1972) *A History of British Trade Unionism*, London: Macmillan.

Pizzorno, A. (1978) 'Political exchange and collective identity in industrial conflict', in C. Crouch and A. Pizzorno (eds), *The Resurgence of Class Conflict in Western Europe since 1968*, volume 2, London: Macmillan, pp. 277–98.

Pollert, A. (1981) *Girls, Wives, Factory Lives*, London: Macmillan.

Procter, S.J., Rowlinson, M., McArdle, L., Hassard, J. and Forrester, P. (1994) 'Flexibility, politics and strategy: in defence of the model of the flexible firm', *Work, Employment and Society*, 8: 221–42.

Przeworski, A. and Teune, H. (1970) *The Logic of Comparative Social Inquiry*, New York: Wiley.

Purcell, K. (1982) 'Female manual workers, fatalism and the reinforcement of inequalities', in D. Robbins (ed.), *Rethinking Social Inequality*, Aldershot: Gower, pp. 43–64.

Rawls, J. (1972) *A Theory of Justice*, Oxford: Clarendon Press.

Reid, A. (1978) 'Politics and economics in the formation of the British working class', *Social History*, 3: 347–61.

Renner, K. (1953) *Wandlungen der Modernen Gesellschaft: zwei Abhandlungen über die Probleme der Nachkriegszeit*, Vienna: Wiener Volksbuchhandlung.

Rex, J. (1986) 'The role of class analysis in the study of race relations – a Weberian perspective', in J. Rex and D. Mason (eds), *Theories of Race and Ethnic Relations*, Cambridge: Cambridge University Press, pp. 64–83.

Ricketts, E.R. and Sawhill, I. (1988) 'Defining and measuring the underclass', *Journal of Policy Analysis and Management*, 7: 316–25.

Ritter, K.V. and Hargens, L.L. (1975) 'Occupational positions and class identifications of married working women: a test of the asymmetry hypothesis', *American Journal of Sociology*, 80: 934–48.

Roberts, H. and Barker, R. (1986) 'The social classification of women', London: City University Social Statistics Research Unit.

Robertson, D. (1984) *Class and the British Electorate*, Oxford: Basil Blackwell.

Roemer, J. (1982) *A General Theory of Exploitation and Class*, Cambridge, MA: Harvard University Press.

Rogovin, V.Z. (1986) 'Social justice and the socialist distribution of vital goods', in M.

Yanowitch (ed.), *New Directions in Soviet Social Thought*, London: M.E. Sharpe, pp. 133–54.

Roller, E. (1994) 'Ideological basis of the market economy: attitudes toward distribution principles and the role of government in Western and Eastern Germany', *European Sociological Review*, 10: 105–17.

Rose, D. and Marshall, G. (1986) 'Constructing the (W)right classes', *Sociology*, 20: 440–55.

Rose, D., Vogler, C., Newby, H. and Marshall, G. (1984) 'Economic restructuring: the British experience', *The Annals of the American Academy of Political and Social Science*, September: 137–57.

Rose, M.A. (1991) *The Post-Modern and the Post-Industrial*, Cambridge: Cambridge University Press.

Rose, R. and McAllister, I. (1986) *Voters Begin to Choose*, London: Sage.

Rossi, P.H., Samson, W.A., Bose, C.E., Jasso, G. and Passel, J. (1974) 'Measuring household social standing', *Social Science Research*, 3: 169–90.

Runciman, W.G. (1990) 'How many classes are there in contemporary British society?', *Sociology*, 24: 377–96.

Rutkevich, M.N. and Filipov, F.R. (1973) 'Principles of the Marxist approach to social structure and social mobility', in M. Yanowitch and W.A. Fisher (eds), *Social Stratification and Mobility in the USSR*, White Plains, NY: International Arts and Sciences Press, pp. 229–40.

Rutter, M. and Madge, N. (1976) *Cycles of Disadvantage*, London: Heinemann.

Sarlvik, B. and Crewe, I. (1983) *Decade of Dealignment*, Cambridge: Cambridge University Press.

Saunders, P. (1984) 'Beyond housing classes: the sociological significance of private property rights in means of consumption', *International Journal of Urban and Regional Research*, 8: 202–27.

Saunders, P. (1989a) 'The question of equality', *Social Studies Review*, 5: 77–82.

Saunders, P. (1989b) 'Left write in sociology', *Network*, 44 (May): 3–4.

Saunders, P. (1990a) *Social Class and Stratification*, London: Routledge.

Saunders, P. (1990b) *A Nation of Home Owners*, London: Unwin Hyman.

Saunders, P. (1996) *Unequal but Fair? A Study of Class Barriers in Britain*, London: Institute of Economic Affairs.

Savage, M., Watt, P. and Arber, S. (1990) 'The consumption sector debate and housing mobility', *Sociology*, 24: 97–117.

Savage, M., Barlow, J., Dickens, P. and Fielding, T. (1992) *Property, Bureaucracy and Culture*, London: Routledge.

Scase, R. (1977) *Social Democracy in a Capitalist Society*, London: Croom Helm.

Scharpf, F.W. (1984) 'Economic and institutional constraints on full employment strategies: Sweden, Austria and West Germany, 1973–1982', in J.H. Goldthorpe (ed.), *Order and Conflict in Contemporary Capitalism*, Oxford: Clarendon Press, pp. 257–90.

Scherer, K.R. (ed.) (1992) *Justice: Interdisciplinary Perspectives*, Cambridge: Cambridge University Press.

Seligman, A.B. (1990) 'Towards a reinterpretation of modernity in an age of modernity', in B.S. Turner (ed.), *Theories of Modernity and Postmodernity*, London: Sage, pp. 117–35.

Shkaratan, O.I. (1973a) 'Social groups in the working class of a developed socialist society', in M. Yanowitch and W.A. Fisher (eds), *Social Stratification and Mobility in the USSR*, White Plains, NY: International Arts and Sciences Press, pp. 63–105.

Shkaratan, O.I. (1973b) 'Social ties and social mobility', in M. Yanowitch and W.A. Fisher (eds), *Social Stratification and Mobility in the USSR*, White Plains, NY: International Arts and Sciences Press, pp. 289–319.

Sinfield, A. (1981) 'Unemployment in an unequal society', in B. Showler and A. Sinfield (eds), *The Workless State*, Oxford: Martin Robertson, pp. 122–66.

Solga, H. (1995) *Auf dem Weg in eine klassenlose Gesellschaft?*, Berlin: Akademie Verlag.

Sørensen, A. and Trappe, H. (1995) 'The persistence of gender inequality in earnings in the German Democratic Republic', *American Sociological Review*, 60: 398–406.

Sørensen, A.B. (1991) 'On the usefulness of class analysis in research on social mobility and socioeconomic inequality', *Acta Sociologica*, 34: 71–87.

Stafford, W.W. and Ladner, J. (1990) 'Political dimensions of the underclass concept', in H.J. Gans (ed.), *Sociology in America*, Newbury Park, CA: Sage, pp. 138–55.

Stalin, I.V. (1955) 'Talk with Emil Ludwig', in I.V. Stalin, *Collected Works*, volume 13, Moscow: Foreign Languages Publishing House.

Stanworth, M. (1984) 'Women and class analysis: a reply to Goldthorpe', *Sociology*, 18: 159–70.

Stent, A.E. (1986) 'East German quest for legitimacy', *Problems of Communism*, 35 (March–April): 79–85.

Stephens, J.D. (1979) *The Transition from Capitalism to Socialism*, London: Macmillan.

Stewart, A., Prandy, K. and Blackburn, R.M. (1980) *Social Stratification and Occupations*, Cambridge: Cambridge University Press.

Strmiska, Z. (1987) 'Social mobility in soviet-type societies in comparative perspective', in P. Kende and Z. Strmiska (eds), *Equality and Inequality in Eastern Europe*, Leamington Spa: Berg, pp. 143–97.

Swift, A., Marshall, G. and Burgoyne, C. (1992) 'Which road to social justice?', *Sociology Review*, 2: 28–31.

Szreter, S.R.S. (1984) 'The genesis of the Registrar-General's social classification of occupations', *British Journal of Sociology*, 35: 522–46.

Teckenberg, W. (1990) 'The stability of occupational structures, social mobility, and interest formation', in M. Haller (ed.), *Class Structure in Europe: New Findings from East–West Comparisons of Social Structure and Mobility*, Armonk, NY: M.E. Sharpe, pp. 24–58.

Therborn, G. (1985) 'The rise of social scientific Marxism and the problems of class analysis', in S.N. Eisenstadt and H.J. Helle (eds), *Macro-Sociological Theory*, London: Sage, pp. 135–67.

Tholfsen, T.R. (1976) *Working-Class Radicalism in Mid- Victorian England*, London: Croom Helm.

Treiman, D.J. (1970) 'Industrialization and social stratification', in E.O. Laumann (ed.), *Social Stratification: Research and Theory for the 1970s*, Indianapolis: Bobbs Merrill, pp. 207–34.

Treiman, D.J. (1977) *Occupational Prestige in Comparative Perspective*, New York: Academic Press.

Treiman, D.J. and Yip, K.-B. (1989) 'Educational and occupational attainment in 21 countries', in M.L. Kohn (ed.), *Cross-National Research in Sociology*, London: Sage, pp. 373–94.

Turner, B.S. (1983) *Religion and Social Theory*, London: Heinemann.

Turner, B.S. (1990) 'Peroration on ideology', in N. Abercrombie, S. Hill and B.S. Turner (eds), *Dominant Ideologies*, London: Unwin Hyman.

Vågerö, D. and Illsley, R. (1995) 'Explaining health inequalities: beyond Black and Barker', *European Sociological Review*, 11: 219–41.

Vågerö, D. and Lundberg, O. (1995) 'Socio-economic mortality differentials among adults in Sweden – towards an explanation', in A. Lopez, G. Caselli and T. Valkonen (eds), *Adult Mortality in Developed Countries*, Oxford: Clarendon Press, pp. 222–42.

Valentine, C.A. (1968) *Culture and Poverty*, Chicago: University of Chicago Press.

Van Velsor, E. and Beeghley, L. (1979) 'The process of class identification among employed married women: a replication and reanalysis', *Journal of Marriage and the Family*, 41: 771–9.

Walby, S. (1986) 'Gender, class and stratification', in R. Crompton and M. Mann (eds), *Gender and Stratification*, Cambridge: Polity Press, pp. 23–39.

Walker, A. (1990) 'Blaiming the victims', in C.H. Murray (ed.), *The Emerging British Underclass*, London: Institute of Economic Affairs, pp. 49–58.

Walton, J. (1981) 'The demand for working-class seaside holidays in Victorian England', *Economic History Review, Second Series*, 34: 249–65.

Weakliem, D. (1989) 'Class and party in Britain, 1964–1983', *Sociology*, 23: 285–97.

Weakliem, D. (1991) 'The two lefts? Occupation and party choice in France, Italy, and the Netherlands', *American Journal of Sociology*, 96: 1327–61.

Weber, M. (1968 [1922]) *Economy and Society*, New York: Bedminster Press.

Webster, J. (1986) 'Word processing and the secretarial labour process', in K. Purcell, S. Wood, A. Waton and S. Allen (eds), *The Changing Experience of Employment*, London: Macmillan, pp. 114–31.

Wesolowski, W. (1988) 'Does socialist stratification exist?', The Fifth Fuller Bequest Lecture, Colchester: University of Essex.

Wesolowski, W. and Mach, B.W. (1986) 'Unfulfilled systemic functions of social mobility, parts I and II', *International Sociology*, 1: 19–35, 173–87.

Westergaard, J. (1992) 'About and beyond the "underclass": some notes on influences of social climate on British sociology today', *Sociology*, 26: 575–87.

Westergaard, J. and Resler, H. (1976) *Class in a Capitalist Society*, Harmondsworth: Penguin.

Wexler, P. (1990) 'Citizenship in the semiotic society', in B.S. Turner (ed.), *Theories of Modernity and Postmodernity*, London: Sage, pp. 164–75.

Williamson, B. (1979) *Education, Social Structure and Development*, London: Macmillan.

Willis, P. (1979) *Learning to Labour*, Westmead, Hants: Saxon House.

Wilson, W.J. (1978) *The Declining Significance of Race: Blacks and Changing American Institutions*, Chicago: University of Chicago Press.

Wilson, W.J. (1987) *The Truly Disadvantaged: The Inner City, the Underclass, and Public Policy*, Chicago: University of Chicago Press.

Witz, A. (1995) 'Gender and service-class formation', in T. Butler and M. Savage (eds), *Social Change and the Middle Classes*, London: UCL Press, pp. 41–57.

Wood, S. (ed.) (1982) *The Degradation of Work?*, London: Hutchinson.

Wooldridge, A. (1995) *Meritocracy and the 'Classless Society'*, London: Social Market Foundation.

Wright, E.O. (1979) 'The class structure of advanced capitalist societies', in E.O. Wright, *Class, Crisis and the State*, London: Verso, pp. 30–110.

Wright, E.O. (1980a) 'Varieties of Marxist conceptions of class structure', *Politics and Society*, 9: 323–70.

Wright, E.O. (1980b): 'Class and occupation', *Theory and Society*, 9: 177–214.

Wright, E.O. (1985) *Classes*, London: Verso.

Wright, E.O. (1989a) 'Women in the class structure', *Politics and Society*, 17: 1–34.

Wright, E.O. (1989b) 'Rethinking, once again, the concept of class structure', in Wright et al., *The Debate on Classes*, London: Verso, pp. 269–348.

Wright, E.O. and Martin, B. (1987) 'The transformation of the American class structure, 1960–1980', *American Journal of Sociology*, 93: 1–29.

Wright, E.O. and Singelmann, J. (1982) 'Proletarianization in the changing American class structure', *American Journal of Sociology*, 88, Supplement: 176–209.

Xie, Y. (1992) 'The log-multiplicative layer effect model for comparing mobility tables', *American Sociological Review*, 57: 380–95.

Yanowitch, M. (1977) *Social and Economic Inequality in the Soviet Union*, London: Martin Robertson.

Index